M000316205

Etna –
A Murder
Out of Time

Michael Mancuso and Eric J. Kerchner

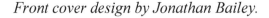

Front cover design by Jonathan Bailey.

"Etna – A Murder Out of Time," by Michael Mancuso and Eric J. Kerchner. ISBN 978-1-951985-65-3 (softcover), 978-1-951985-66-0 (hardcover), 978-1-951985-67-7 (eBook).

Contents

About the Authors

Michael Mancuso

Mr Mancuso has practiced law in Monroe County Pennsylvania for nearly 30 years. He has worked in many different fields within the law. For over 15 years he practiced in the firm of Mancuso and Mancuso with his wife, the Honorable Colleen Mancuso. Mancuso focused on all types of civil litigation including commercial disputes, personal injury, and will contests. Throughout the entirety of his career Mancuso also worked extensively in the field of the Criminal Law. He worked as Chief Deputy Public Defender for over six years. During that time he represented hundreds of criminal defendants charged with the entire range of crimes, from retail theft to Murder. During his tenure as a public defender Mancuso learned the trade of criminal jury trials, often called into multiple jury trials on short notice. Since the year 2000 Mancuso has served as an Assistant District Attorney and since 2004 as the First Assistant District Attorney.

The position of First Assistant District Attorney is a statutory creation which requires Mancuso to serve as second in command of the District Attorney's Office and to assume the duties of District Attorney during the DA's absence or unavailability. As a prosecutor Mancuso specializes in the investigation and prosecution of murder and suspicious death cases. In that effort Mancuso spearheaded the creation of a standing Investigating Grand Jury focusing on cold cases and what he calls 'Equivocal' death investigations. In other words, deaths where the manner of death i.e., natural, accident, suicide, or homicide is not readily apparent. Despite the modest size of the county, Mancuso has worked on hundreds of death investigations. Additionally he has tried to verdict nearly fifty murder defendants. The defendants prosecuted represent all backgrounds and walks of life. The victims have been killed by all sorts of means, including gunshot, blunt force trauma, sharp force trauma, asphyxiation, neglect, fire, and poison. Many of the cases tried by Mancuso have been cold cases. The oldest cold case murder he tried before a jury took place in 1968 but was not brought to trial until 2015. Many cases have been based entirely on circumstantial evidence. Oftentimes there was not an identifiable murder weapon. On occasion Mancuso has prosecuted murder charges where the body of the victim was never recovered.

Mancuso is married to Colleen Mancuso and has four children. He currently resides in Monroe County with his family, not too distant from the scene of Etna Bittenbender's murder.

Eric J. Kerchner

Mr. Kerchner is the chief of the Monroe County Office of the District Attorney's Criminal Investigations Division under E. David Christine, Jr., District Attorney. Graduating from Marple Newtown Senior High School in 1973 Eric joined the United States Army, attending the United States Army Military Police School at Fort Gordon, Georgia. Eric served as a military police officer in Butzbach Germany for the next three years as a patrol officer and then as a traffic accident investigator after attending Northwestern University's Military Police Traffic Accident Investigation School in Vilseck, Germany in 1975. While in the military, Eric completed additional law enforcement training while attending the University of Delaware and Central Texas College.

In 1982, Eric established and operated a Monroe County based private security and investigations firm, Kerchner Associates, Inc. with annual revenues of 1.4 million dollars and employing more than 70 officers. That company was sold in 1998. Eric operated as a private investigator through 2001.

In 2001, Eric was retained as a special investigator by the Monroe County District Attorney's Office focusing on housing mortgage fraud. In 2002, he was appointed as a full time detective.

Eric attended and completed police academy training at Lackawanna College. Over the years, Eric received specialized narcotics training with the Middle Atlantic Great Lakes Organized Crime Law Enforcement Network (MAGLOCLEN), the Pennsylvania Narcotics Officers Association (PNOA), the Drug Enforcement Administration (DEA), and the Montgomery County, PA Drug Task Force. In 2006, he received the Monroe County Drug Task Force Officer of the Year award and in 2007, Eric received the Pennsylvania Narcotic's Officers Association's Unit Citation Award.

In 2009, Eric was promoted to the position of Chief County Detective.

Eric resides in Monroe County with his wife, Gloria. Both of his children, Michael and Suzanne, are graduates of Pleasant Valley High School and reside in the area with his three grandchildren.

Foreword

"Oh mysteries, thou shalt not elude me; my wisdom and strength shall cast aside all darkness. You will not blind me nor lead me astray; the light will find me and shall unto me deliver the truth."

Unknown

From beyond our hunter-gatherer origins down through the ages, the need to seek out and solve mysteries has been one of humanity's persistent preoccupations. The desire is always with us, whether in the form of whispers around an ancient camp fire concerning what monsters may be hidden just beyond the flickering light, to our current quest to scientifically unravel the mysteries of the universe. So too is a common thread that weaves itself into and through every society and era; the need to find and hold evil doers accountable for their actions in order to protect the innocent and maintain a sense of order and safety in the world. Every religion, belief system or set of laws throughout history, have included concepts of justice, retribution, accountability, and punishment.

For a certain few, the intersection of these two great forces, the desire to seek justice, and the need to solve a mystery, creates an irresistible type of passion and devotion. Although this book is centered on a journey to find truth about the ultimate wicked and sinful act, a wanton and brutal assault and slaying of an innocent life that occurred long ago, it is also about public servants like Mike Mancuso and Eric Kerchner, whose passion and devotion knows no bounds. They have taken the sacred duty of seeking justice to a new and admirable level. Their mantra is leave no stone unturned and find answers no matter how long it takes. They have circumvented all obstacles, never gave up, and at long last the darkness has been cast aside, and the truth has been revealed.

Read on!

Hon. E. David Christine, Jr., Esq.
District Attorney Monroe County
Commonwealth of Pennsylvania
Stroudsburg, September 11, 2020

Dedication

Michael Mancuso - "This book is dedicated to my loving wife Colleen, for her patience, encouragement, and yes, constructive criticism; and to my children Callie, Julia, Emilia and Anthony. Enjoy!"

Eric J. Kerchner – "Michael and I began this historical investigation more than eight years ago. Since the investigation was 'unofficial' we had to complete our research after work and on weekends. I dedicate this book to my patient wife, Gloria, for tolerating my enthusiastic focus on such a topic. I also dedicate this book to my father and mother, David and Barbara, for giving me the tools necessary to accomplish such a task".

Introduction

"… there is nothing truly hidden; with hard tenacious work, everything can be known."

Detective Giuseppe Dosi, Rome,
Rivista di Polizia, August 1, 1929 pg. 118

On Sunday October 31st 1880 a murder occurred in Hamilton Township, Monroe County, Pennsylvania. The victim was Etna Bittenbender, 17 years old, the oldest daughter of Samuel and Margaret. She was raped and brutally beaten with stones and a club. Her body was found the next morning on the side of a road next to a path and a low wall of field stones. No one remembers it today, but back then the murder terrorized and shocked the rural county. The place was turned upside down. Vigilantes roamed all over, women were afraid to go out at night or alone. At any point a lynch mob might spring up. A large reward was raised for information that would lead to the arrest of anyone involved. A great deal of suspicion lay on several local people. Suspicion also fell upon strangers passing through the area. Many arrests were made but none stuck and those arrested were let go. The famous Pinkerton Detective Agency was hired to help the investigation. Detectives were dispatched from New York and Philadelphia to solve the crime. Despite so much hard work no-one was ever brought to trial. The case was never solved.

Why would anyone want to write about this today? To take it one step further, why would anyone write about a murder of some forgotten farm girl from 140 years ago? The answer is different for Detective Kerchner than I. For my part, the answer goes back to what I do, my line of work for the last 20 years. I am the First Assistant District Attorney for Monroe County. I work on murder cases. I'm called out to homicide scenes. I talk things over with the detectives, help analyze the case, provide advice, see if there is enough evidence for search warrants, and if appropriate decide whether there is probable cause to approve charges. I take the case through all the proceedings and jury trial.

I work on cases that are pretty bad actually, just horrible, horrendous, and brutal. Many of the cases are very difficult to solve, very hard to prosecute, entirely circumstantial. Often there is no murder weapon, no confession, no direct evidence, no eyewitness, and sometimes no body. This line of work could leave a guy jaded, bitter or down in the dumps; shocked by the inhumanity of it. But there is a draw to it. What really gets me in all these cases, no matter how ugly, is that moment when the truth starts coming out. Even the ugliest case takes on a kind of beauty when you realize the truth. Sometimes that happens early in a case; maybe even in the first hours of the investigation, sometimes it takes longer, a heck of a lot longer. You know the old-timers would say that there's a certain beauty in the truth, no matter how bad. I do believe that people are naturally drawn to the truth. That's what draws me. I really want to know the truth. That remains the reason why I stay in this line of work.

Everything I said about some murder cases being tough is multiplied when you're talking about cold case murders. When people talk about cases being 'cold' they mean that something went wrong, or something was left undone, and now nobody can really figure out how to get things back on track. In other words, there's no plan, there's no angle, there's no way that anyone can think of to find out the truth. The longer this goes on the colder the case gets. It could get to the point where people start to forget, family members move on with their lives, thinking that no one cares anymore, and the guilty keep their dark secret under wraps. Eventually witnesses start to pass away and the case gets so cold that it is considered hopeless and dies a quiet death, its files forgotten in some storage room, or even worse, discarded. It's a shame to say, but a lot of the cases, the murder cases that I do are cold case murders. About a third of the cases I have brought to jury trial have been 'cold'. Once in a while a cold case will turn hot real quick, but most of the time it is a long tedious process; trying to breathe life into a cold case.

The coming alive of a cold case is one of the most beautiful things that somebody in my position could experience during the course of their career. For example, two years after a tragic car accident blamed on a deer jumping out on the road, Reverend AB Schirmer was arrested for murder. The 'good' Reverend beat his poor wife Betty to a pulp in their home next to the United Methodist Church in Reeders. Schirmer put Betty, unconscious but still alive, in his car, drove a short distance, and slammed into a guard rail to stage her death as an accident. But it took the suicide of Joe Musante, who took his life in Schirmer's own office, which led the investigators to take another look at the case. Mr. Musante's wife was having an affair with Schirmer.

I still remember the look on the detective's face when he came to see me with a handful of photographs he managed to find that were taken the night of the car crash. It was clear that the blood in the car did not get there as a result of the crash; that Betty Schirmer was bleeding heavily before Mr. Schirmer put her into his car. Mr. Musante's suicide opened up a big background investigation into Schirmer. That investigation led not only to charging him for the murder of Betty Schirmer, but also for the murder of his first wife Jewel, which happened down in Lebanon County. Jewel was also beaten to a pulp, but her death was staged as a fall down the cellar steps while she was vacuuming. The time between Jewel's murder and the arrest was 11 years. For his crimes, Schirmer is spending the rest of his life in prison.

An example of a cold case getting real hot goes back to August of 2001. A fellow named Randy Huegel went missing. His landlord Tom Cook was a person of interest but there was no evidence connecting him to Huegel's disappearance. Six years later Cook's neighbor came to the authorities. He was troubled by a secret he was keeping, something Cook told him. Troopers VanLouvender and Sebastianelli convinced the neighbor to wear a recording device and chat with Cook. It worked. Cook, who was packing up to move down to Tennessee, spoke in a carefree way about the murder and how he buried and reburied the remains of the victim several times over the years. You see he was upset with Randy, who he believed had burglarized his dad's cabin. So he forced him to walk into the woods at gunpoint and, after Randy refused to dig his own grave, Cook shot him in the head. Seven years after the murder, Cook pled guilty. That day we brought him into the woods and he showed us where the remains of Huegel were buried. I remember how grateful Randy's elderly and sick parents were; since they finally were able to know what happened to him and bury their boy properly. They passed away a short time later. It seemed like they could let it go finally.

In October of 2005 David McEntire disappeared; gone without a trace. His work van found in front of his business with the keys in the ignition, the doors locked, and the battery dead from the headlights being left on. We had some phone records that connected him to a drug ring run by a despicable fellow named Anthony Caiby. Mr. Caiby was David's drug dealer. David, an addict, owed a lot of money to him. Worse than that, Caiby suspected that David stole drugs from another associate of his. So Caiby lured David to the house he was dealing out of. When David arrived he was attacked, beaten, shot with a .22 rifle in the legs, not enough to kill him, blindfolded, tied to a pole, and then injected with a 'hot shot', a mixture of cocaine and bleach. He finally died. Caiby and his people burned the remains and dumped them somewhere.

Hard work and determination kept the investigation alive. Eventually, one of those involved, a female prostitute of Caiby's, provided information about a 'guy named Dave' who was missing. She gave the info in an effort to get out of a shoplifting charge. This allowed us to get a search warrant for the scene. The search itself didn't produce anything staggering. But the same day of the search, a partner of Caiby, a one legged man called 'Beans' gave us a confession. We had enough now to go after the whole group. I'm happy to say that all those involved in the murder have been brought to Justice. Mr. Caiby is currently serving a life sentence. Sadly though, Mr. McEntire's remains have never been found.

Most cold cases move forward not because of a sudden revelation or something unusual making them hot again, but just the persistence of the team working day in and day out, collecting details, putting together bits of circumstantial evidence; piece by piece, like a jigsaw puzzle; until enough of the picture is presented to see what happened. That kind of effort is the essence of what we do. One example is the murder of a kind and gentle man named Benjamin Amato. Mr. Amato was found bludgeoned to death after being sprayed with mace in his home. Looking at the scene it appeared that he walked up the steps to his house from the garage and when he opened the door he was maced in the face and beaten with a blunt object all the way down the steps, dying at the floor of his own garage. His body was found four days later after his friends, concerned that they hadn't heard from him, asked the authorities to conduct a welfare check. His ex-lover, Cheryl Kunkle, was suspected in the murder. The motive was a bitter child custody case. But it took several years of patient hard work by the dedicated team of investigators, including Troopers Shawn Williams and Tom MacAndrew that developed enough evidence to finally bring charges against her. Cheryl Kunkle was convicted of first-degree murder and solicitation to commit murder. She is currently serving a life sentence.

There are many cold cases that remain unsolved. In my County we have at least two dozen unsolved murders. They run the gamut from suspected domestic violence murders, missing person cases, unidentified remains, and murders which appear to have been committed outside the county but the body dumped here. For example back in April of 1983 the body of 43 year old Doris Ace was found submerged in a portion of the Bushkill Creek in Middle Smithfield Township. She was dressed only in a bra. But she did have a diamond ring on her left hand. An autopsy was performed and it was determined that she was killed by a combination of blunt force trauma and manual strangulation. Although the original investigators had a suspect and the investigation has been continuing on and off over the years, to date no one has been brought to justice.

Back in March of 1979, a 25 year old man named Satya Gupta was found dead on a unpaved road in a private development in Pocono Township. He had been a precious gems dealer. According to his family he would typically carry $300,000 worth of precious stones. He worked in Manhattan. Within days of his murder another precious gem dealer was found dead. Although his body was found in New York he also was known to carry hundreds of thousands of dollars' worth of precious gems. The two men were similarly killed i.e., bludgeoned and strangled by a ligature. The case remains unsolved and frankly doesn't appear to have gotten the attention it deserves.

In November of 2005 the body of 50 years old Carlos Alamo was found shot to death in his room at the Wine Press Inn in Bartonsville. Although suspects have been developed the case remains unsolved. In 2014 on the berm of a road in Price Township, a human torso was found. The remains had been previously stored elsewhere. Genetic phenotype testing was performed after a DNA profile was obtained. No progress has been made to date on the identity of the Torso.

The list goes on. We have created an investigating grand jury in the county. One of its main purposes is to advance the investigations of cold cases, to ferret out the remaining evidence, follow up on previously unknown or ignored leads, to continue to give attention to these cases, and hopefully solve them. Part of my job description is to investigate homicides through the grand jury where that resource has been requesting by law enforcement. The Monroe County Investigating Grand Jury has been instrumental in solving a good many cold cases in our County. The grand jurors vary from year to year, but all have shown a great interest in the work and should be commended. No matter how cold a case may appear it is my experience that clues remain and work can be done to ferret out the Killer.

In October of 1968 the murdered body of Alfred Barnes was found with multiple gunshot wounds, lying face down in a lonely field in Chestnuthill Township. Mr. Barnes had worked as an executive secretary for Bethlehem Steel Corporation. He had just bought a brand new Ford Thunderbird 1969 Edition Deluxe and fully loaded. His car was found about a week later in a rural area of New Jersey just over the Delaware River. The early investigators had great intuition that helped develop the profile of the Killer. The profile included a homosexual connection and the phenomena known then as 'cruising'. However it wasn't enough to

6

arrest. Tragically, both of the original investigators passed away within months of the murder. The case went into limbo. As part of a new protocol implemented in 2002 Pennsylvania State Police cold cases were given yearly reviews by having them assigned to members of the various State Police barracks in the county. During a review in 2014 a trooper, a young guy, was able to follow up on a lead that had previously eluded the investigators. They had been looking for a Mr. Richard Keiper but had lost track of him somewhere in Florida in the 1970s. Using modern databases that didn't exist back then, the trooper was able to locate Mr. Keiper living in the state of Texas. The trooper reached out to a Texas Ranger dedicated to cold case investigations to contact Keiper and try to interview him. The interview, a masterful work, eventually led to Keiper giving a 'semi' confession; blaming the killing on self-defense. Keiper was charged, extradited, and brought to trial 47 years after the murder. Using the law from the old penal codes the jury convicted Keiper of first-degree murder. He is serving out a life sentence. The Keiper prosecution is the oldest cold case prosecution in the state and among the oldest in the country. The Case shows that no one should ever lose hope with these cases.

Getting back to the murder of Etna Bittenbender, every now and then I would hear about a young girl who was murdered over a hundred years ago somewhere in Hamilton Township. I heard that the case was never solved. The old time gossip wasn't even consistent as to who did it. Some talked about an old boyfriend who then left the state, moving out west. Other gossip mentioned some crazy guy who eventually killed himself. There was a split between the killer having come from outside the area versus some local person. But there was never any detail or real substance to these rumors. I wouldn't even call them rumors. They were more like the echoes of rumors spread in the days, weeks, and months following the murder; echoes of rumor only.

There were also tales of a ghost, some shadowy figure veiled in white; a female haunting the area where the murder took place. Apparently, young lovers parking in a lonely spot nearby were the frequent victims of the apparition. Local lore also held that horses passing through the area would hesitate, slow, and stop before being urged forward. But I never really got a handle on the facts. I wasn't even sure where it happened. I didn't know the victim's name. I didn't know how she was killed. I didn't know about any kind of motive for her death. Really, it was at best a curious ghost story. So after finding out her name I started to look into it. It was more or less just curiosity; nothing really prompted me to dig deep. Once I got the name 'Etna Bittenbender', the next step involved figuring out where it happened; that was much harder than it sounds. Once I found that place, and realized that I drive by that spot almost every day to and from work, it started to really bother me. Right here, practically in my backyard, a horrible murder happened that nobody even remembers anymore; let alone knows the truth of what happened to the girl.

So at that point I was bitten by the bug. I had to find out more. Part of me figured there could be a chance to actually solve the murder. But I knew that everybody involved in the case was long dead. For another thing, back then the police and detective work that I take for granted wasn't even invented yet. But I did enlist the help of my friend Chief County Detective Eric Kerchner to see if he was interested in lending a hand. He was. He's a curious fellow to begin with and he enjoys history and mystery. So he and I set about gathering the facts; wherever we could find them, both official and unofficial. This took on a life of its own as we dove into the littlest details, not only of the murder and its investigation, but of how living was back then, how things were dealt with, how records were kept, how technology or its lack affected things; all of it led to this Book.

It's been fascinating work; a lot of evenings and weekends spent figuring out things we would normally take for granted about a case. For one thing, there is no case file, if one ever existed it remains lost, or even worse, thrown away. There are hardly any official records of the murder, a Coroner's Inquest, a Grand Jury's mandate, financial records archived in the county, and the Pinkerton Collections. Local historians over the years provided some helpful things. The Census from the year 1880 provides invaluable information. The Archives of the Eastern State

Penitentiary have also been a great help. Old maps and aerial photos have been helpful. There are numerous newspaper accounts that provide a good amount of detail about the case, the scene, the suspects, and the progress or lack of progress of the investigators.

One of the most compelling reminders of this terrible crime is carved on Etna's grave stone itself. Her body lies in the Mt. Zion Cemetery in Hamilton Township. She lies right next to her parents, who died decades later. There's an inscription carved into the stone that serves as a remembrance not only of Etna, but of what happened to her. The stone records that Etna was: "Murdered by some person unknown on Sunday evening October 31st 1880 between the hours of 4 and 6 O'clock. Aged 17 years 1 month and 8 days." Although only a few words, the inscription gives both clues and questions that helped our investigation.

The details uncovered have shed light on this horrible crime and provide valuable evidence and insight into the hearts and minds of those suspected, the investigators, and the people of that time and place. This work gives a snapshot in time; a picture, an image that gives answers to a murder mystery worth remembering. It has been a journey into the darkest inner recesses of the human soul. Maybe this work can bring some comfort to the girl and her family; some solace in knowing that neither she nor the horrible things done to her have been forgotten.

Chapter 1

Finding the Location

"One who knows the lay of the land can unravel its mystery"

Michael Mancuso

The location of a Murder, which is the scene of the crime, is, in itself, a very important piece of evidence in a murder case. The scene of the crime, its mere location, gives valuable clues helping to figure out important details; details about the crime, about the killer, and about the victim. Sometimes the location of a crime gives you a look inside the mind of the killer. Why that location? What's the importance of that location to the crime; to the killer? Depending on the crime, it's planning, how well thought out it was ahead of time, how the killer thought it through, the scene of the crime can shape the details of the murder. For example, in the case of Reverend Schirmer, he had already killed his first wife Jewel in their house in 1998. He staged the scene to look like it was an accident, a fall down the stairs while cleaning. Then in 2008 he attacks his second wife Betty in their house. He couldn't leave her in the house to die; he couldn't blame it on another fall down the steps or similar household tragedy. So the fact that he fatally injured his second wife in their house required him to move her from that location, to avoid everybody wondering what the odds were that he had two wives die accidentally in their homes. He took Betty out of the house, put her in his car, drove down the street, and intentionally crashed the car; blaming her death on a deer jumping in front of his path.

Examples of where the scene helped shape a murder, giving the investigators a peek into the killer's head are pretty common. It seems that when both the victim and the killer live in the same house, or have equal access to the location of the murder, you tend to see more evidence of staging the crime scene; that is making it look like something it isn't.

11

It's just common sense. If the killer and victim live together, the killer's options are limited. He can try to make it look like an accident. He can blame it on someone else; to make it look like some other person came in and did a murder, such as a bogus home invasion. He can also make it look like a suicide or even make it look like a natural death. An interesting example on the effect of location on a murder is a case I brought to trial in 2015, the Tedesco case, John and Tina Tedesco, husband and wife. They were charged with the third degree murder of an elderly woman named Barbara Rabins, who they were supposed to be taking care of. The woman was intellectually disabled, so her father, a wealthy dentist, had set up a lucrative trust account designed to allow Barbara to live comfortably after he passed away. Somehow Mr. and Mrs. Tedesco weaseled their way into Barbara's life and began taking advantage of her. While they lived high on the hog with her money, they allowed Barbara, who was partially paralyzed by a stroke, to waste away in her own filth. Under their care she was caked in feces, covered in deep sores, dehydrated, and starved. She actually choked to death on a piece of food she couldn't swallow. The Tedesco Case is an example of how the location of the death itself was staged. They tried to make it look like Barbara died in their home instead of in the filthy crummy apartment they rented for her. When John Tedesco stopped by that apartment and found Barbara's dead body, he was in a quandary; what could he do? If he left her there eventually the landlord would of course find out, the police would have to get involved, and the whole sick scheme would come to light. So as every responsible caretaker would do, he took the corpse, in the middle of the night, wheelchair and all, put it in the back of his pickup, drove home, and wheeled the body into his living room. He called 911. The ambulance personnel arrived, followed by a deputy coroner. The body was removed. That would have been the end of it; but noticing that the filthy deplorable condition of the body seemed so out of place in the immaculate home of Mr. and Mrs. Tedesco, the deputy coroner didn't feel comfortable and arranged for an autopsy. The police got involved. Eventually, we presented the case to the investigating grand jury; which, after a full investigation recommended that homicide charges be filed against the couple. They went to trial, were convicted and are serving lengthy jail terms for third-degree murder. This is an example of how the aftermath of the crime, the staging of the scene, was affected by the initial location of the death. In fact, it took several months of investigating before information about the apartment even surfaced.

When the killer has no connection or real control over the crime scene, you don't usually see evidence of the kind of staging that is designed to hide the true nature of the crime. You can see attempts by the killer to try to separate, erase, or cut off any connection he may have to the scene and victim. Such a killer will try to destroy all evidence that could link him to the victim. On October 31, 2001, Halloween, Helen Biank was found dead in her Barrett Township home. She died by a single gunshot wound through her head. She was found lying on a couch in her living room by firefighters battling the flames of her burning house. The fire was set by the killer to destroy evidence that connected him to the crime. It was a tough case. There were several men who had motive and opportunity, but in the end Mr. Mark Miller, the killer, made a few big mistakes. His biggest mistake was to assume that the house would be completely consumed by the fire, and along with it the murder weapon, a stolen rifle. He had approached Helen as she lay on the couch and shot her once through the head. He then wrapped the rifle in a towel, left it next to the body, and set the couch and living room on fire. Because the fire was poorly vented, not enough oxygen fed it, the fire petered out. In fact, by wrapping the gun in a towel, Mr. Miller actually preserved the evidence. The towel protected a 'tonal reversal' on the stock of the rifle. A tonal reversal is an inside-out fingerprint; it happens when during pressure, the ridges and valleys of a fingerprint distort and the ridges become valleys and the valleys become ridges. The tonal reversal was enhanced by fingerprint examiners of the Pennsylvania State Police, including my friend retired Trooper Phil Barletto, and a match was made to the left middle finger of Mark Miller. Miller, on the eve of trial, pled guilty to murder in the third degree and is serving a sentence of 20 to 40 years in State Prison.

Fire is a frequent tool of a killer trying to erase evidence connecting him to a murder. In the Caiby Case I mentioned before, the killers did the deed in their own space, the house where they were living and dealing drugs. They couldn't leave the victim there, at least not for long, and they also couldn't leave any clues connecting them to the murder. So after they burned his body they were careful to remove all the pieces they could find and dump the burned flesh, ashes, and bone bits very far from their residence. They scrubbed down the house, repainted the walls, used bleach, and even shampooed the carpets. You typically don't expect such a level of housekeeping by drug dealers. Years later the scene was searched, some evidence, in the form of latent blood, that is invisible blood, was detected. The investigators were able to spray a chemical called 'luminol' throughout the house. When luminol comes into contact with blood; even blood you can't see with the naked eye, it will glow in the dark. The glowing reaction took place in the same areas of the house described by some of the participants and coincided with the details of the brutal assault and murder.

So I wondered if the location of Etna's murder might give us some insight into the crime. Before that could happen we had to figure out precisely where the murder occurred. It was very important for us to look at all the surviving information that mentioned the scene. The starting point had to be one of the few remaining official records of the murder, the Coroner's Inquest. A Coroner's Inquest is an investigation into the cause and manner of a death. They have been around a long time; back to the Middle Ages. In Etna's day, 1880, Pennsylvania had a coroner system very much like the system in effect today. The coroner was the official who determined the cause and manner of death, kept records of those findings, and put the information into a death certificate. The investigation a coroner does is not the same as that conducted by the police or the district attorney; those are criminal investigations. A coroner does not have the power to charge someone with a crime. A coroner in an inquest can subpoena witnesses, records, and conduct a hearing; all of which is in front of a jury of six people. Back in Etna's day they had to be 'good and lawful men of the county'.

In today's law the coroner presides over the inquest but the district attorney runs the inquest, presents the evidence and questions witnesses. In Etna's day the coroner had more power over those things than today.

However, a district attorney would often request certain evidence or information be obtained by the coroner at an inquest. I saw a few notes in one of the old inquest files from Etna's time where the district attorney requested that a post-mortem examination be made on a young wife thought to have been beaten. There is no indication in the record of whether that was done. But in any case it was nice to see that even in the 1870s the district attorney and other authorities would work together on these types of cases. Coroner's Inquests were much more common decades ago than they are today. Indeed, in my job as First Assistant, I ran an inquest into the cause and manner of the death of an elderly gentleman. The death was staged by an abusive caregiver. The poor gentleman was actually beaten to death, dressed in different clothing, set in a wheelchair, with food, canned peaches, jammed down his throat to suggest an accidental death. The inquest was very helpful, covered several days in length, and allowed us to gather enough evidence to convict the caregiver of murder. This was the first inquest held in my county in about 35 years.

There was a coroner's inquest into the death of Etna Bittenbender. That inquest was conducted by a Justice of the Peace. There was a law back then that called for a JP, today's district judges, to conduct inquests when the body lay more than a certain number of miles from the county seat. Indeed, even when the body was found in the county seat, Stroudsburg, the inquests I've read all appear to have been conducted, not by the coroner, but the various justices. The inquest into Etna's death was presided over by a fellow named Eugene Marsh, designated as a 'special justice of the peace. The regular JP for the Township of Hamilton was John Fenner. There is no recorded reason about why John Fenner did not conduct the inquest.

Eugene Marsh had presided over only one inquest prior to Etna's. That was in May of 1879 and involved the death of a man who had gone into the woods to chop lumber. Through a mishap, a tree that had been propped up to the tree he and his friends were cutting dislodged, fell on him, and crushed his skull. The victim, George Azor was killed instantly. At the time of Etna's inquest, Eugene Marsh was in his mid-30s and lived in Sandhill, Hamilton Township with his wife and young children. Today Sand Hill is just a collection of a few houses with an old stone bridge over the Creek. In 1880 there was a busy foundry there called the 'Marsh Foundry' which made good quality agricultural implements and parts. Eugene had been running the foundry, which was set up by his father.

Figure 1- Sand Hill Foundry site circa 1946; opened in 1848 by John Marsh. When John retired the Foundry continued under Eugene Marsh. In 1904 the Foundry burned down. It was rebuilt. After a second fire in 1914 the Foundry was moved to Stroudsburg. Notes of William Lesh Landmarks of Hamilton Township.

The old fashioned language, handwritten by Eugene Marsh states: "...[The] good and lawful men of the county... who being sworn to inquire on the part of the Commonwealth when, where, and after what manner ...Etna Bittenbender came to her death say upon their Oaths that some unknown person or persons not having the fear of God before his, her, or their eyes but being moved and seduced by the instigation of the devil on the 31st day of October 1880 between the hours of 4 O'clock p.m. and 11 O'clock a.m. the 1st day of November with force and arms on the **public road leading from Snydersville to Woodville about 2 miles from Snydersville** … Etna Bittenbender then and there being in the presence of God ... feloniously violently and of his, her, or their malice aforethought made an assault on ... Etna ,,, [and] with club and stone did violently beat ... Etna … upon the head with the stones and club ... and that Etna … came to her death at the time and place aforesaid by the force of blows of the club and stones…" . It's not the easiest read, but clear enough.

So the first clue is of a 'public road' and according to the Inquest it is there, right on the road, where Etna is attacked and murdered. That, if true, shows us a wild, brazen, reckless crime; a total lack of worry on the part of the killer or killers that they might get caught in the act. It's a public road, one of the few in the area. It connects two population centers. How busy of a road was it? We are not talking about a drive-by shooting, or a murder that would take seconds to complete. This is about killing a young girl in the prime of her life with stones and a club. The fact that this may have happened on a public road and during daylight hours is astonishing. It certainly would narrow possible suspects down to those who would fit an extreme uncontrollable mindset or a very emotionally disturbed person. But such people leave a lot of clues that connect them to the scenes of their crimes. There's usually not any real effort to clean up; so there's all kinds of transfer evidence that can be found. It is Dr. Locard's 'Exchange Principle'; whatever the killer contacts leaves traces on him and deposits something from him. Here we could expect a great amount of bloodstain and human tissue transfer, hairs, fibers, possible bodily fluids, DNA, fingerprints and maybe he would have taken belongings of the victim. There is also a whole discipline devoted to the study of sick people like that suggested by the Inquest. People, who kill for some twisted need, thrill seeking, or other dark motive. These usually build up over time. They start by fantasizing over murder or some other violent felony. They plan out the details in their minds over and over. They may reflect their fantasies in writings, drawings, music, books, movies, pornography, or similar items. They might have a history of violence in their lives. Some began by torturing other things, like small animals, slowly working their way to humans.

I have several experiences with such people in cases that we have investigated and prosecuted. One of them was the brutal murder of 21 year old Michael Goucher in 2009. Michael, a young gay man, had been seeing another young man named Shawn Freemore. Shawn and Michael had been together. Michael wanted to see Shawn again. Shawn arranged to meet Michael at a lonely spot in Price Township on Snow Hill Road. Michael drove to that spot around midnight. Shawn was waiting and got into Michael's car. Michael wanted to have sex with Shawn. Shawn agreed but told Michael they should walk under the bridge they were parked near; telling Michael they could be intimate and not worry about anyone coming up on them. Michael agreed and they exited the car and went under a bridge. The only lighting was from Michael's cell phone. Shawn had Michael sit down and he did so. Michael didn't know that Shawn's best friend Ian Seagraves was waiting for them armed with a knife and a meat cleaver. Shawn knew because he was part of a plan to kill for the thrill of it. Shawn also was armed with a knife and cleaver. Michael was brutally attacked, stabbed in the neck from behind. He struggled to break free; gaining the road he ran toward a nearby community, guided, no doubt by the single street light at the entrance to the community. He never made it; they caught him, stabbed him again and forced him into the snow covered woods, away from the light. There they stabbed and slashed him dozens of times, even after he was dead. They tried to move his car but didn't get far because they thought it ran out of gas. They took stuff from his body and his car. The stuff included a digital recorder; Michael, an organist at his local church, had recorded music he played on the church's organ. They did throw away their clothing, but not all of it. They kept the sneakers. In the days that followed they would visit the body and reflect on what they did. Eventually, they set the murder to a poem and then they turned the poem into a rap song, which they recorded on Michael's digital recorder. Both Ian and Shawn had histories predicting they were capable of such violence. They had juvenile court records and school records with disciplinary and attendance problems. There was also drug and alcohol abuse. The crime was quickly solved and the proof overwhelming because the efforts to cover their tracks weren't a real priority for them.

In Etna's murder, more work needed to be done to determine where exactly on this road the crime occurred. How busy of an area was it? Where were the nearest homes? Are there places easy to hide in nearby? Why was Etna there, at that place and time? Was it part of a routine of hers? Or was it a spur-of-the-moment decision? Where was she going and why? Did anyone know what her plans were? Why did the Inquest give such a large gap of time for when the murder had occurred; remember 4pm October 31st all the way through 11 a.m. November 1st?; that's almost a whole day, 19 hours. Was she reported missing? Did people begin to search for her? The questions go on and on. Now back in 1880 most people were unaware of the importance of trace evidence.

However, it's true that the detectives of the time, and there are examples of this in the literature, did collect subtle pieces of evidence to connect them to offenders. In fact, there are examples of that level of sophistication used by the detectives working on Etna's case. DNA was unknown, fingerprints; or at least their significance and individual characteristics, were unknown. Photography was only just beginning to be used to document scenes in more urban areas; so it's likely that many murders lacked the sophisticated clean-up efforts seen in the modern day.

The Inquest tells us the road runs from the town of Snydersville to 'Woodville'. Snydersville exists today, but Woodville does not, at least by that name. There are today about a half a dozen roads that lead from Snydersville. All those roads are public, so it is important to know whether Woodville can be identified. In Jackson Township, a few miles from Snydersville there is a small cemetery sometimes called the "Woodville Cemetery". The gravestones date to around the time of Etna's murder. The cemetery is in a small town called 'Neola'. Could Woodville be today's Neola? Sure enough, a *Pocono Record* article from 2003 talks about how old homesteads developed into towns and became hubs of industry and commerce in the county. Speaking of Jackson Township, the article relates that the towns of 'Rinkerville' and 'Woodville' became the town of Neola around 1833. Why the Inquest uses Woodville instead of Neola is unknown. Since the Woodville referred to in the Inquest is in fact Neola, we can now identify the "Public Road". The most direct road from Snydersville to Neola today is Pensyl Creek Road. It winds its way, more or less following the creek, heading northerly and westerly uphill from Snydersville. About a mile along it reaches Sand Hill, where the JP Eugene Marsh lived and worked. After a little over two miles from Snydersville it runs into Effort Neola Road. Neola is about a quarter mile from where Pensyl Creek Road runs into Effort Neola Road. So at about the two mile mark from Snydersville, identified in the Inquest as the scene of the crime, on Pensyl Creek Road, is the area where the men of the Inquest gathered to view Etna's dead body back on Monday November 1, 1880. To view the dead body at the place found was a requirement for an inquest back then. That is from the Latin term, 'in visu corporis, meaning 'upon view of the body.

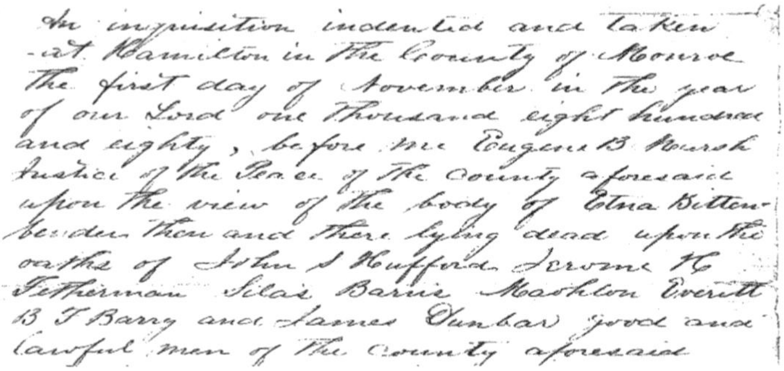
An inquisition indented and taken
at Hamilton in the County of Monroe
the first day of November in the year
of our Lord one thousand eight hundred
and eighty, before me Eugene B. Marsh
Justice of the Peace of the County aforesaid
upon the view of the body of Etna Bittenbender then and there lying dead upon the
oaths of John S Hufford Jerome K
Fetherman Silas Barrie Mahlon Everitt
B. F Barry and James Dunbar good and
lawful men of the County aforesaid

Figure 2 – An Excerpt from the Inquest

It must have been a terrible sight for them; after all they would have seen her often, perhaps in church or other gatherings, watched her grow up from a little girl to the beautiful young woman described in the accounts of the crime. It is also something that they probably would never forget. Indeed, one juror's wife, Mary Barry, sister to the Justice of the Peace Eugene Marsh wrote a poem about Etna and the murder.

The area today is thickly wooded and rises, at places steeply, on the Northern side of the road away from the Creek. On the other side of the road, towards the Creek, there is a fairly narrow strip of level land, maybe about forty yards wide. The land then drops to the Creek. Crossing the Creek the land rises steeply then levels out and borders another road called today Neola Road. Although there are a handful of houses on Pensyl Creek Road that appear to be as old or older than the time of the murder; the nearest of those houses is just outside of Sandhill, about three-quarters of a mile from the scene.

Figure 3 - The image above is a Google map close up view of the area around 2 mi from Snydersville along Pensyl Creek Road. The creek itself is not the Pensyl Creek which lies east of this location. The present day name for the creek is the Appenzell Creek. In Etna's day it may have been called the 'Little McMichaels' as it is labeled on a map from 1875. At the location of Smiley Lane intersection there would have been a bridge over the creek and then a roadway leading up to Neola Road. The portion of the road past Smiley Lane was only built after the Flood of 1955.

There is no doubt that the contours of the road are changed from Etna's day. In fact, an elderly gentleman, 88 year old John Haney told us that his dad worked for the Township and widened the roadway as part of a work crew after the floods of 1955. The two mile mark on the road is near a bridge that crosses over the creek. The road then continues toward Neola Road. I am told that bridge did not exist in Etna's day.

Figure 4 – The crime scene area as it appears today, nearly 140 years later. Etna's body was discovered just below the level of road near where the sign '599' appears. This photo can be compared to that in figure 20 taken of the same area in the 1940s. The former owner, Tom Bilheimer, recalled that his grandmother, who lived on the property for decades, often spoke of the murder and pointed to a stone marker, now removed, which memorialized the spot where Etna's corpse was found. Courtesy of Trooper Jesse Bachman, Pennsylvania State Police Forensic Services Unit.

Figure 5 – View from ground level looking up and across Pensyl Creek Road. The remains of the old stone fence are visible. Again, the body would have lain in the area of the sign. Courtesy of Trooper Jesse Bachman, Pennsylvania State Police Forensic Services Unit.

Rather, there was a different bridge, an old stone bridge that was right at the intersection of 'Smileys Lane' and Pensyl Creek Road. The old stone bridge crossed the creek then cut uphill joining Neola Road. The old bridge washed away in the flood of '55. The road system after the flood was altered. This is borne out by the remains of an old road bed and ruined bridge north of Pensyl Creek Road across Neola Road in the woods. The basic topography of the land remains the same. The hill north of the road coming all the way down to the berm, the road, the narrow level strip of land which then drops down to the creek bed and then continues up a steep hill before leveling out at Neola Road. The area is much more wooded today than it would have been in 1880. The countryside isn't as open today as it was then. Hamilton Township was very rural. Most of the population was farmers. Although the fields were much more abundant and open spaces more prevalent, there were dense patches of woods. The area of the hillside bordering Pensyl Creek Road was wooded in 1880 as it still is today.

Monroe County had two weekly newspapers circulating in 1880. The *Jeffersonian Republican* came out every Thursday and, as the name suggests, catered to the Republican residents of the county. The other paper, the *Monroe Democrat*, was printed every Tuesday; as its name suggests, had a Democrat bent. The democrats were the majority party. All the office holders in 1880, Judges, District Attorney, Sheriff, were democrats. Unfortunately, the *Monroe Democrat* newspapers have not been totally preserved. There are many years in the late 1800s which are missing from the various collections. Fortunately, we have been able to recover most, if not all of the articles written about the murder in the *Monroe Democrat*. This was in large part thanks to a bookstore owner in Stroudsburg who explained to me the practice of 'correspondence'. Correspondence involved the various newspapers sending copies of their editions to the other so that, if someone publishing in Easton was taken by a story from the *Monroe Democrat*, they could add that to their printing presses. So by researching all the archives of nearby newspapers, Easton, Bethlehem, Honesdale, Scranton etc., we were able to find more details about the case. There were also other papers from further away that took an interest in the story and even sent reporters. One of the better and most detailed of these stories was from a former correspondent with the *Reading Eagle*, a Mr. JL Guinther. At the time of the murder Mr. Guinther had been living nearby in Saylorsburg. When he got word of the horrible deed he travelled to Snydersville and the scene. He spoke to people first hand and sent the story, "Monroe County Horror", by telegraph to his former employer, the *Reading Eagle*, on Thursday November 4, 1880.

Figure 6 - This is a view of the front of the old Bittenbender farmhouse. The same house Etna visited that Sunday, October 31st 1880, to spend time with her family; the last day of her life. Her body would be brought here the following day.

Mr. Guinther writes about how Etna was found: "... the victim was a young daughter of Samuel Bittenbender. She was a little over 17 years of age. She left her parent's home about 4 last Sunday afternoon to go to the place where she was hired as a maid servant. She had to pass through the woods ... the corpse was found on Monday morning between 8 and 9 by her own sisters. They were going to school and passed the house where she was hired, when the woman of the house asked the girls where their sister was. The girls replied that she left home on Sunday afternoon to come over, and being informed that she had not been there the girls started back to inform their parents, when to their horror they found their murdered sister lying in a fence corner by the side of the public road."

Stroudsburg's *Jeffersonian Republican* in their article about the Murder titled 'Foul Murder' gives us more clues as to the location of the crime:" ...the body was found about a mile from her father's home." She had been working at the 'house of Jacob Marsh' as a housekeeper. Jacob Marsh's house was 'close by the schoolhouse' her sisters were going. The *Jeffersonian* also provides the following:"... passing through a piece of woods by a path and a road when the deed was committed."

Figure 7 - The above photograph depicts the Old Stone Barn, part of Sam Bittenbender's Farm as seen from the roadside of the modern subdivision along Dragon Head Court. It's one of the oldest Barns in the area.

From these accounts we can pinpoint with much greater accuracy the location of the crime. The key language starts with the victim being found about 1 mile from her father Samuel Bittenbender's Farm. We are told there was a 'piece of woods', a 'path', and a 'public road'. We are also told that the body was found in a 'fence corner'; that is a dry stone wall common in the area. Dry stone walls are all over the county. Farmers would pile up the stones they ploughed up, year by year on the boundaries of their fields. The area is so full of stones that they are known as 'Pocono Potatoes'. We are told that Etna was on her way to the house of Jacob Marsh that Sunday, the last day of October, and that it was 'close by' a Schoolhouse. So the question is; does the location on Pensyl Creek Road, about two miles from Snydersville, match the scene of the crime? Does this location fit the description?

First, is it a mile from the house of Samuel Bittenbender, Etna's Father? To start, we turn to the Census for the year 1880.

Figure 8- 'Milton Bittenbender 7/6/42'.

The Census that year was an incredible undertaking. During the month of June 1880, census-takers travel-ed throughout Hamilton Township, house-by-house, street by street, they recorded, by hand, the names of the people living in each home, their relationship to one another, their occupations, and ages. Also, because they went house by house we could 'canvas the neighborhood' so to speak, and get an idea of who the neighbors were. 1880 was also an Agricultural Census year. The Agricultural Census included Hamilton Township. These records are highly detailed and cover the owner of the farm, it's acreage, how many acres were dedicated to certain crops, what livestock was on the land, what part was forested, what was the value of the farm, how many crops harvested, what else was produced on the farm, such as milk and butter etc.;. These records are two very wonderful sources of information for us.

The 1880 Census tells us a lot about the Bittenbender family, Etna's family. It's a snapshot in time, the summer of 1880, the season before the murder. There we find Samuel Bittenbender, age 46, born in Pennsylvania back in 1834. The head of his household, married to Margaret, age 42, also born in the Commonwealth. Sam is by occupation a farmer. Sam and Margaret have 12 children, Eugene the oldest is 19, Sylvester 17, Etna, the oldest daughter, is 16, Ella 15, Milton 12, Tacy 13, Peter 10, Malinda 8, Alda 7, Samuel 6, Annie 4, and Little Jenny, just 2 years old. Also living with the family is Margaret's mother, 82 year old Sarah Neyhart. Sam had a very prosperous Farm; nearly 200 acres, 146 acres were under cultivation, 7 acres devoted to pasture and orchards, almost 40 acres were forested. Sam didn't show any payments to hired labor for the preceding year, apparently relying upon his numerous progeny to carry out the daily chores. The farm was incredibly productive. In 1879 he harvested 12 tons of hay, 107 bushels of Buckwheat, 112 bushels of Indian corn, 129 bushels of Oats, 100 bushels of Rye, 28 bushels of wheat, 90 bushels of potatoes, 50 bushels of apples, and cut 74 cords of wood. They also produced 250 lbs. of butter, and 50 dozen eggs from 30 chickens. They also raised pigs and cattle and had about a half-dozen horses. All their neighbors were farmers, men such as William Fleming, Solomon Rinker, John Stackhouse, Alexander Harps, and Amos Frantz.

Sam's father George was still alive in 1880. According to the census George Bittenbender senior was 70 years. He gave his occupation as a 'gentleman' and lived along today's Pensyl Creek Road about one mile from Snydersville. The house he owned still stands. Sam had several brothers and sisters, including a twin brother named George who lived in Snydersville in 1880. Unlike his twin, George was not a farmer, but a shopkeeper, selling groceries and other things right in Snydersville. The shop also had a telegraph. A newspaper article from Easton the day of the discovery of Etna's body reports, in its evening edition, that a telegraph was received from George Bittenbender announcing the murder and warning surrounding areas to be on the lookout for suspicious persons.

Figure 9 - This is a photo of the farm circa 1946 provided by the present owners of The Farmhouse. The countryside would have been remarkably similar to how it appeared in Etna's day with wide open fields.

Figure 10 - The Rees School from the photo taken by historian William Lesh circa 1946. It is located on Neola Road in the extreme Northwestern part of Hamilton Township close to the Jackson Township Line.

So, all this information points to the farm being located in Hamilton Township, nearby the suspected crime scene. His father lived on Pensyl Creek Road about a mile from Snydersville, and his twin brother living in Snydersville; but where is the farm? Remember, according to the reports it should be located only a mile from the scene. In the archives for Monroe County there's a wonderful series of maps drawn in 1875, included is a map of Hamilton Township. Luckily the map lists many of the farms and other homes in the area as they existed in 1875. For instance, the home of George Bittenbender is depicted on the map as a small black square alongside the road. The Map also shows the locations of the homes of William Fleming, Solomon Rinker, Amos Frantz, and Alexander Harps, the neighbors of Sam Bittenbender from the Census records. Right in the middle of them is a house belonging to a person named 'J. Starner'. Sam hadn't owned his farm for a long period of time before the murder. In fact, according to the deed of ownership he only purchased the property in 1877, three years before, from 'Joseph Starner and his wife'. Therefore by 1880, the location on the Map attributed to the house of 'J. Starner' had become the farm of Etna's father, Sam. So we are able to pinpoint the Bittenbender Farm on the 1875 map under the name of its previous owner, Mr. Joseph Starner.

During our investigation we were able to locate the actual farmhouse. It still stands, surrounded by a planned community of quite nice houses with well-kept yards. The house sits back a ways from the road, hidden from view, but a very old stone barn gives it away. The present owners, a young professional couple, were very helpful. Among other things, they showed us around and pointed to a stairwell with names carved into its side, many names dated to the 1940s and '50s. One of the names shown to us was that of 'Milton Bittenbender', one of Etna's younger brothers, only 12 years old at the time of the murder. They also allowed us to copy a photograph printed on a postcard from the 1940s, in black and white, showing the farm from the air. This was very helpful because the farm was still working at the time and the countryside was not crowded with suburban sprawl and fields overgrown with woods, but wide open like it would have been in Etna's day.

Figure 11 – To the right is an aerial view with a GPS overlay showing the straight line distance from the area were the body of Etna Bittenbender was found on November 1st 1880 and the Rees School House which was 'close by' her intended destination that Sunday afternoon or evening. The distance is only 920 feet, about three football fields.

The area on Pensyl Creek Road is less than a mile from the Bittenbender Farm. Indeed, a Google Maps GPS calculation puts the distance, for walking purposes, at slightly more than a mile, but that's if one was to take Smiley Lane down to Pensyl Creek, make a left and continue a bit further. It's even shorter in a beeline or as the crow flies. Do the other clues about the location of the crime scene match? In the newspaper accounts, from both the *Reading Eagle* and the *Jeffersonian Republican*, a school house was nearby. They mention Etna's destination that afternoon or evening as the house of Jacob Marsh 'close by' the school. The search for a nearby school house from Etna's time wasn't difficult at all. In fact, if you drew a straight line from the scene on Pensyl Creek Road, across the creek, and up the hill, you would run right into a one-room wood-framed schoolhouse; it is only about 300 yards away. It is painted red today, although in Etna's day it probably would have been painted gray or yellow. The school didn't close until the 1950s. The

Jeffersonian refers to the name of the school house as the 'Rinker' School. However, a local historian, the late William Lesh, refers to it as the 'Rees' School House. It does appear on the Map from 1875. It is the closest Schoolhouse to the scene and would have been the destination of Etna's brothers and sisters that Monday morning, November 1 1880; when the dreadful discovery was made.

Figure 12 - Bittenbender farm as it appears today.

What about the house of Jacob Marsh? That house is supposed to be close by the school. That is the house that the poor girl was heading to at the time of the murder. Was there a Jacob Marsh? Who was he? What was his connection to Etna? Let's start with the 1880 Census. The census for Hamilton Township lists a Jacob B. Marsh, age 46, married to Emma Marsh, age 37. The couple had several children, two still living with their parents. The oldest child at home was Wilson Marsh, almost 16, followed by his brother Curvin age 11. The prior census from the year 1870 shows that the Marsh family had an older son named Edwin. By 1880, Edwin was living in the state of Iowa. Further genealogical research shows that Jacob Marsh and Sam Bittenbender were first cousins. Jacob's mother was Anna Bittenbender, a sister of George, Etna's grandfather. Emma Marsh's maiden name is 'Rees', the same name as the school house. Even if we refer to the name' Rinker' School for the structure, it is also interesting to note that Emma's mother was a Rinker.

Emma and Jacob were members of the 'Gospel Shop', an Evangelical Church, the remains of which are located today on the property of Julia Gum just off of Neola Road. A bit further on Neola Road is a very small graveyard. It serviced members of the Gospel Shop who went on to the great beyond. Jacob Marsh lies there. Jacob died relatively young, at 48, in 1881. His widow Emma placed a poignant remembrance of her husband on the stone; "Sleep on dear husband thy work is done..."

Figure 13 - St. John's Cemetery and the headstone of Jacob Marsh located just down the road less than a quarter of a mile from the school house.

These are all good clues that the home of Jacob Marsh must have been close to our scene. In the census Jacob is listed as a farmer. However, there is an article from the 1930s out of Penington South Dakota. It deals with the life of one of its premiere and original ranchers, Wilson Marsh. Wilson recalls that his father Jacob was a 'Cooper' by trade, which is a barrel maker. Perhaps that trade along with farming is how he made a living. The 1880 Agricultural Census shows that Jacob had a modest farm where he grew crops of buckwheat, corn, some potatoes, kept a few pigs, chickens, and a couple cows for milking; not close to production levels of his cousin Sam's farm, but still a working farm in 1880.

Figure 14 - The site of the Marsh residence as it appears today, to the left is the schoolhouse, and to the right is Neola Road. This location is only 300 yards from where Etna's body was found.

The couple had no daughters which may explain why Emma Marsh needed Etna to help with keeping house.

The records of the County show that Jacob died in much debt. One of his creditors, a man named Silas Barnes, petitioned the court and obtained control over Jacob's Estate so that he could sell its assets and satisfy the debt; Mr. Barnes was also one of the inquest jurors. It is interesting to note that in 1882 Barnes sold some of the land to Eugene Marsh. Years later, in 1910 some more of the land was sold to Hamilton Township. The Deed of that transaction specifically mentions the Rees School. It would appear that in 1880 Jacob Marsh owned the land the school stands on.

So does our location match the crime scene? The final piece of that puzzle is the 1875 Map of the area. You'll recall that many of the houses in the community were drawn in with little black squares and alongside the squares, the names of the owners were written. The same was done for the Marsh home. The map shows that the house of Jacob Marsh and his family was right next to the school; on the same side of the road, first the house, and then the school.

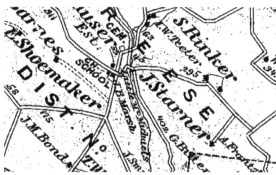

Figure 15 - This is a close up focusing on the 1875 Map of Hamilton Township, notice it lists, side by side the School and house of Jacob Marsh. It is very close to the Bittenbender home (Marked J.Starner), little over a mile away. The Creek Road, right at the bend, across from the 'le' of Little McMichaels is the area where the body was found. The distance to the Marsh residence is under 300 yards. Also depicted is the configuration of the bridge over the Little McMichaels which was straight across from Smiley Lane. The bridge crosses the stream then turns to the left and goes up Neola Road. Just beyond the bridge is a cemetery where Jacob Marsh lies buried.

The final connection that needs to be made is finding the path described in the accounts. They are quite detailed; the body was alongside the public road and a path, lying in a stone fence corner. Our scene is along a public road. It matches the distance from her family's farm and Etna's intended destination. But is there evidence of a path? A path at that location would have saved Etna about a half of mile or so of walking. She could have decided to walk along the road to the Marsh house. She could have avoided the woods leading down to the Creek Road. She could have walked along Smiley Lane down the hill, over the bridge, and arrived at the Marsh residence. Instead, Etna took a shortcut; a fateful decision; one memorialized in a poem of the tragedy written by Mrs. Mary Barry.

Detective Kerchner and I walked all around the scene looking for signs of a path. We assumed that the many Bittenbender children would have used that shortcut going to and from school. Because the school was operating into the 1950s, we believed that a path would have been fairly well worn through the patch of woods.

Figure 16 – The gap in the stone fence marking the end of Sam's fields looking back toward the Bittenbender farm.

Figure 17 – This is the approximate location where the old stone marker was set up to commemorate the spot where Etna's body was discovered. Compare the photograph taken by William Lesh (figure 21) which depicts the stone. Courtesy of Trooper Jess Bachman, Pennsylvania State Police Forensic services Unit.

One of the first things we did was walk the former fields of Sam Bittenbender's Farm; leaving the house and walking through what were once apple orchards and fields of buckwheat, Indian corn, rye, and potatoes. We could see where the original wood line was located, because the area was bounded by a fairly wide dry stone wall or fence; representing season after season of plowing the fields. Then we came upon a gap in the wall of about four feet; where Sam's fields ended and the patch of Woodland began. This spot had to be where the Path first entered the woods. We walked through the Gap and made our way down the slope. Most of the trees are evergreen. However, many of them are dead or dying of some kind of blight. Many fallen trees blocked our path. It was hard to discern, after all those years, the way the path would have taken. But we proceeded on the assumption that it would be a path of least resistance. In other words, where the slope was most gentle in its descent; along that line we proceeded down the hill arriving at Pensyl Creek Road.

Figure 18 – A closer view of the crime scene area. Note the remains of the stone fence, the level of the road is higher than the foreground. This area is also close by the location where the foot path crosses the road and continues down to the creek. Courtesy of Trooper Jesse Bachman, Forensic Services Unit, Pennsylvania State Police.

Once we reached the road we looked across to Tom Billheimer's land, the narrow strip between the road and the creek. It seemed to us that the most natural exit from the patch of woods was directly across an access path made, according to Tom, by the workmen who put an in ground pool on the property. It seems like the path would have been where the pool is today. We saw stones piled up in that area. Although now they supported the road bed, we knew the road had been widened. The stones were field stones, indistinguishable from those that would make up a stone fence. We then walked straight across the level stretch of ground to the creek. Detective Kerchner, who intensely dislikes the outdoors and is naturally sweaty, even during inactivity, was very happy to have finished our walk. It was a good drop down to the creek bed. Someone could easily hide in that place. Certainly people on the road wouldn't be able to see someone several feet below down in the creek. The whole place has a gloomy and dark aspect to it. It is strange, but the walk started out bright and open as we crossed Sam's fields; but once we left those old fields, it grew somber and darker the closer we got to the creek. Looking across the creek bed we could see how one would make their way up the hill toward the schoolhouse and the site where the home of Jacob and Emma Marsh once stood.

It isn't easy to figure out in your mind's eye the scene as it appeared almost a hundred and forty years ago. We saw much evidence, still on the land, but we wanted to search further back in time for any documentation of the area. We found some. One of the most helpful was from a website put out by Penn State University which contains aerial photographs of Pennsylvania. Multiple years are available for these photographs, but the oldest of our area is dated October 31st 1938, 58 years to the day Etna was last seen alive. The population census and statistics told us the population of the area didn't change much between 1880 and 1938. The area was still rural and the ground cover that characterizes the area today was absent. The photograph is high quality. As we studied it we saw the Bittenbender Farm. At that time the land was owned by Milton Bittenbender, Etna's younger brother, the same Milton who carved his name into the stairway of the farmhouse. We could see the orchards, the fields, and the patch Woodland. We could see the road and the course of the old bridge. We could see the schoolhouse; the Marsh home was already gone by then.

Figure 19 – This is an aerial photograph of the scene taken October 31st 1938. The landmarks are labeled. On the following page we provide a closer view of the path Etna took on October 31st, 1880.

Figure 20 – This photograph shows the path Etna took starting from her home and ending at the crime scene. The red line marks Etna's walk, beginning at the Bittenbender Farm (far right corner of photograph) and trailing westward (Path through Woods), ending at the "Crime Scene". The red line which continues beyond the 'crime scene' shows the route Etna was intending to take to the Marsh Farm before her travels were brutally ended and her life snuffed out.

As we looked closer, we could make out a faint line traveling from the Bittenbender farmhouse, over the fields; it became more pronounced down through the woods to the road, across the creek, and tracing up the hill to the school. This was the path taken by Etna on her last day. Alongside that path and the road was where Etna's body was found.

Figure 21 - The Triangular Stone marking the scene today. Perhaps someone some years ago recognized the significance of this place and arranged the large stone as a remembrance so the scene's connection to the terrible crime would not be forgotten.

Examining the scene from a distance gives us insight into potential leads. Among the first thoughts; was the murder triggered by opportunity? In other words, was Etna just in the wrong place at the wrong time? Did someone take advantage of the situation and attack the girl leading to her rape and then murder? The belief that this was a random attack was one of the most prevalent theories of the first investigators. What if the killer or killers were passing through the area when they saw the pretty farm girl, all alone, with night coming on, and decided to take her? This theory came to be known as the 'Tramp Theory'. Tramps were all over the place in those days. Tramps were landless men, drifters, traveling the countryside looking for work or stealing to survive. The newspaper accounts are full of stories about the crimes they committed or at least were accused of committing. The Tramp Theory is supported by evidence found at the scene and witness accounts. The other thought that comes to mind looking at this scene is that this was some kind of inside job. In other words, the killer was local or at least local enough to know Etna's comings and goings. What are the odds that at the same time she's making her way back to the Marsh Farm, taking the isolated route through the woods, she would be attacked and murdered? Well the odds are a lot lower if you figure the killer was aware of her plans. The fact that this could have been an inside job was the other predominant theory; the local theory is also supported by evidence.

One thing is clear, regardless of which theory is right, the killer or killers were very reckless and bold. They would have had to take the victim by force, fairly close to her intended destination, the Marsh home. They would need a secluded enough place to rape her; somewhere she would not be seen or heard. It doesn't make sense for the rape to happen in the same spot where her body was found. It was too open; practically up on the road within sight of the bridge looking north and fifty yards or so looking south toward Sandhill.

Figure 22 - The above photo also from William Lesh's pamphlet. It shows a stone marker just below the level of the road marking the site where the body was found. When describing the scene as it appeared in the 1940s Lesh also notes the bold, daring, and reckless location for the crime. But he believed the assault and the murder happened in the same place, something the authors disagree with. The stone marker no longer exists; apparently it was removed when the road was widened in the 1950s.

One thing the original detectives agreed upon was that whoever did the crime, whether 'tramp' or local, it was premeditated. She was stalked, ambushed, and murdered. This belief is borne out in Ms. Barry's Poem, set to the tune of Sweet Home, the sad poem, taken from Mr. Lesh's pamphlet on the Landmarks of Monroe County, which has been modified somewhat to correct apparent typos (*poem follows*):

T'was on a Sunday evening, the autumn winds did blow,
A patch of woods lay on her way, through which she had to go
And what was lurking in those woods, the poor girl, she did not know.
She said, "This path is lonely, but I will venture through;
There is nothing there to harm me; my heart is young and true."
A cruel thought deceived her, a girl so young and fair,
For a fiend more cursed than Satan soon had her in the snare.
In vain she cried, "Oh father and mother do come near,
My anguish is so very great, much more I cannot bear."

No father or companion came; no helping hand was near,
The torture of this dreadful work, the lonely girl must bear.
And then she called on Jesus, on Jesus name alone,
And her request granted he saved her by his love.
And now she rests in Paradise, in that bright land so fair,
No wicked man can harm her more, no sin can enter there.

Figure 23- This is one of William Lesh's photos taken around 1946 of the crime scene. The slope of the hill on the upper left as it comes down to the road and the existence of the guardrails line up nicely with the present day scene. The photograph shows the clear line of sight coming from both directions. For someone to carry out a prolonged crime such as a rape in this open area just doesn't pass the common sense test. Although the body was found here the assault and rape must have taken place in a more secluded location nearby.

Figure 24 – The gravestone of Mr. and Mrs. Barry at the Kellersville Methodist Church Cemetery.

Chapter 2

The Crime Scene

*"A crime scene may appear static but is
replete with the expressions of movement
which replay the murder, its prelude, and its
aftermath."*

Michael Mancuso

The crime scene, the place where a murder happens, is usually the heart of a case. There is so much that can be learned about a crime from looking around the scene that is hard to put it in words. You can get all kinds of information about the crime, about the killer, the motivations, the state of mind, premeditation, the number of killers, the method or means used; the possibilities really are endless. I have visited many scenes where you pick up valuable information that you would never have without a first-hand look. We are lucky there was such good and detailed coverage about the crime scene of Etna's murder. Knowing the scene, its layout, what was nearby, the terrain, and using that knowledge and comparing it to the details collected in the old accounts of the crime, helps us tie up a lot of loose ends. It helps in answering important questions about the case, its investigation, and it points us in the direction that will lead to the guilty party.

I have seen how, overtime, as the evidence is being processed, documented, examined, talked about, and analyzed, you really start getting a picture of what happened. During a murder trial I always try to show the jury, step-by-step, how the investigation unfolds. How each piece of evidence at the scene is documented and examined, how it relates to the big picture; it's subtle, almost imperceptible; the build-up through the trial of pieces of evidence shown to the jury, talked about, connected to other pieces of evidence. It creates a kind of net that traps the guilty party. Many times they don't even realize it. A criminal defendant can sit in prison waiting for their murder trial for a couple years. They will get copies of all the reports, videos, photographs of the crime scene, evidence logs, lab results, witness statements, you name it, but for some reason they don't see the significance of it all. A lot of times they really think their defense will be strong or that the evidence against them is very weak and inconsequential. So as the trial goes on and the same evidence is walked through, step by step, usually in a different way than the defendant may have thought it would be, by the end of the trial the picture is pretty clear. A lot of times a defendant won't even know the total effect of the evidence until closing argument. It is one of the favorite parts of preparing for a trial; hard work, painstaking work, frustrating work, but in the end satisfying. Not only does the jury convict, but you have the satisfaction of knowing that they did so because of the truth. You see 'verdict' comes from Latin and means simply for the jury 'to speak the truth'.

As we examined the old accounts of Etna's murder we analyzed the details and clues that the early investigators noted. Are the things they saw what we would expect to see? In other words, does the crime scene square with what we would expect? What was in place and expected versus what was out of place or missing? A lot of times what is expected but missing proves critical to a case. Take for instance the Nicolosi case, sixty nine year old Eleanor Nicolosi was charged with killing her husband Francis. His body was found in an apple orchard on their property just a couple hundred yards from their home. Ironically, the home was located off of Devil's Hole Road in Paradise Township. Francis or 'Nicky' as he was known to his friends was shot multiple times. It looked like he tried to run from his killer while being shot and eventually fell dead. The murder weapon, a .38 caliber revolver, was never recovered. The killer had covered the body with carpet taken from Nicky's pickup truck. Also lying next to the body was Nicky's baseball cap emblazoned with the Knights of Columbus Chapter he belonged to. The defense claimed that the killer or killers of Mr. Nicolosi were outsiders; maybe drug addicts entering the property illegally and looking for loot, or people with whom he had problems. But in any case, the defense maintained that the killer came from outside the property; this would have naturally excluded Nicky's wife, the elderly Eleanor Nicolosi.

A victim's body is also part of the crime scene. In the Nicolosi Case there was a problem with the victim's right big toe, not his toe specifically, but what wasn't on it but should have been; you see something was missing. Through the trial I had the state police investigators identify photographs of the body at the scene. These included close-up shots of the sneakers Nicky had on when his body was discovered. Later we displayed autopsy photos, including pictures of his socks and even bare feet. I also put into evidence Nicky's sneakers and socks. The sneakers, white in color, were clean and free of stains. When the right sneaker was removed and we looked at Nicky's white sock there was a nice round blood stain over the big toe. However, when the sock was removed the toe was uninjured, no cut, no blood, no damage at all. How did his sock have a blood stain on the toe; a stain caused by a single drop of blood, what's called a passive blood drop, the kind of drop that's made when blood, through the process of gravity, falls uninterrupted onto a surface, and yet the sneaker was clean and the toe uninjured? Although the basic facts were brought out during the trial, this big toe mystery wasn't explained, not until closing argument. Then the jury was shown how these pieces of evidence connected. The only conclusion that made sense was that the shoe was off when the blood dropped onto the sock. It was used to show that the killer was not an outsider but somebody who still had feelings for the victim. It was in line with the fact that the body was covered with pieces of carpet taken from Nicky's own pickup truck. Somebody who didn't want Nicky's body to lie exposed to the elements would have been motivated to cover him. When someone dies a violent death, say shot multiple times while running, it is not uncommon for them to lose a shoe. The twisting, the contorting, the dynamics of a killing often result in a shoe coming off. No outsider would bother to put the sneaker back on Nicky's foot; but his wife Eleanor would. The evidence when viewed in context showed that during the murder Nicky's shoe came off and as he laid there dead Eleanor put the shoe back on; covering the blood-stained sock with the clean sneaker. The jury found Eleanor Nicolosi guilty of murder in the first degree. But this wasn't the last time I had to try her for murdering Nicky.

The Pennsylvania Superior Court granted her appeal and reversed the conviction based upon hearsay evidence. A close friend of Nicky's, a man named Mario Caltabiano had testified that Nicky came to visit him a couple weeks before the murder and confided to him that recently he had been walking in the orchard with his wife. He was a bit ahead of her when, as he turned around he saw her pull out from her brassiere a .38 caliber revolver. He was startled. He asked her why she had the gun. She told him she had it for protection and asked him to show her how to shoot it. He then took the gun and showed her how to shoot it, firing a couple rounds at a tree. The Superior Court felt that the story denied the defendant a fair trial and so we were back to square one.

In preparing for the second trial I felt like something was missing, something that would also show that the killer was not from the outside. The defense was now aware of the connection between the bloody sock and the murder that was made in the first trial. They would try to counter it in some way. But one thing I kept looking at were the photographs; over and over of the scene, the evidence at the scene, the condition of the body. Something didn't seem right. Something I had not noticed before. During the first trial, the defense had put into evidence a photo album of Nicky and Eleanor. It was clear that Eleanor put the album together after Nicky's death. The album contained many photos of the couple and all were happy. The idea was to show that since she loved and missed him she did not kill him. I looked over the album at the time of the first trial and thought it was not a big deal. But other than that I didn't give it a thought. Then, when getting ready for the retrial, as I was looking over photos of the body at the scene, something struck my eye, something that wasn't there; where was Francis Nicolosi's wedding ring? What happened to it? I thought I saw photos of him wearing his wedding ring? So I went back, I got the photo album and I poured through it. There, in every single photograph, Francis Nicolosi was wearing his wedding band. But when his body was found there was no ring to be seen. One of the initial responders to the crime scene had contact with Eleanor the day the body was discovered. He had the good instincts to take photographs of Eleanor Nicolosi that very day. This was done to document whether or not she was injured, her general appearance, that sort of thing. There was one photo in particular, of Eleanor with both arms outstretched that caught the eye. There I saw that on her left hand she was wearing not one but two wedding bands. There it was another piece of evidence to show that she, not an outsider, killed her husband. It was like part of a ritual; she put the sneaker back on, covered the body with carpet to keep it from being exposed, and took his wedding band for safekeeping, placing it with hers. Mrs. Nicolosi was convicted a second time of murder in the first degree. This time her appeals were denied.

Etna's murder was a brutal sight to behold. The seventeen year old girl with long black hair, who was described as 'beautiful', 'stylish', and 'quite the belle', now lay dead and battered. The scene was by all accounts a disturbing, disgusting, and bloody mess. "She was lying beside the fence on a heap of stones by the roadside, the club which laid near the victim stained with blood and spotted with brains, even the stones and fence were spattered with blood and brains." (A Horrible Murder: *Hackettstown Gazette*, Friday November 12, 1880). "Her brains scattered over the fence and stones were she lay" (*The Evening Gazette*, Port Jervis New York, Tuesday November 2, 1880). "Her head was completely smashed the cracks of such size as to make the brain visible." (*Hackettstown Gazette*, November 11, 1880). "Her head was nearly mashed and full of holes made by a club with a knot in it and by a sharp pointed stone, both of which were lying near the body with the hair of her head sticking to them." (*Jeffersonian Stroudsburg*, November 4, 1880). "... [t]he girls started back to inform their parents, when to their horror they found their murdered sister lying in a fence corner by the side of the public road. They ran home and told their father that their sister was shot. He immediately ran to the scene and found his daughter had been most cruelly murdered. Her head was lying on a stone, and lying near her were stones and a club, which had been used to kill her. Her head was fearfully battered and broken; five or six different gashes were in the skull, so that a person could look right into it and her brain was lying out..." (Monroe County Horror: *Reading Eagle*, November 5, 1880).

The district attorney, David Stokes Lee, called for an autopsy, or post-mortem examination, as they were often called, to take place. The post-mortem report is lost to history. Luckily its main findings are detailed in the press accounts. "The post-mortem examination revealed the following facts: there were several large wounds on the forehead and scalp ranging from 1 and 1/2 to 4 and 1/2 inches in length, all penetrating to the skull, and three of them penetrating the brain. On removing the scalp the whole of the right side of the skull was found to be crushed and also the brain was found to be wounded in four places, and the right side engorged with blood. No disease of any of the organs in the chest or abdomen was discovered. Some indications of an attempted outrage were discovered, but the opinion of the physicians on this point has not been made public. The report circulated that the murdered woman was enceinte (pregnant) is not true, as shown by the post-mortem. The post-mortem examination was made by doctors JP Mutchler of Stroudsburg, assisted by doctors Rogers Levering, Hagerman and Gregory of Hamilton Township in the presence of the Squire Fenner of Sciota. All Physicians fully agreed in the above report." (*Jeffersonian Republican*, Thursday November 4, 1880).

The murder weapons were found on the ground right next to the body. The club with the knot in it had been 3 feet in length but was found broken into pieces. (*Wayne County Herald*; from *Monroe Democrat*, November 11, 1880). The broken club was obviously used in the victim's murder. It was also documented in the Coroner's Inquest. The blood, brain, and hair sticking to the weapon showed that it was used to batter the victim's head. It was collected in evidence and stored for many decades in the Monroe County Courthouse, waiting the day when it would be needed in court for trial against the guilty party. There were also signs of an additional weapon or weapons used; namely, either one or more rocks were used to batter Etna's head. One of the stones is described as 'large', 'pointed', and bloodied. The Inquest also mentions not just a club but also a 'stone' or 'stones' used in the murder. These

48

too were found lying next to her body and collected in evidence and stored in the courthouse.

It is a common feature in murder cases that juries are instructed that they may presume that a killer had the intent to kill where the evidence shows that a deadly weapon was used on a vital area of the victim's body. Repeated blows to the head with a club and stones clearly shows that Etna's killer or killers had the specific intent, desire, and purpose to kill her. I have only had one experience where a stone or large rock was used to kill in a case that I prosecuted. Luis Vasquez had planned to murder Bertoldo Velez and his friend Joe King. Velez had been loan sharking, and Vasquez had owed him money. At some point Vasquez decided to kill both men rather than face the consequence of not paying the debt. The murders were premeditated, Vasquez, wearing latex gloves, walked up to the men, defenseless, sitting in their car, and opened fire with a 9mm handgun; emptying the gun into both King and Velez. He then walked around the car, to the driver side, and pulled the dying Velez out of the car; he got a large rock, then straddled Velez, and repeatedly struck him in the head. Blood, brain, and skull covered the stone and what is referred to as 'cast off' and 'impact spatter' was found throughout the parking lot. The top of Mr. Velez's head was gone.

The massive skull and brain injuries weren't the only injuries found on Etna's body. Her body bore evidence of a 'severe struggle' (*Wayne County Herald*, November 11, 1880). In fact, the blows to her skull were only the final act, a coup de grace, in a horrible ordeal for the young girl. Etna may have been killed in that fence corner, but the crime scene was much larger than that area. The investigators had followed a long blood trail; the length of which varied with the accounts, but all are consistent with one thing; that the blood trail began in the patch of woods where the path first left the open fields. "From all appearances there was a terrible struggle for it was about 200 yards or over from the public road where the body was found to the place back in the woods where they traced the first drop of blood." ('Monroe County Horror', *Reading Eagle*, November 5, 1880). "... [t]he side of the highway for about 300 yards shows evidence of a terrible struggle and there is a track of blood from the point where the girl is supposed to have first been struck to the spot where her dead body was found."(*Easton Daily Free Press*, from Stroudsburg, November 18, 1880).

What happened between the initial attack in the woods, and the brutal murder? How much time was there between the attack and the murder? What was the motive for the attack? How many people were involved? What was the time of her death? These are all questions that need to be answered in order to forward the case. We need to go back to the evidence at the scene and the circumstances of finding the body in order to answer these questions. Like I said the scene is the heart of the case. All the signs point to a sexual assault. The old saying is that someone will be known by their deeds. In this case the signs of sexual assault are clear and point to the motive. But can we say that Etna was sexually assaulted, raped somewhere nearby after she was attacked? The doctors at the inquest did not make those findings public. But the *Jeffersonian Republican* reported that the doctors found signs of an 'attempted outrage.' 'Outrage' was the word commonly used for a sexual assault. The doctors don't detail what signs of an attempted outrage were found. Was Etna a virgin? Was her hymen found to be intact during the post-mortem? We don't have the answers to those questions. We do know that there was a rumor in the community falsely claiming that she was pregnant; that was debunked by the autopsy. It is also possible that by reporting only signs of an attempted outrage the doctors were trying to avoid the details of a horrible personal tragedy and spare the family. They would be acting out of a sense of modesty and in keeping with the times. The accounts about rape are split. Some accounts stick to the attempted rape angle. Other accounts, without question conclude that Etna was raped and then murdered.

"She had to pass through the woods and she was watched, as is supposed, by some person who knew of her coming. He attacked her about two hundred yards from the public road, undoubtedly for the purpose of outrage; but from all appearances he did not accomplish his design, and then probably, upon her threatening that she would betray him, he committed the murderous deed." (Monroe County Horror, *Reading*

Eagle, November 4, 1880). "No motive is known for the commission of this crime, unless the bloody-handed outlaws attempted to violate her person and outraged by her resistance and cries for help and from fear of discovery or pursuit committed a cold-blooded murder." (*The Gazette Hackettstown*, Friday November 12, 1880). "It is presumed that Miss Bittenbender while passing along the highway at a lonely spot was confronted by her assailant, who made indecent proposals which she disregarded, when he dealt her a blow on the head with a stone felling her to the ground. Medical examination has revealed the fact that the villain then succeeded in his designs." (*Somerset Herald*, Tracking a Murderer, Stroudsburg November 18, 1880).

The issue of whether Etna was raped is important to the investigation. Somebody might wonder why it is important if she was raped or if it was only an attempted rape; why that would matter. In today's day and age whether she was raped would be critical. Obtaining a DNA sample for instance during the autopsy, or upon her clothing, could lead to the identity of the rapist and therefore the murderer. That was not an option for the original investigators. Knowing if she was actually raped helps answer other important questions. Concluding that the attack was only an attempted rape presupposes that Etna resisted being raped to the point where she either was killed outright or managed to flee briefly, was caught, and then killed. In other words, we're talking about a crime that happens relatively quickly, maybe in a matter of minutes. On the other hand, if she was raped and then murdered we're talking about a longer period of time; a sustained attack. It's even longer if more than one person is involved. So for one thing the question of rape versus attempted rape helps determine the time of death. There are very disturbing signs that show this was not an attempted rape followed by an impulsive quick murder, but a vicious sustained sexual assault and a murder that can be likened to an execution.

We had to figure out the time of death. There are clues which indicate that an interval of hours occurred between the initial attack upon Etna near the wood line and her murder. Certainly her family would not want to imagine the horror of her rape and suffering prior to her death at the hands of her killer or killers. Etna's family had inscribed certain clues onto her gravestone. The language is unique because it gives an actual time of death, not only the day or day of the week, but the actual time of day. Further, the time inscribed on the gravestone is much narrower than the official findings from the Inquest. On the gravestone, right below the family name, Sam and Margaret had the following inscription carved into the stone: "Murdered by some person unknown on Sunday Evening October 31st 1880. Between the hours of 4 and 6 O'clock."

Figure 25 - Engraved on Etna's cemetery head stone.

This is the narrowest time for the murder; just two hours; four to six p.m., late afternoon on October 31, the Sunday that she spent with her family. Basically, the Bittenbender family put the time of their daughter's murder right after she walked off her father's fields into the woods heading towards the home of Jacob Marsh. "The girl left her father's house shortly after 4 p.m. to return to her employer, this being the last time that she was seen until she was found weltering in her own blood." (*Wayne County Herald*, from the *Monroe Democrat*, November 11, 1880). How could they be so sure? Or was it merely a hope, a prayer that their beloved daughter didn't suffer for hours. Compare that time frame to the finding of the Inquest. The official Inquest notes that the murder occurred between 4 p.m. on October 31 and 11 a.m. on November 1.

This is the widest swath of time for the murder. It takes the time 4 p.m., which undoubtedly is the time that Etna's family believed she left the farm to head back toward the Marsh House and eleven a.m. the next day. One of the duties of coroners is to pronounce death and they record the time for that. But the time of pronouncement of death is not the same as the time of death. The official pronouncement of death occurs when the coroner, in this case the special Justice of the Peace Eugene Marsh, arrived at the site where the body lay and began his official inquiry. The summoning of the jurors, the swearing of the jury, its view of the body would have commenced the inquest. That is the time when the death would be pronounced. That would have happened at 11:00 a.m. on November 1, 1880.

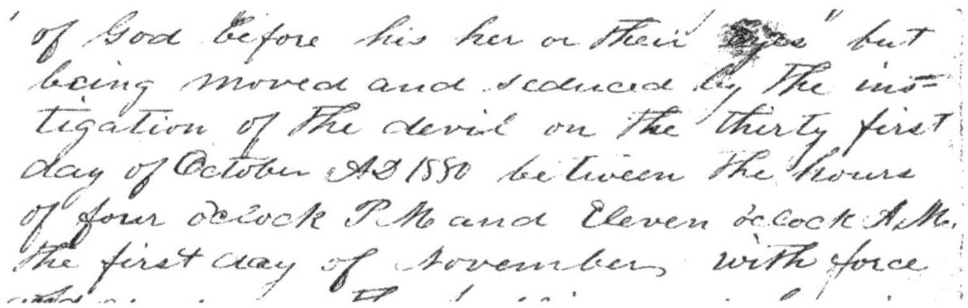

Figure 26 – Part of the Coroner's Inquest; "...on the thirty first day of October AD 1880 between the hours of four o'clock PM and eleven o'clock AM the first day of November..."

We know from the accounts that Etna's body was discovered between eight and nine that morning by her little sisters who, going to school, turned back after being told by Emma Marsh that Etna had never showed up the night before. On their way back home to tell their parents what Emma Marsh told them, the children came across their sister's body battered in the fence corner. "The corpse was found between eight and nine by her own sisters." (Monroe County Horror, *Reading Eagle*, Friday November 5, 1880). Although the *Jeffersonian* puts the discovery at 11 a.m. as the children are returning from school. This appears to be an error in that it makes no mention of the discussion Emma Marsh had with Etna's sisters which prompted them to head back home having just arrived for school. So if we exclude the time after the discovery of the body by Etna's little sisters, that still gives a time of death as anywhere between 4 p.m. Sunday till 9 a.m. Monday morning; basically, a window of 17 hours. Here's the problem with that, not so much a problem but a disturbing clue; from the blood trail traced back to the path through the woods, beginning at the edge of Sam Bittenbender's Fields, we know

Etna had to be attacked shortly after she left home. Is it possible that even though she was attacked around four in the afternoon she wasn't murdered until many hours later?

Figure 27 -Emma Marsh as she appeared circa1900 from RH Marsh. "They were going to school and passed the house where she was hired, when the woman of the house asked the girls where their sister was. They replied that she left home on Sunday afternoon to come over, and being informed she had not been there the girls started back to inform their parents, when, to their horror they found their murdered sister lying in a fence corner by the side of the public road..."(Monroe County Horror Reading Eagle Thursday November 4, 1880).

Now figuring out the time of death is a tricky thing. Forensic pathologists hate to get pinned down on a time of death. They cry foul every time you try to get them to talk about it. They will tell you there are too many variables; the weather, temperature, the age of a victim, the body type, the specific cause of death, all those things and more make it speculation to try to pinpoint the time of death based on the condition of the remains and stages of decomposition. But in my job the tighter the time frame of when a murder victim died, the more you can show who had the opportunity to do the deed, what story or alibi can hold water, and what doesn't. But we never go by just the condition of the remains to figure time of death. Instead we look at any evidence that might help pinpoint the time of death. Traditionally this includes retracing a victim's last known activities. In today's age that would usually include cell phone extraction, social media activity, surveillance cameras, computer forensics, 911 recordings, and all the other trappings of modern life.

Nevertheless, the body of a murder victim is evidence; if the body is found at the scene of the crime that body is part of the scene. After death there are certain changes that happen to a body, changes that are measurable; things such as' lividity', 'rigor mortis, a cooling of the body, 'marbling' of the skin, infestation by insects, etc.; all follow predictable patterns. By no means can you pinpoint exactly to the minute or hour the time of death, but you do get a time frame.

Sometimes this evidence is highly important. Take for instance the cold case murder of twenty seven year old Kristen Wagner. In 2011 her body was found in a broken commercial 'reefer' trailer in a scrapyard at Crowe Road, East Stroudsburg. The yard was owned by James Bidwell who ran a garbage hauling business called 'Christian Waste'. Wagner's body was found hanging from the ceiling of the trailer. Industrial heating/cooling wire was fashioned into a loop and wrapped around some aluminum caging and used to suspend the body. The first investigators called it a suicide and that's how it stood for over five years. We brought the case through the grand jury. Detectives Rich Luthcke and Wendy Serfass both did a great job building the case. Eventually, Mr. Bidwell was brought to trial. The jury found him guilty of first degree murder.

One of the key pieces of evidence was the condition of the body at the scene. Luckily, some of the original investigators took multiple photographs of the body as it hung from the caging. In these photographs lividity was noted over her lower back. Lividity or 'livor mortis' has been described as a purple or similar coloring to the skin from the settling of blood in a deceased person. The settling of blood into the skin results from gravitational forces. Lividity only occurs after a person is already dead and only to those areas which, depending on how the body lay after death, would be subject to gravity. It can be noticeable as early as twenty minutes after death. There was no reason for Ms. Wagner's lower back to show signs of lividity if she died by hanging. The sign was unmistakable. It showed that Ms. Wagner wasn't hung until after death. In fact, she must have lain on her back for at least twenty minutes or so before her dead body was suspended by the wire. This is an example of how a murder victim's body while at the scene is part of the crime scene. Also, the lividity on her lower back was not fixed. This meant that by the time of her autopsy the next day the lividity had already shifted and was gone. If detailed photographs of the scene with the body in situ were not taken, this key evidence would never have been captured and a murderer may have escaped justice.

One of the saddest things that I do involves the investigation and prosecution of child deaths. In some of these parents or caregivers sometimes provide information about when they last saw the child alive that doesn't match the condition of the body. For instance, if a parent says less than an hour went by since he or she last checked on the baby and the baby was fine and now, an hour or so later, the baby is dead, there shouldn't be a stiffening of the limbs suggesting rigor mortis. Rigor mortis is like a bell curve of sorts where the muscles contract, stiffen, and then gradually the stiffness subsides. Rigor mortis usually takes 3 to 6 hours to set in with a maximum stiffness at about 12 hours. The rigor then will subside over time disappearing by degrees until no sign remains after about twelve hours. Although many factors affect the onset and duration of rigor, that's the general rule; 12 hours from death to maximum rigor and another 12 hours until the absence rigor mortis.

56

It is of keen interest that there is no mention of Etna's body showing any signs of rigor mortis. There is a mention of her body being 'cool to the touch'; but no rigor mortis. The doctors of the day, including Dr. Mutchler of Stroudsburg who was the lead physician at the autopsy, would have known the significance of rigor mortis and its usefulness in establishing a tighter time frame for death. Why wasn't that mentioned here? Is it because there were no signs of rigor mortis? The fact that the Inquest gives such a wide range for the time of death and fails to mention any evidence of rigor mortis, leaves us with two possibilities; one is that the body had been dead for so long that rigor had already come and gone, which would have required around 24 hours or so. That is not possible if Etna was last seen alive at 4 pm on October 31. The second is that the body had been dead for only a few hours; not enough time for rigor to set in.

Because the body was cool to the touch, we wanted to know the temperature that night from Sunday late afternoon October 31, 1880 to Monday morning November 1, 1880. There was no real way to look into historical records on weather stations, that sort of thing didn't exist back then, at least not locally. One of the things that we found interesting was that there were evening edition newspapers in nearby communities. Some of those papers recorded the temperatures that morning. One of the papers was Easton's *Daily Free Press*. Its Evening Edition recorded an early morning temperature for November 1, 1880 at 46 degrees Fahrenheit. Based on the fact that Monroe County typically experiences cooler temperatures than in the Lehigh Valley, we estimate the temperature to be in the low 40s or so that Sunday night into Monday morning. If Etna had been alive and exposed to those temperatures for hours on end she would have been cool to the touch, even if she'd only been dead for a few hours prior to discovery.

This evidence so far suggests that Etna was alive for longer than the two hour time frame written on the grave stone. But it's possible that her corpse reacted outside the norm, developing rigor quicker and its dissipating quicker than the normal curve suggested in the illustration above. It's also possible she was killed soon after she entered the woods. But this is at odds with the circumstances. Not only the condition of the body, the absence of finding rigor mortis, the blood trail starting up in the woods; but at odds with witness accounts as well. I don't mean eyewitnesses; but people who were in the area, more than one, who should have seen or heard something. After all, Etna's body was found lying alongside a well-used path and a public road, close to an intersection and a bridge.

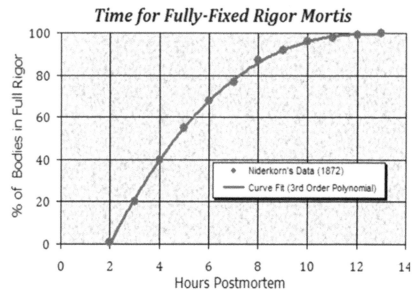

Figure 28- An old Rigor Mortis Curve Chart incorporating data from an 1872 Study. The significance of rigor to the case would have been recognized by the investigators.

There's a church in Woodville, today Neola, a Methodist Church, which dates back to Etna's time. In 1880 a young reverend, only 26 years old, was assigned there. His name was Francis A. Gilbert, married to Sally, 21 years old, no children. Reverend Gilbert was traveling that Halloween evening, Sunday October 31, 1880. "Reverend Gilbert of the M.E. Church passed within one quarter of a mile of the scene of the tragedy at about 6 p.m. and while thus passing along heard faint groans and cries, supposing that some little girl was being whipped, he paid no further attention to the same." (*Wayne County Herald*, from *Monroe Democrat*, November 11, 1880).

Figure 29 - Reverend Gilbert's Church as it looked in his day.

The late William Lesh relates a similar story: "The writer remembers hearing it said that Reverend Francis Gilbert, Methodist preacher at Neola, was traveling from his home in Cherry Valley and at the time the deed was committed was on the road leading from Miles Kirkuff, to the Sciota-Neola Road. He reported having heard screams, he thought a family lived near and made no investigation." (*'Landmarks of Monroe County'*; William S. Lesh, Compiled and Edited by Henry C. Hoffman, Brodheadsville Pennsylvania).

Figure 30 - The late William Lesh local historian and educator.

Mr. Lesh was writing in the 1940s. The Miles Kirkuff he mentions lived in Kellersville, Hamilton Township, just down the road from Snydersville. In fact Mr. Kirkuff is buried in the Kellersville Methodist Church Cemetery off Keller Road. The road leading to Mr. Kirkuff's house from Neola Road would be Greenview Drive. The only place in that area that would be within a quarter of a mile from the scene of the murder would be on that stretch of road where Neola Road first runs into Greenview Drive. In other words, the good Reverend would have been passing the Marsh Home and the school house as he was approaching Greenview Drive. There at around 6 p.m. he heard either screams or crying from a girl; but didn't think it was worth investigating. Sadly, times were different back then. Maybe it was normal for 'little girls' to be 'whipped' without raising suspicion. Or perhaps Reverend Gilbert felt uncomfortable or afraid to investigate or even issue a challenge, something like 'hey what goes on there?'

The account of Reverend Gilbert seems a bit defensive. His excuse for not investigating because he thought it was a simple case of corporal punishment isn't credible. Maybe the young reverend wasn't too familiar with the area and was feeling a bit intimidated. He was, after all, alone and it was dark by then. The phase of the moon for that night was barely a sliver. Autumns get very dark in the Poconos. His carriage would have been his means of transport. For lighting he would have had only a lantern to guide him. The reverend did characterize the calls as cries for help or a little girl being whipped. But it is odd that he never mentions hearing other sounds, other voices. If a child is being whipped, a common form of corporal punishment back then, why wasn't a parent's voice heard?

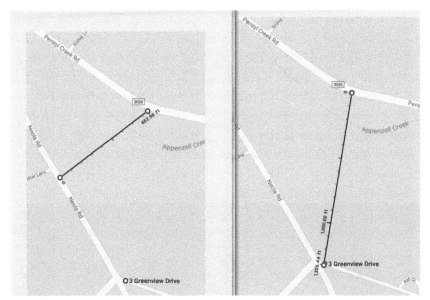

Figure 31 - The figure above shows two distance calculations along Reverend Gilbert's line of travel Sunday October 31, 1880 around six pm. A quarter of a mile equals 1,320 feet. The Illustration to the left is at the point where the Reverend passed the Home of Jacob Marsh. On the right is at the point of entering Greenview Drive.

The fact that Etna was still alive and suffering at 6 p.m. is terrible, but that's not all, it seems that the road, today's Pensyl Creek Road, was a busy one that Sunday night into Monday morning. Based on the accounts, at least five or more people passed by the exact spot where her body was found and yet did not see anything. "... [o]ther parties passed that very spot at different times between 4 and 9 p.m. without noticing anything unusual." (*Honesdale Herald*, from *Monroe Democrat* November 11, 1880). "Her father passed the place on Monday morning with a load of wood without noticing her". (*Reading Eagle*, 'Monroe County Horror', November 5, 1880). "Her father went for a load of wood in the morning and passed by where she was lying without seeing her; one of her uncles and several others also passing by her body without discovering it". (*Jeffersonian*, 'Foul Murder', November 4, 1880).

What are the odds that all the people passing by her body between 4 p.m. and 9 p.m. didn't notice her? What about those who pass by later, even her own father on Monday morning and her uncle who also didn't notice the body? The odds are great if her body wasn't there yet. The early investigators saw this as a problem too. They had to account for the lack of an earlier discovery of the body. They had to account for the observations by Reverend Gilbert of a female crying down in the vicinity of the crime scene as late as 6 p.m. They had to account for the blood trail that began practically the moment Etna would have stepped foot in the woods.

Figure 32 – A place of cover, convenient for 'decoying' Etna. This is along the banks of the creek just yards from the spot where her body was found. Across the creek, up the hill is Neola Road where the Marsh residence was located and the Rees schoolhouse still stands. Courtesy of Trooper Jesse Bachman, Pennsylvania State Police Forensic Services Unit.

They were aware of a gap in time, a gap that would have been filled with horror for the girl. Some accounts even speculate that the killers removed Etna to a place of isolation in order to rape her. The theory is that Etna was 'decoyed' into the woods; kept there till about 6 p.m., when she was raped. The 'hellish' purpose was accomplished but then Etna in, 'some way', made her escape. They followed her striking 'severe blows'. Eventually, she reached the fence and attempted to cross it; but there received the 'death blow'. (*Wayne County Herald*, November 11, 1880). Some of the ' decoyed in the woods theory' is at odds with the crime scene evidence; not the fact that Etna was 'decoyed' for a period of time, during which she was raped, but the fact that she received a death blow while trying to climb over the stone fence. That doesn't square with the evidence. Remember, there was evidence of a severe beating with blood spatter on the rocks and ground around the body, blood, brain, and hair covered the suspected murder weapons; a broken club and a stone or stones. Anyone looking at the body would know that she suffered repeated fatal blows to the head while lying on the ground. This was born out by the autopsy as well. "The assailant, judging from the wounds on the head of the victim must have struck her a dozen times." (*Somerset Herald*, Tracking a Murder, Stroudsburg November 18, 1880).

The location of the crime scene now becomes even more troubling. The spot where her body was found is right up against the public roadway. Anyone could come right up to the killer or killers before they even knew they were there. This is bold and reckless; a total disregard for the ability to get away. That type of a mindset leads us to believe that the location was not random or accidental but chosen; that Etna's final resting place was chosen by her killers. The accounts also mention that her head was 'lying upon a rock', like a pillow, and that there were other rocks under her body so she was a little above the ground. The location was also at the junction of the well-worn footpath and Pensyl Creek Road. There is a statement there, in that choice of location; a statement that says: 'look here, look what has been done!'

That leads us to conclude that one person alone did not commit the crime. It would be a very difficult thing for one person to do; attack the girl, keep her for hours on end in some nearby location, hidden from people passing by, raping her, and then, hours later, bringing her to the stone fence corner and bashing her head in with 'stone and club'. That type of effort shows us clearly that at least two people were involved in her rape and murder. This conclusion was also shared by some of the early

63

investigators. It only seemed natural that this type of a crime and its duration needed more than one perpetrator. So the picture that the evidence paints is truly a horrible one. In that tiny stretch of land, only a couple hundred yards from her destination, Etna is attacked, raped, and abused for hours until viciously murdered. This was something alluded to by Mrs. Barry in her poem: "In vain she cried, 'oh father and mother do come near. My anguish is so very great much more I cannot bear.' No father or companion came, no helping hand is near. The torture of this dreadful work the lonely girl must bear."

Figure 102 - The above is an overall depiction of the crime scene based on the detailed accounts from the Inquest and newspapers. Etna's body lies alongside the stone fence bordering the 'Public Road'. The level of the road is higher than the field where her body was found. The stream would be off to the right across the narrow strip of land. The right was also the direction of the Marsh Farm and the Rees Schoolhouse. Across the road on the left is the wooded area going uphill and ending at the Bittenbender Farm. This patch or 'piece' of woods is where the investigators first traced the blood trail. Courtesy Trooper Jonathan Bailey of the Pennsylvania State Police.

Figure 103 - A closer view of the body and the weapons, "stone and club" arrayed around her. Courtesy of Trooper Jonathan Bailey Pennsylvania State Police.

Figure 104 - The closest view of the scene; Etna's battered skull along with the broken club and pointed bloody stone. The premeditated nature of the murder is inescapable. Courtesy of Trooper Jonathan Bailey Pennsylvania State Police.

Chapter 3

The Reaction

*"Who could describe, even in words set free of
metric and rhyme and a thousand times retold,
the blood and wounds that now were shown to
me! At grief so deep the tongue must wag in
vain; the language of our sense and memory
lacks the vocabulary of such pain."*

Dante Alighieri, Inferno Canto XXVIII

N ews of the murder, as it usually does, travelled very fast.
Confusion, panic, and fear took hold as rumor grew and spread;
"The Township of Hamilton thrown into the wildest excitement
this morning." (*Jacksonville Republican*, Jacksonville Alabama,
November 2, 1880). The brutality of the murder was shocking. "One of
the most fiendish deeds ever committed in that portion of the state".
(*Jacksonville Republican*, Jacksonville Alabama November 2, 1880).
"Women are afraid to go out or stay home alone. Hundreds of people
visited the afflicted family." (Monroe County Horror, *Reading Eagle*,
November 5, 1880). Parents wouldn't send their children to school or
even let them out of the house. Women were not to go out alone. Men
armed themselves, carrying their weapons openly. There was no police
force to speak of. The Borough of Stroudsburg didn't get a police force
until 1906. The Pennsylvania State Police weren't in existence either,
only created in 1905. The usual authorities included the sheriff, who had
certain arrest powers, but by no means a large force of deputies. There
were also constables for each of the townships. They would serve arrest
warrants and oftentimes act as police. There was the district attorney,
called the chief law enforcement officer of the county, but he did not
have a regular detective or assistants. There was also the 'Horse Patrol',
men called upon to apprehend horse thieves, often traveling many miles

chasing down the would-be thief. These men could be quickly mobilized in times of emergency. People would also take matters into their own hands; vigilantes could spring up at any time.

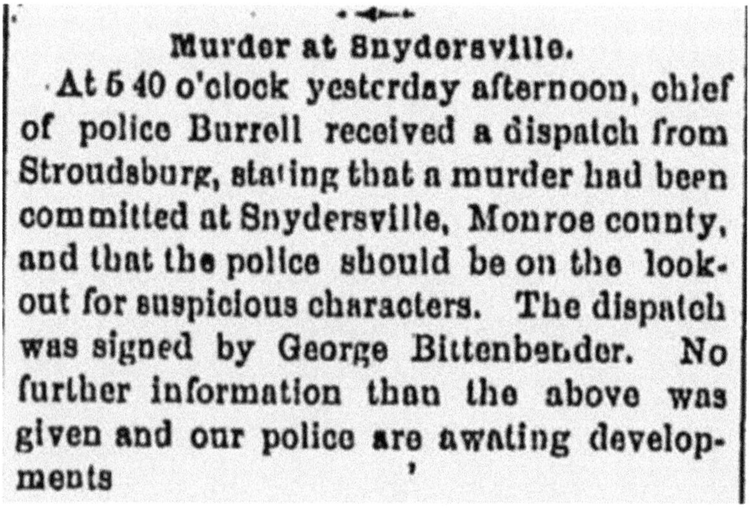

Murder at Snydersville.

At 5 40 o'clock yesterday afternoon, chief of police Burrell received a dispatch from Stroudsburg, stating that a murder had been committed at Snydersville, Monroe county, and that the police should be on the lookout for suspicious characters. The dispatch was signed by George Bittenbender. No further information than the above was given and our police are awaiting developments

Figure 33 - Easton's Daily Free Press mentioning the telegram sent by Etna's Uncle George, the earliest official or at least public mention of the murder.

When news of Etna's murder spread all these various groups came out in one form or another. There were no telephones, no 911 centers; there was word of mouth, swift horses, and telegraphs. The news had to be sent as quickly as possible. Not only did locals need to be informed, but also the surrounding areas. Numerous telegrams were sent within hours of the grisly discovery. Many of these telegrams were reported in evening newspapers on the very day the body was discovered. "There were several tramps seen in the vicinity early in the morning and it is supposed that they committed the atrocious crime. Telegrams have been sent to all points east, west, north, and south to head off the supposed murderer." (*Evening Gazette*: Girl Killed by Tramps, Port Jervis November 2, 1880). One such article, printed in the evening edition of Easton's *Daily Free Press*, was based on a telegram sent by Etna's Uncle George, the twin of her father who had a grocery store in Snydersville. The telegram was sent to Chief Burell, Easton's chief of police, telling of the murder and asking him to be on the lookout for suspicious characters. Many papers

68

picked up the story immediately. Articles of the murder and the fact that tramps were suspected appeared all over the United States, as far away as California, and all points in between.

The authorities were quick to mobilize. An Inquest was summoned that day by Special Judge Eugene Marsh. Marsh sent constables bearing subpoenas issued by Marsh for delivery on the men he selected to serve as jurors for the Inquest. The men gathered at the scene to view the body. The District Attorney, David Stokes Lee was notified. A post mortem examination of Etna's body was performed. Dr. Mutchler of Stroudsburg was the lead physician. A location in Sciota, probably the Sciota Hotel, was chosen for the inquest. Potential witnesses such as Reverend Gilbert and Wilson Marsh were identified and brought in front of the Inquest for questioning. While this was going on people came forward claiming to have seen suspicious men nearby. The descriptions were noted and word was put out to find the 'suspicious characters.' There were so many rumors that the investigation would soon be hurt by the number of conflicting leads. The resources of the small community were taxed to their utmost.

Figure 34 - Members of the County's Horse Patrol, posing in front of Stroudsburg's famed Indian Queen Hotel circa 1884. Undoubtedly many of these men would have been involved in the investigation into the murder, searching for suspicious persons, drifters referred to in the vernacular of the time as 'tramps'.

The people of Hamilton Township, Etna's friends and neighbors, raised the sum of $900.00 Dollars and offered it as a reward for the arrest and conviction of those responsible. Sheriff William Baker added another $200.00 to the reward and printed reward posters describing two men of interest. This was a hefty sum for a farming community back in 1880. The buying power in 1880 of $1 Dollar was the equivalent to nearly $24 Dollars today. Sometimes rewards can backfire. The Bittenbender Murder Investigation was jammed up by a lot of false leads, innuendo, rumor, suspicion, and multiple layers of hearsay. There was a belief that some people were providing information just in the hopes that they might be the lucky winner of the reward. But the descriptions given, the same ones Sheriff Baker put out in reward posters throughout the area, was a tangible and believable early lead of the investigators; one that helped define and shape what came to be known as the 'Tramp Theory'.

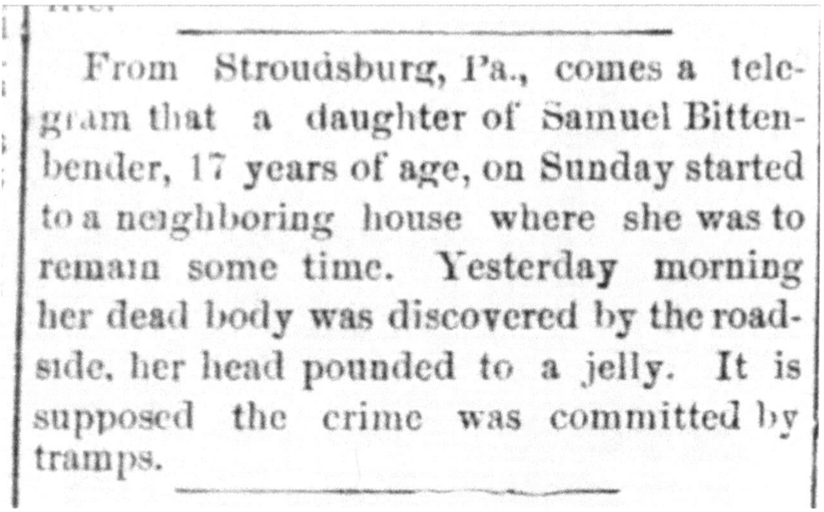

From Stroudsburg, Pa., comes a telegram that a daughter of Samuel Bittenbender, 17 years of age, on Sunday started to a neighboring house where she was to remain some time. Yesterday morning her dead body was discovered by the roadside, her head pounded to a jelly. It is supposed the crime was committed by tramps.

Figure 35 - A clipping from a newspaper out of Davenport Iowa November 2, 1880.

"[t]wo tramps were seen in the neighborhood on the day of the murder, the theory is found that these tramps were in the woods on the afternoon of the 31st of October, and they committed the terrible deed." (*Honesdale Herald*: The Hamilton Murder, from the *Stroudsburg Democrat*, November 10, 1880). Tramps were all over; men without homes, drifters roaming from place to place, not welcome, they were frequently suspected when bad things were done. Tramps were a phenomenon in those days. They were a concern for law enforcement as

70

$200.00 REWARD!

Two tramps answering the following description, were seen in the vicinity where Edna Bittenbender was murdered on Sunday, October 31st, in Hamilton township, Monroe county, Pa:

One man, 5 feet 10—weight 180—40 years of age, with brown hair—did not see beard, but may have one. Gray sack coat—pants like the coat, and black soft hat.

Second man, 5 feet 7—weight 150—30 to 35 years old, with smooth face and light colored clothes. Had on a cap, think it used to be dark blue.

If seen and circumstances warrant, arrest and hold them, and notify

WM. T. BAKER, Sheriff,
Stroudsburg, Monroe Co., Pa

Nov. 8th, 1880.

Figure 36 - Reward offered by Sheriff Baker along with the descriptions.

well as the general population. A number of states passed laws against these men. These varied from state to state. The Pennsylvania law is as follows: "Wandering about without a home, and living by begging constitutes one a tramp." (Pa. Laws 1879 (April 30), 33, No. 31 Section 1). Pennsylvania made certain exceptions to the definition of a tramp. Among those who couldn't be prosecuted under the Tramp Law were females and the blind. Tramps could be arrested and either required to work on public projects or could be hired out privately. The laws also set a time limit for such compulsory work, usually 30 days. (The Year Book of Jurisprudence for 1880, Abbott, Benjamin Vaughn pp. 417-418). The fear and concern over these wanderers was real.

THE TRAMP ACT.

A bill is pending in our state senate, having passed the house, that provides for the severe punishment of tramps. We notice that some papers in the state object to it as needlessly severe, if it happens to be administered by harsh officials. We do not consider this a valid objection to a law. It is to be presumed that laws will be justly and humanely enforced, and not made the

Figure 37 - From the Valley Sentinel Pennsylvania April 4th 1879. The article goes on in great detail to justify the pending bill over criticism that it would be too harsh. The writer reminds that 'Tramping' or 'vagrancy' would be a misdemeanor punished by not less than 6 months nor more than 18 months in prison. Stronger penalties would apply if any tramp entered a dwelling against the will of the owner or 'kindled' a fire on the public highway or property of any person without his consent.

The writer of the piece justified the need for the law to protect society and discourage that wandering lifestyle because it leads to crime. "We see no harshness in all this. Much of the crime now committed is traceable to tramps. They enter houses, against the will of the owners, and commit outrages where they deem themselves safe. Incendiary fires, theft, and even murders are traceable to them. An entire system of begging and wandering, that constitutes the essential features of tramp life, tends to crime. And to avoid the tendency, the system itself must be broken up. It is said that the Panic of 1873, and the enforced idleness consequent upon it, drove many out to the tramp life, this is partially true, at least. But it does not justify the unnecessary continuance of what was originally a necessity, possibly. The trouble is that many having once cultivated the reckless independence of tramp life are disposed to continue it, and prefer it to honest work, even where employment may be had. They have laid the foundation of criminality, and the tendency will be to follow that career. It is against this that the law is directed. Crime must often be fought in its incipiency. Prevention of evil is often better than its cure. Hence the importance of meeting this evil, that so rapidly tends to crime. The opportunities for employment are greater than when the tramp nuisance began, and there is little reason for it now, founded on lack of employment. It is also, the bad quality of increasing, if unrestrained. Tramps become more abundant as time passes. Example and the propensity to viciousness contribute to the enlargement of the number of tramps, and hence the tendency will continue unless it is broken up. The experience of other counties proves that tramping becomes a popular profession while unchecked. Such are the evils that we have, and they must be treated as such and rooted out under the strong hand of the law. The real trouble with this new sense is that it has been treated so kindly that is it has flourished and grown. We regret to think that institutions founded for benevolent purposes unintentionally encourage tramps by giving them shelter, night after night for weeks. It is said that Pittsburgh has a larger number of tramps who find better quarters here than elsewhere and so are wintering among us. And observation teaches that their morals are of the lowest. They beg, because it is safer and easier; but that failing, they steal without hesitation. Some go farther than this into the more refined forms of rascality. Hence the conviction is impressed on our minds, that few if any tramps are honest. Their surroundings and associations tend to crime. In order, therefore that it may be rooted out, and it must be treated as crime producing, and proceeded against as such. This is the theory on which the legislature is acting. It defines tramping as a crime, and tramps as vagrants. If they are merely tramps, the punishment is not great, and has a tendency to break up the evil. If they go farther and commit depredations, the punishment is more severe, the idea of being, continually, to stamp upon every phase of tramp life, the impress of criminality. The law is wise and proper. Industry and intelligence are the basis of good citizenship. The opposite qualities take from it. As a result we must, in order to limit the production of criminals, put our hand upon this evil and suppress it. (*Valley Sentinel*, Pennsylvania April 4, 1879).

A popular handgun descriptively styled the "Tramps Terror" was widely advertised for sale during this time period. This .22 caliber revolver weighed seven ounces. The weapon, manufactured by Western Gun Works of Chicago, sold for $3.00 Dollars; included in the sale price, 100 cartridges. Part of the sales pitch states: "Tramps, Burglars, and Thieves infest all parts of the country. Everyone should go armed".

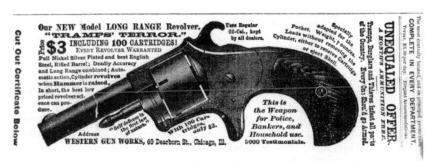

Figure 38 - Quite the sales pitch from Frank Leslie's Illustrated Newspaper, April 7, 1877.

So early on in the investigation what we call the 'Roundup of the Tramps' began. Guys were arrested, questioned, and eventually released. The accounts include men being arrested not only in Monroe County on suspicion of murder, but also the surrounding counties; Carbon, Pike,

Lackawanna, Luzerne, and Northampton. "Edward Graham, a tramp was arrested at Pittston yesterday on suspicion of being an accessory in the murder of Etna Bittenbender, near Stroudsburg a short time since. He has been taken in charge by the authorities." (*Lancaster Daily Intelligencer*, November 10, 1880). "A tramp of suspicious appearance was arrested by the police yesterday and locked up. We could not learn his offence. A girl was murdered in Stroudsburg some time ago, it is supposed by a tramp, and the police are keeping a sharp look out for these wanderers. A description of the supposed murderer has been furnished the police." (*Wilkes-Barre Record* November 5, 1880). Many of these men were arrested because they were thought to be coming from Monroe County or just because they were tramps. Several of the accounts talk about holding these men until the authorities from Monroe County came to question them. The tone of many of the articles is one of certainty that the tramp then in custody was in fact the killer. Much effort went into ferreting out whether a particular man in custody was connected to the murder. The accounts mention witnesses, people, or at least a person who saw suspicious characters around the scene of the crime being brought to view a detained suspect. The whereabouts of the suspected men at the time of the murder was also carefully investigated. This process was referred to as the 'tracing' of the tramps; that is trying to see if they were connected in any way to the murder. There was a lot of work involved in the process.

Perhaps as early as the first day, DS Lee, the District Attorney, knew he needed help. One of his first decisions was to hire the Pinkerton Detective Agency. Lee would have been familiar with the Pinkertons. The agency was famous and the founder, Mr. Pinkerton was held in the highest regard. Lee also knew that the Molly Maguire prosecutions several years earlier, some of which were presided over by Lee's mentor, Judge Samuel Dreher of Stroudsburg, relied heavily on an undercover Pinkerton Agent who infiltrated the Irish gang. Lee was forward thinking and looking for help where he could find it. The Pinkertons weren't cheap. Lee sought and obtained the approval of the County Commissioners to fund the detective expenses.

Figure 39 - The man behind the moustache is David Stokes Lee or 'DS' as he liked to be called. He was born on August 19, 1840 in Stroud Township. He became a school teacher at 17. When the Civil War began, Lee enlisted as orderly sergeant of the 166th Regiment, Company H, Pennsylvania Volunteers. He served most of his term in South Carolina before being honorably dis-charged. Later he served as a school teacher in Mauch Chunk and as the principal of the Strouds-burg Academy before getting into the law; in 1867 he was admitted into the Monroe County Bar. He was regarded as a talented and successful trial lawyer. He served as a defense counsel in the murder trial for the death of Daniel Brodhead and the wounding of his brother. He was married to Martha Posten, eventually they had four children. Lee enjoyed playing baseball on a local team. He belonged to the Stroudsburg Presbyterian Church. Apparently, his membership was put on probation for a time in the late 1870s due to appearing publicly intoxicated in town. He became DA in 1872 after a tough fought campaign involving several candidates. At the time of Etna's Murder, Lee was just finishing his eighth year as DA. This was his last term. He had never prosecuted a murder. Eventually, in 1898 he ran and won a seat in the state senate. On Tuesday July 14th, 1908, he returned home from a busy day in court complaining he was not feeling well and collapsed. He lingered on for a couple of weeks as his condition worsened. At one point he told Martha, "he was about to depart from this life and enter another realm". After lapsing in and out of consciousness he called for his daughter Nellie, who came to his bedside. Lee tried to speak to her, to say farewell, but unable he passed out and died; he was 68.

So the belief that a 'Mr. Tramp', as he was sometimes referred by the press, was responsible for the brutal murder was compelling for many people in the area, not just lay people, but those in authority as well. Yet there were some who did not find comfort in the Tramp Theory; I say comfort because it was comforting to the people of the community, and Etna's Family, to believe that outsiders did the foul deed. As opposed to someone living among them, someone who they spent time with on a daily basis, attended functions together, worked together, or perhaps they were even related to.

There was another group who thought that the perpetrators were among them; perpetrators who were familiar with Etna's routine and habits; able to stalk her, to anticipate when she would be leaving her parents to go to the Marsh residence, and based on that knowledge waited and watched until she was alone and vulnerable. This theory was never given a formal name, we call it 'The Local Theory', and it was talked about in the accounts quite often. The Local Theory was based on the reasonable assumption that the guilty party had to know Etna's comings and goings. Otherwise, the odds would be great that at the precise time she was heading back to the Marsh House and just as she entered the woods she would be randomly attacked. " On Sunday morning she expressed the wish to spend the day with her parents, which request was granted by her employer, and she immediately left for home, arriving there in due time without noticing anything unusual along the path. After spending the day in innocent enjoyment, the girl left her father's house shortly after 4 o'clock P.M., to return to her employer, this being the last time she was seen until found weltering in her own blood… and while Mr. Tramp is receiving his share of abuse, etc., we are inclined to think that parties familiar with the location and probably acquainted with the girl, are the guilty parties." (*Monroe Democrat*, November 11, 1880 from Wayne County Herald).With every twist and turn of the investigation one theory or the other would be in the ascendancy. One day it could be the Tramp Theory and everybody was working hot and heavy toward solving the case on that basis. Then, something unexpected happened, perhaps a witness came forward, or a piece of evidence was found, or some other incident happened nearby and the investigation would be thrown off course, and the focus would now be on an insider, a local as the guilty party. "For a few days after the finding of the body the neighborhood adjacent to the scene of the murder was in a terrible state of excitement and rumors of every description were floating around and numerous theories existed as to how and when the murder was committed and who was the perpetrator." (*Monroe Democrat*, November 10, 1880 from *Honesdale Herald* November 14, 1880).

Looking back at the information, the facts, and evidence that was being gathered, it's a shame the way things came together; how often the two views clashed on an almost daily or weekly basis and kept stalling or derailing the investigation. Don't get me wrong, there were strong reasons, based on fact and circumstance that supported both the 'Tramp Theory' and the 'Local Theory.' Any investigator worth his salt is going to pursue any and all evidence, tips, and leads, ferreting out the case, no matter what direction it takes.

One of the objects of this work is to determine if any of those in authority might have had what today we would call conflicts of interest, but then was simply known as 'relations' or ties of friendship or kinship with possible suspects. That possibility certainly did not escape DS Lee. Perhaps it is one of the reasons why he was so quick to seek the hiring of the Pinkerton Agency. The possibility of conflicts of interest is not at all far-fetched. The population of Hamilton Township was at most several thousand people. The community was small and tight knit. Most of the people were of Pennsylvania German extraction, although many of the families had emigrated from Central Europe generations before, German was still spoken commonly in the area. At the time of her murder, Etna's Church, Christ Hamilton, offered alternating German and English sermons. I remember Elmer Christine, a fine man and an attorney, my good friend David Christine's father, telling me that when he was solicitor of nearby Eldred Township in the 1950s and 60s the people still, at the beginning of each meeting, recited the Pledge of Allegiance in Pennsylvania Dutch.

The 1880 Monroe County census discloses that the population of the entire County was but 20,000 people; Hamilton would have been a fraction of that. One estimate, by counting the number of entries for Hamilton Township in the Census, gives the figure of approximately 1,875 people. There are signs of possible conflicts of interest. For some reason the regular Justice of the Peace, Mr. John Fenner did not preside over the Inquest, although he did observe the post-mortem examination. Eugene Marsh, who presided over the Inquest, bears the same surname as Jacob Marsh; whose house Etna was traveling on her last day alive. A review of the 1850 Census shows that Jacob Marsh, then age 17, was living in the same household as Eugene Marsh, then age 3. A further review of the genealogical records shows that Jacob Marsh's father, Johannes, may have been Eugene Marsh's grandfather. Also, Sam Bittenbender and Jacob Marsh were cousins; Jacob's mother was Sam's Aunt, his father's sister.

One of the things you want to do in a cold case is get to know things about the original detectives or investigators; figuring out their 'M.O.' that is modus operandi, how they conducted themselves, their reputation for thoroughness, thinking outside the box, imagination, in short their character. Knowing things like that about the original investigators can give you a better sense of the case, analyzing the leads and their reasons for choosing one course of action over another. Getting inside the head of the original detective brings that connection that you need between the case and its possible solution. Knowing the shortcomings of the detectives involved allows you to do things that they either couldn't know about or were too quick to discount. In the 1968 Monroe County homicide of Alfred Barnes, a case that went unsolved until 2015, one of the original investigators was a state police detective, named Bernard McCole. McCole was known to his colleagues as 'Ole Stone Face'. He didn't often crack a smile. He was all business and detective like. Reading his old reports and examining his theories on the profile of the killer, the motivations that brought the victim and killer together, turned out to be one hundred percent correct. The way Ole Stoneface analyzed the evidence and the way the case turned out were nearly identical. A good detective will do that for a case, even if the identity of the killer eludes him.

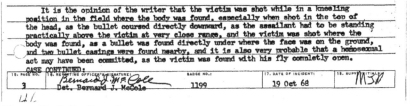

It is the opinion of the writer that the victim was shot while in a kneeling position in the field where the body was found, especially when shot in the top of the head, as the bullet coursed directly downward, as the assailant had to be standing practically above the victim at very close range, and the victim was shot where the body was found, as a bullet was found directly under where the face was on the ground, and two bullet casings were found nearby, and it is also very probable that a homosexual act may have been committed, as the victim was found with his fly completly open.

CASE CONTINUED:

15. PAGE NO.	16. REPORTING OFFICER'S SIGNATURE:	BADGE NO.:	17. DATE OF INCIDENT:	18. SUPV INITIALS:
3	Det. Bernard J. McCole	1199	19 Oct 68	MSP

Figure 40 - Police Report.

This is a portion of detective McCole's report where he figures that the victim was killed execution-style; that is while kneeling with the shooter standing above him. The circumstances of the victim being alone at night with a fancy brand new car and apparently in the company of another male, coupled with the victim's fly being found open raised questions of a homosexual connection between the victim and the killer. This connection would not be confirmed until much later. Also, at the time detective McCole made these initial observations the victim's car had not yet been located.

It is the opinion of the investigating officer that the victim was shot while slumped down or in a reclining position, and that he was definitely in the drivers seat, and was shot by a person who was in the right rear of the car, and that his head was turned towards the criminal when he was shot, as according to the course of the bullet that entered the right cheek and exited from the left side of the neck, the person that did the shooting would have to be to the right rear, and higher than the victim.

It is also the opinion of the writer that after the criminal shot the victim once in the car, he got out and removed the victim from the car(Victim would have been alive and partially mobile at this time), and upon leaving the car, the victim apparently slumped to his knees, where the assailant placed the gun above the head id face of the victim, and fired two more shots into the victim, while the victim was on his knees, as indicated by the direct downward shots and course of two bullets.

CASE CONTINUED:

15. PAGE NO.	16. REPORTING OFFICER'S SIGNATURE:	BADGE NO.:	17. DATE OF INCIDENT:	18. SUPV INITIALS:
3	Det. Bernard J. McCole	1199	19 Oct 68	MSP

Figure 41 - Police Report Once the car was located and the motor vehicle examined the detective revised his earlier opinion with a supplemental report.

Eventually this basic scenario was proven correct when, 47 years later, the killer, Richard Keiper, admitted in a roundabout and intentionally misleading way that Barnes was shot first in the car and then pulled out of the car and shot again. Keiper didn't appreciate being questioned about a homosexual connection, but the emotional response he provided both to the Texas Ranger and the Pennsylvania state troopers who questioned him confirmed their suspicions.

One of the things a good detective needs is instinct. During the interview with Richard Keiper, Texas Ranger Bill Holland kept up a cat and mouse game with the cagey Keiper. Keiper wasn't going to just admit he killed Barnes all those years ago. Holland needed leverage, a hook. Since he didn't have one, he made something up. Now trickery is something allowed during an interview. There are boundaries though. You can't type up a fictional report or statement and use that to get a guy to admit to bad things; but you can allude to knowing things you don't. In speaking with Keiper, Holland found out that he was a fan of the TV series Cold Case. He watched it every week. No doubt he often compared his own cold case murder with the ones he saw on TV. So Holland found his hook. Bringing up the show he told Keiper how the police in Pennsylvania still had the victim's car all these years later. He told Keiper that a smart trooper had samples taken from the steering wheel, the seat covers, and anywhere the killer might have had contact with. The lab, according to the Ranger, was able to extract DNA and test it through a 'familial' analysis. The Ranger knew that Keiper had a brother who was in and out of state prison. The Ranger told Keiper that the DNA was a 'familial DNA match'; meaning it was either his, or his father's, or his brother's. The Ranger said that since his father died before the murder, the DNA was either Keiper's or his brother's. Keiper's head was spinning. He believed it. His belief in the capabilities of DNA made him believe the Ranger's tale. The defining moment in the interview was this ruse. At that point, after a brief pause, Keiper looked up at the Ranger and said; "If it's mine, it was an accident." Now he had to explain all about the 'accident'. The 'explanation' was an utter failure. At trial, Keiper's statement to the Ranger was the most important piece of evidence leading to the Jury's guilty verdict. Keiper was convicted of first-degree murder and is serving a life sentence without parole. By the way, the police returned Mr. Barnes' car to his family back in 1969, decades before the discovery of DNA.

Another example of where the insight and effort of a particular detective made a big difference in a case is the troubling murder of 87 year old Joseph De Vivo. Mr. De Vivo was a well-known educator in East Stroudsburg. He had taught for many years. Now this World War II veteran, in the twilight of his life, suddenly turned up missing. His house was eerily silent, his heating blanket turned on and warm, his bed sheets turned down. Both he and his car, a fancy Lincoln, were gone. Nothing else was disturbed. There was no sign of a struggle, nothing was in disarray. The OnStar unit of his motor vehicle was activated and the car was located travelling in the Charlotte North Carolina area. Through a telephone call from OnStar to the car's phone, an individual claiming to be Mr. DeVivo complained that he was 'just trying to enjoy his vacation.' DeVivo's adult children, listening to the call, quickly pointed out that the man was not their father. After a chase that person was taken into custody. His name was Rico Herbert. He was a known sneak thief who had pending charges in Monroe County for the burglary of a bar. Herbert denied any knowledge or involvement, claiming he didn't do anything to 'some old man.' While he was incarcerated in Charlotte North Carolina, Herbert was interviewed by a detective there by the name of Phillip Rainwater. Rainwater's interview was highly insightful and patient. Every time Herbert lied, beat around the bush, trying to mislead, the patient Rainwater would, in his own folksy way, cast doubt on the story and Herbert would eventually agree and proceed one step closer to the truth. It's common in these types of cases for a killer to create an alter ego, somebody else to blame for their heinous acts. Herbert was no different. He blamed everything on a mysterious guy named 'TJ'. At one point during the lengthy interview Detective Rainwater told Herbert that 'TJ was about as 'real as the Easter Bunny.' Rainwater gave his theory of the case directly to the suspect starting with the fact that there was no 'TJ' but that Herbert himself forcibly took the car from the victim, killing him and dumping his body.

Eventually, the badly decomposed remains of Joseph DeVivo were found partially submerged in a ravine down in Lancaster County South Carolina. The body was so badly decomposed the forensic pathologist couldn't medically determine the cause of death. Herbert was still maintaining that he did not do anything to harm the victim. On the eve of trial Herbert took a guilty plea to murder in the third degree, robbery, and burglary. During the lead up to the guilty plea Herbert admitted that after sneaking into the victim's home and getting ready to steal his car the victim confronted him. Herbert, a whopping 6-foot 4 inch, nearly 300 lb man, simply placed his hands over Mr. DeVivo's mouth and smothered him. Herbert is serving an aggregate sentence of 31 to 62 years in State Prison.

To investigate Etna's murder, early on we found out that the county had paid for detectives to work the case. In the County's 1880 budget of money spent and received there was an item for a payment in the amount of $98.63 designated for "Detective Expenses (Bittenbender Case)." (*Jeffersonian Republican* February 3, 1881).That was our first real clue that detectives were engaged. That amount, nearly $100, would have been used entirely in November and December of 1880. That was a sizable amount in 1880. There's no similar case that year that cost nearly as much money. Indeed, that amount is over 1/3 of the entire money spent on housing inmates at the county jail for the whole year. Other news accounts corroborated the fact that a detective or detectives were working the case. "A detective from New York is here investigating the matter which has created great excitement all over..." (Monroe County Horror, *Reading Eagle* November 5, 1880). "A detective from Philadelphia is here and endeavoring to get a clue..." (*Daily Free Press*, Easton November 19, 1880). "Detectives are engaged in working the different clues and astonishing revelations may shortly be unearthed." (*Monroe County Democrat*, through *Honesdale Herald*, November 11, 1880). "The work of the detectives has not for a moment ceased." (The Bittenbender Case Again, *Jeffersonian Republican*, December 9, 1880). "A detective has been employed for several days endeavoring to unravel the mystery." (*Monroe Democrat*, through *Honesdale Herald*, November 18, 1880). Even six months later the accounts related that detectives continued to investigate, albeit without success. "Despite the work of the detectives the Bittenbender murder still remains a mystery..." (*Jeffersonian Republican*, May 5, 1881).

Unfortunately, nowhere in the local accounts or the newspapers was any detective mentioned by name. Detective Kerchner and I searched the entire courthouse for any record, including the county archives, all the storage areas of the courthouse, attic, basement, evidence vaults etc., yet we could not find what detectives were employed, let alone case notes or investigation reports. On a hunch we requested any record of the case from the Pinkerton Archives located in the Library of Congress Washington DC. The result was bittersweet. The Pinkerton Agency was in fact hired by none other than DS Lee the district attorney of Monroe County to investigate the murder of Etna Bittenbender. The date of hire was November 4, 1880, only three days after the body was discovered. The agreed-upon rate was $8 a day. A detective was dispatched by train from New York to Stroudsburg that very afternoon, Thursday November 4, 1880. That detective was identified as Pinkerton Agent John S. Wood of Brooklyn New York.

Figure 42 - The Pinkerton Ledger Book indicating the identity of the detective, the client and the case.

Yet surprisingly the researchers were unable to locate the Pinkerton case file for the Bittenbender murder. In fact, much of detective Wood's work was not included in the archives. This was repeated when searching lesser archives containing Pinkerton records in cities such as Philadelphia and Chicago. Even though we were disappointed that we couldn't find out more, we still knew who the lead detective was; and that we must learn more about him, his methods and compare that to the direction and course of the investigation.

The Pinkerton National Detective Agency was by 1880 the first and foremost detective agency in the world. Its founder Allen Pinkerton was legendary. The exploits of the Agency paved the way for counter intelligence and law enforcement worldwide. Pinkerton's work during the Civil War cemented his reputation. As police forces came into being in the various cities and large towns across the country, they often worked hand in hand with Pinkerton agents, operatives and detectives. The training of the Pinkerton men was rigorous.

Figure 43 - Allen Pinkerton

There was a lengthy period where 'shadowing' was required. They would surveil suspects or targets for days on end. Oftentimes, non-descript ordinary men or even boys were employed to shadow; you couldn't use somebody too tall or too short or odd in appearance, anything that might stand out. Average or non-descript would not draw attention. Sometimes, disguises were employed, but rarely during the day. Shadowing might require wearing layers of clothes and several soft hats that could be changed quickly to help confuse the suspicious. A good 'shadower' was patient, discrete, and a keen observer. Similar to shadowing, but requiring more finesse, was working as a plant. Agents would attend social events of the rich and famous. They would blend in and socialize with the guests, but were hired to lookout for thieves and hopefully catch them in the act. Plants were also used to elicit confessions from suspects incarcerated on various charges. The plant would pretend to be recently incarcerated, perhaps on some minor or relatable charge, he would then buddy up to the suspect and through conversation and manipulation gain his trust. The most famous example of a plant would have been the agent who infiltrated the Molly McGuire Gang, which eventually led to the arrest of multiple gang members and their executions.

Another aspect required of an agent was to investigate crimes. This function is the one most similar to the work that we do; to be called to the scene of a crime look for clues and decide which course the investigation needs to take, what methods need to be used. Only the brightest made it to the level of investigator, but there was an even more elite group, men called 'Ropers.' These combined the skills of the Shadow, the Plant, and the Investigator, into a master detective whose skills, experience, and knowledge of human nature could tie a suspect to the crime and deliver the case. "The Roper must to speak plainly, rope men in. He comes nearest to the dime novel detective of any in the list ... The Roper is simply a gentlemanly person, social, of good address, able to form excuses for anything he may do or say, and able to turn the conversation in any way he pleases. He must have traveled, must have a good knowledge of men, must be an easy talker but a better listener." (*Potter Enterprise* Coudersport Pennsylvania November 9, 1881, from an interview with Allen Pinkerton).

Figure 44 - Robert Pinkerton in his Office

Michael Mancuso and Eric J. Kerchner

In 1880 Detective John Wood lived in Brooklyn New York at 23 Sterling Place, in a brownstone home. He was 32 years old and married to Josephine, or 'Josie', as he liked to call her. The couple had a beautiful two year old girl, named Estella, their only child, the apple of her father's eye. Wood's mother in law, Lucy Bates, age 70 lived with them. Wood wasn't born or raised in Brooklyn. He wasn't even a city boy. Wood was born in 1847 in Scipio just south of Auburn, Cayuga County New York State. His father died when he was young. Wood was raised by an uncle, a house painter. By the start of the Civil War, Wood was working on a farm. He wasn't tall, about five feet five inches in height, black haired, blue eyed, and fair in complexion. Wood enjoyed riding. He would enlist in a cavalry unit and served as a bugler, until he was transferred to the 192nd New York Volunteers, where he served the rest of his enlistment until honorably discharged. After the war he was appointed as 'Keeper of the Prison' at the cutting edge state prison in Auburn New York. There he learned a great deal about the criminal mind, and was considered very effective in maintaining discipline and managing the inmates. He worked at the prison until he sought and obtained a position with the Pinkerton Detective Agency in the City. Already married to Auburn native Josie Bates, Wood and Josie relocated to Brooklyn in 1877. The next year Estella was born. Wood quickly ascended the ranks in the Brooklyn Office working directly under Robert Pinkerton, Allen's son who ran the New York Office. It wasn't long before Wood proved his abilities and obtained more important assignments.

Detective John Wood did in fact possess all of the essential qualities of a master 'roper.' The cases he was involved in show a guy who was very dedicated to his job, hard-working, thorough, with a lot of energy. He could make very subtle distinctions that could change the outcome of a case, moving it closer to the truth. His resume included uncovering the guilty parties in a fraudulent land deal concerning the sale of an Ice Pond. Wood had placed an advertisement in a newspaper seeking to purchase an ice pond knowing that a suspect who had recently defrauded an unsuspecting buyer would reach out to him. Wood setup the fraudster in a sting style investigation and he was convicted. In another case, Wood tracked down a fence who had received possession of a very rare scale used for weighing precious metals. There was only one other like it in the entire country. Through tireless effort Wood traced the burglary to 'river thieves". He spent weeks getting to know the fisherman and other members of the River Community along the Hudson. The method of the river thieves became known to him and allowed him to identify the likely fence. Wood then traveled to the store that the fence operated posing as an innocent purchaser. Wood must have had the Gift of Gab because even though the scale had only been stolen for a few weeks and wasn't in the store, the fence actually brought Wood to his house to show him the object.

Figure 45 - Pinkerton Detective Agency Building Brooklyn Office. This is the Office where Detective Wood worked.

A good example of the merit of John Wood as a detective stems from his work in convicting Charles Rugg for a series of murders. The story begins on November 17, 1883. Shortly after 4 pm, in the small farming community of Brookville Long Island, Queens County, the neighbors of the Maybee family heard the blind and disabled patriarch of the family, Mr. Gerrit Maybee screaming over and over the word 'murder.' Neighbors, many of whom hastily armed themselves with shotguns and other weapons arrived at the house and saw by the light of a lantern Mr. Maybee covered in blood. He was asking where his wife and adult daughter Annie were. Some searched the rest of the house, other neighbors went to the outbuildings. In the barn they found mother and daughter both dead. Mrs. Maybee's body was covered in leaves and was cold to the touch. The daughter Annie, who was a 'strong and powerfully built' woman lay on the barn floor. Her body felt 'blood warm.' Neither woman showed any outward signs of injury, but there was evidence of skin and blood under Annie's fingernails. After the discovery was made, two of the neighbors, Jacob Fitting and Edward Tappan, returned to the main house. Mr. Maybee asked, 'tell me the truth are they dead?' When told the fate of his family Mr. Maybee became inconsolable. Mr. Maybee would eventually testify that the family was getting ready to eat supper. Annie just finished setting the table. As was her habit, Mrs. Maybee went into the barn with two pails to get some milk from the cows there. When she did not return, Annie went to the barn to check on her. As Mr. Maybee sat in the dark of his own blindness, he heard footsteps approaching and then the door to the house opening and closing. The sound of the footsteps was not familiar to him. It sounded like someone walking without shoes. They certainly were not those of his wife or daughter. He called out in alarm asking who was there; a male voice, trying to disguise itself as female replied; "it's me." At that point someone approached him and said; 'old man where is your watch? Tell me or I will kill you.' Mr. Maybee replied that he had not worn his watch in two years since becoming completely blind. Maybee felt hands rummaging through his clothing and his pockets. Then the disabled man was struck four or five times in the head with an old cane of his. As Mr. Maybee sat bleeding he heard the killer walking through the house, room by room, rummaging through things. After a while, when he heard the killer leave, Mr. Maybee began to scream.

FINDING THE BODIES.

Figure 46 - "Murder Most Foul" National Police Gazette December 8, 1883.

Suspicion almost immediately fell on a tramp named Eddie Doyle; a dark sinister looking fellow who was seen nearby at around 6 p.m. that evening. A local man even came forward claiming that he had seen Doyle entering the barn shortly before the murder. People wanted to hang the tramp. The district attorney of that place, a Mr. Fleming, questioned Doyle during the coroner's inquest. He told Doyle that if he believed he would be hurt by any question he would not have to answer. Doyle responded by stating that no questions could hurt him and he gave a very straightforward account of his actions. Despite the so-called witness statement, Fleming did not feel comfortable pinning the crime on Doyle. Doyle was cleared of suspicion.

Figure 47 - The tramp Eddie Doyle initially suspected in the murders of the Maybee family. (National Police Gazette).

What happened next just about 'solved' the case. A neighbor of the Maybee Family was 52 year old John Tappan. Less than two months after the murders, John Tappan was arrested for a violent home invasion robbery of James and Aurelia Townsend in their home in Oyster Bay. Both husband and wife were beaten severely. It was believed that Mr. Townsend would not recover from his wounds. A hammer had been used in the assaults and was left in the house. A pair of bloody overalls was found just behind the house on a wooded slope. The hammer and overalls were identified as belonging to John Tappan. John Tappan had a younger brother named Edward. Both men, neighbors to the Maybee Family, were married and had children.

The brothers were friendly with a man named Halstead Frost, identified as a detective in some accounts, and as an auctioneer and local newspaperman in others. After his arrest on the Townsend Case, John Tappan sought Frost's advice saying: "I wouldn't be surprised if I was arrested on that Maybee Case." Frost responded: "I guess you will be John."(John Tappan the Man, *New York Times*, January 19, 1884). Based on that, District Attorney Fleming questioned Tappan's brother Edward.

Ed Tappan became so nervous he was gripped in fear, turned purple, and needed large amounts of brandy and peppermint to calm down. (id). Later Frost convinced Ed Tappan to visit him in his home. Frost claimed that Ed said "Hal I can't rest. I want to make a confession." (id) Frost falsely told Ed that John had flipped on him and was accusing him of the Maybee Murders. Frost told Edward that the only way out would be to finger his brother. Frost assured Ed that if he admitted to what they did, he would only be used as a witness; he even gave him $10 Dollars to hire a lawyer. Ed Tappan then provided a very detailed confession. Frost had the confession reduced to writing. Ed Tappan signed it, swearing that his confession was made 'unsolicited' and believing it was his 'duty to make a complete confession in regard to the part he took in the murders'. Ed Tappan's Confession:

> I know who took the lives of Lydia and Annie
> Maybee on the evening of November 17th- it was
> John B Tappan, my brother. He was in the barn
> when Mrs. Maybee came in but I was not in the
> barn. I saw John go in the barn; he went in the
> double doors; I was at the front side of my house
> when he went in feeding pigs. When John choked
> the old lady to death I was at the front door of the
> barn. I saw him he choked her to death on the barn
> floor; he caught her by the wrist with one hand
> and then took her by the throat with the other. I
> saw him do it; I was looking through the door; it
> was light enough for me to see in the stable. When
> John had her by the throat she was on the ground.
> When she came in for leaves John was standing in
> the stable where the leaves were. It took from 10
> to 15 minutes to choke her to death. After she was
> dead John picked her up and laid her in the back
> stable. I saw him throw some leaves over her. I
> was standing on the barn floor very near the
> opening in the door that goes down in the stable.
> I saw the whole thing myself. After she was dead
> John said: 'I am going to wait for Annie. I am
> going to choke her too. If I choke her to no one
> will know about it then I can go to the house and
> get the money.' Annie opened the barn door about
> 2 feet wide and when she stepped into the door

John grabbed her by the right arm and threw her down on the floor about three feet from where he grabbed her; held her by the right wrist and put his knee upon her left arm, and with his right hand took her by the throat. She tried to get away from him. When he grabbed her by the arm she grabbed at his face. She reached his face. I saw her hand close to his nose and mouth. She said;' let me go', that is all she said. He held her by the throat until she was dead. She died in about 10 or 15 minutes. He carried her in the stable near her mother and covered her all up with leaves and said now I am going to the house. We both went into the kitchen door. Old man Maybee said: 'Who is there?' John said: 'It's me', and then went upstairs to Mrs. Maybee's room. When Mr. Maybee knocked on the floor I stood by the door. I saw him do it, then John came downstairs, went in front of Maybee very close to the hall and ran his hand up and down Maybee's breast and said: 'I want that gold which you had two years ago.' Maybee said; 'I ain't got it. I am blind; can't see to get it.' 'I know' said John .John then said; 'I must kill you'; then he snatched the cane out of Maybee's hand and struck him twice on the head. John went upstairs again and came back. He said I have all I want; we came out; he went to the Cedars by the spring and went home. I suppose he gave me $10. I have it now but not with me. I will bring it to you; I will bring it today if I can. John showed me the pin and the watch by the door outside. I could see them. 'I got them upstairs', he said. He did not tell me how much money he got, he did not tell me what he was going to do with the watch and pin. I do not know what he did with them. I have not seen my brother John alone to this day.... After John showed me the watch and pin I went home by the old bridge. This was about 5:45. I know it was not six; I am sure of it. My wife asked me where I had been and I told her down the road. My wife does not know I had a hand in the Maybee Murders. (The Times, Philadelphia, January 19, 1884).

Ed Tappan's confession was considered conclusive. The case was solved. The Tappan Brothers would be placed under arrest for the Maybee murders. A great amount of Ed Tappan's confession matched the evidence at the crime scene just right. Lydia Maybee's body was cold to the touch, unlike Annie's body. This suggested that Lydia was the first killed; just like Ed Tappan said. Skin and blood was found under Annie's fingernails. Eddie Tappan sees Annie's hands going toward his brother's nose and face. The confession suggests that there was some injury to John Tappan's Nose. Ed Tappan's confession matched old man Maybee's testimony, the killer searching his pockets, asking for gold, Maybee's answer, and the assault with the cane. Money, along with a cameo and a watch were taken, all things Eddie Tappan claims his brother showed him. Sure Eddie keeps himself out of any violence toward the family, but that kind of self-serving statement was as common then as it is now. Human nature and experience tells us that a criminal defendant will often try to blame his partner in crime. Frost delivered Eddie Tappan to Detective Wood, who along with a cop from Flushing named Smith took custody of Tappan. Arrangements were made to get the Brothers together. John Tappan was told of Edward's confession; but John seemed unmoved. "Edmund was taken into the room where John was. The two brothers simply said "How do you do?" to each other. "Ed" said John after a moment, "do you say that I did that Maybee business?" Ed said "Yes and you did it and you know it." "Ed can you look me in the face and say I murdered the Maybees?" asked John. "Yes I can." said Ed. "That settles it I do not want to say anything more to you." John said. (*New York Times,* January 19, 1884).

The public was relieved. Families up and down Long Island could now sleep in peace. The New York press praised District Attorney Fleming for his hard work and diligence. Fleming showed an ability for sniffing out the truth; rejecting efforts to pin the crime on the tramp Doyle. The Maybee killer was much too knowledgeable of where to look in the house for valuables; going right to where the family hid the valuables. That was an insider's knowledge, not that of a stranger to the household. Simply put, how could anyone disbelieve Ed Tappan's confession? Further, Detective Ayers from the railroad company on Long Island spent weeks undercover infiltrating the families of John and Edmund Tappan. He passed himself off very well as a recently arrived laborer and gained the trust of the family members. He recalled how at dinners he attended, when asked about the murders and the prospect of catching the killer, he stated that all the time in the world remained and told stories of cases solved years later, sometimes through the ghostly intervention of the murdered victim. In each of these conversations Detective Ayers noted how nervous Ed Tappan became.

Wood was aware of all this and more. But something bothered him about Edward's confession. He could not find the stolen items or even show they were ever in John Tappan's possession. He spent hours searching the residences of both Ed and John Tappan. He tore up carpets and floor boards and checked the outbuildings; but nowhere could he find any of the items stolen from either the Townsend or the Maybee residences. Then he went back over Ed's confession. Ed claimed that earlier on the day of the murders he was hired to slaughter pigs. The owner of the doomed pigs was sure that Ed Tappan was with him through 6 p.m. on the day of the murders. That, if true, meant he could not have taken part in the murders. Some of the detectives thought the owner was mistaken, but Wood wasn't sure. Another part of the confession bothered him. Ed Tappan said that from his side yard, that vantage point, he could see right into the Mabyee's barn and claimed from there he saw his brother strangling Lydia Maybee. When Wood made an on-site examination he realized that you couldn't see the barn from Eddie Tappan's side yard. So Wood doubted that they had gotten their man. The other thing that bothered Wood was Mrs. Townsend's original description of her attacker. John Tappan, a white man, could not be confused for a black man. Mrs. Townsend said that when she realized somebody was by the door, she asked, who it was, and a man answered, "Simon". She asked him to come in. It was at that point that she was assaulted. She originally assumed the man who assaulted her was Simon Rapeleye, a black man that the family hired to do work for them. Mrs. Rapeleye had also done the wash for the Townsend family. Only after Mrs. Townsend was interviewed by detectives and they apparently lead her along with the facts connecting John Tappan to the hammer and the bloody overalls did she change her story. Wood was not happy with the change. In short order, he became convinced that neither John nor Ed Tappan killed the Maybee women.

The break in the case wouldn't happen until the end of January 1884. On the 25th of that month, out in Hempstead Long Island, in the morning hours, a farmer named Sealey Sprague, age 40 was viciously assaulted in his barn. The assailant used a 'strap'; an 18 inch bar, made of iron, pointed, it had leather straps on the ends and sides. It was used to connect railroad ties. The Long Island Railroad line was not too far from the scene of the assault. The concerned neighbors who first arrived at the scene saw so much blood in the barn that it looked to them like a slaughterhouse. Mr. Sprague's skull, the parietal bones were shattered. His face was bloated and black; yet he was alive. The doctors didn't give him much hope for survival. His wife, tall and slender, was in her home at the time her husband was assaulted. She had no idea what was happening. She was about to step outside, to check on her husband, when her small dog started barking. At that point she saw a man, he was wearing a felt hat that actually had a cover that draped his face; but the cover had openings at the eyes which revealed to her that the man was a 'negro'. He told her he wanted her money. She yelled for her husband and tried to get past the man, who grabbed her by the hair and yanked out a chunk of it. He then struck her in the face. He forced her back into the house. She gave him her purse which contained a total of $38; gold pieces, some silver pieces and bank notes. The man then fled. Mrs. Sprague ran to the nearest neighbor, about of a quarter mile away to get help. Eventually, search parties scoured the countryside. At one point the man was almost caught but made an escape. The next day, January 26, 1884, the man, identified as a light-complected 'negro' or 'mulatto' by the name of Charles Rugg, was apprehended. He was almost lynched. But the authorities arrived in time and transported him to a nearby jail. From there he was brought to Mrs. Sprague who made a positive identification.

Wood was hired to see if there was a connection between this man and the attacks on the Townsend and Maybee families. Wood traced Rugg's trail from the Sprague Farm to a store where Rugg bought a new set of clothes, a very fine fancy set of clothes. The amount he spent on the clothes, plus the money he had remaining in his possession equaled $38, the sum taken from Mrs. Sprague. Wood traveled to the jail and began to question Charles Rugg. Wood noted that the strongly built Rugg, with his whiskers and flaring sideburns, dressed as a dandy in fancy colorful clothes, closely resembled Simon Rappleye. Both men were the same size and similar in features, except that Rugg was lighter in complexion. Wood believed Rugg tried to fool Mrs. Townsend into believing he was Rappleye. Wood learned that Rugg knew Simon Rapeleye. Rugg also knew Ed and John Tappan. Wood found out that two years before, in 1882, Rugg had worked for the Maybee family; even staying in the room above their kitchen for period of time. Rugg also knew the Townsend family. Before Mrs. Rapeleye did their laundry, Rugg's own wife did their wash. Charles Rugg had a violent reputation. He was feared in the black community and suspected of robberies and sexual assaults. In fact, at the time of his initial arrest, it was a black man named Amos who brought rope in an effort to lynch Rugg. Although Rugg was married he was carrying an affair with a 'mulatto' prostitute named Mollie. Mollie liked expensive things, especially jewelry. When Rugg was arrested he had several pawn tickets in his possession. These were from pawn shops in New York City. It was thought that Rugg had help fencing stolen items. Wood planned to travel to the city and interview the keepers of the pawn shops in an effort to locate the property stolen from the Maybee and Townsend families.

Wood spent a lot of time questioning Rugg. Wood knew what buttons to push and got 'Charlie', as he called him, to talk. Rugg knew that they had him dead to rights on the Sprague case so he talked about that the most. Rugg claimed that he was lost, cold, and hungry. He saw a barn in the distance and planned to sleep there for the night. He looked around for a stick, he was worried that he might meet up with a dog. He didn't see a stick but he saw an iron bar near the railroad track and picked it up. Although the barn door was locked, he reached through a hole, unfastened the lock and went inside. He got a horse blanket and fell asleep. At daybreak he heard a dog barking and heard footsteps coming.

He picked up the iron bar and waited by the door. Capturing Rugg's vernacular Wood wrote, Rugg's words verbatim, "De do was opened jest a little bit, an in popped a little dorg. I made a hit at him, an missed. But sho as yo's bo'n, a man put his head into de do' that same minnit, an he got the blow instead of de dorg." (The Story Rugg Tells, *New York Times*, January 30, 1884). Rugg then described how he struggled with Mr. Sprague, minimizing the amount of times he struck him in the head; trying to make it seem accidental or just impulsive. He also denied punching Mrs. Sprague, although he did admit he may have pulled her hair, but that was only because he had reached out because he slipped on the ice. The confession was enough to lock in Rugg for the Sprague attack. But Wood wasn't finished. He knew Rugg was passing himself off as a simple, uneducated, not too bright fellow. Wood was doing his homework and learning that Charles Rugg was highly intelligent, devious, and totally lacking in empathy.

The next day, Rugg was to be brought to court for arraignment on the Sprague robbery. "The District Attorney is working very hard to sift the wheat out of the bushels of chaff which are thrown onto his threshing floor; but he seemed very much perplexed yesterday. Rugg's hearing was set for 10 am, but when all was in readiness at the courthouse, it was discovered that the prisoner had again succumbed to the seductive Wood and was relieving his conscience of another load. It was soon whispered around among the swarm of country constables in the hallway that new and important evidence in either the Maybee or Townsend cases was forthcoming. An hour passed and Rugg was still talking. The hearing was put off till two O'clock and the Justice and one or two constables whiled away the interim by playing draw poker....At noon Mr. Wood hurried off to New York and the District Attorney's Office was full of mysterious whisperings. It was said on good authority that Rugg had dropped the information that he disposed of Mrs. Maybee's watch in this City..." (Id).

Detective Wood was sure that he would be able to convict Rugg not only for the attack on the Sprague and Townsend families but for the murders of the Maybee women as well. Indeed, within several weeks the district attorney had filed seven separate indictments against Rugg; three for the murders and robbery of the Maybee family, two for the vicious attacks against the Townsend family, and two for the attacks against the Sprague family. The cases wouldn't be tried together. Rather each of them, even if the victims were of the same family, would be tried separate. The district attorney brought the first case to trial in April of 1884. He selected the murder of Annie Maybee to go first. His thinking was that since Annie was killed after her mother and Annie wasn't killed until nearly an hour later, the killer had to have waited for her; a strong case of premeditation could be made out. If Rugg was convicted of killing Annie he would be executed and there would be no need for any of the other charges. Charles Rugg was represented by three top notch defense lawyers. The lead attorney was John Quarles, a black man; along with him an ex-judge name Richard Busteed, The third attorney was William Shiels.

Wood was busy preparing for the trial tying up loose ends, developing last-minute leads, strengthening the case. Wood was developing pieces of circumstantial evidence that when linked together would form a compelling case for murder. Charles Rugg denied killing the Maybee women. In speaking with Detective Wood, Rugg did admit that he had possession of Mrs. Maybee's watch and brought it to a pawn shop in the city. But he claimed that the watch was given to him by none other than Edward Tappan at around 8 pm the evening of the homicide. He told Wood that he was given the watch while on the road to a town called Greenville. But Rugg's times did not match the facts. Wood had interviewed dozens of witnesses who said that they were with Edward Tappan at 8 pm; he was at the Maybee residence actually helping to carry the bodies of the murdered women from the barn into the main house. Wood also cultivated a source, a black man named Alanson Conklin from Glen Cove Long Island. Conklin was a friend of Rugg. Conklin took Wood to a pawn shop in the city where he said Rugg got rid of items he had taken from the robbery. He even supplied a motive for Rugg's actions. Rugg had been in a sexual relationship with a 'mulatto' woman named Mollie Kennedy. Kennedy and Rugg worked on the steam ships in the summer seasons that plied the Long Island Sound. They had different jobs aboard these ships but apparently made even more money committing petty thefts.

Wood learned that Charles Rugg was born in Long Island and when he was 15 he went to sea on a whaling ship. He was gone for nearly 7 years; had seen much of the world, Europe, South America, Asia and became an expert swimmer. He also was well known as a masterful handler of teams of horses. After his return to the Long Island area, Rugg worked at various jobs, including a hotel maître d, a driver, and a jack of all trades. In fact, Wood located several witnesses who were able to place Rugg at the Maybee residence at various times, doing odd jobs, and even staying there in a spare room for a few weeks. These witnesses would testify that Rugg knew the inside and outside of the residence like the back of his hand. In a very modern view of such things, Wood brought Rugg and six other African-American men with him, all of whom looked similar to Rugg to the various owners of the pawn shops to see if they could identify Rugg. The identity included not only Rugg's appearance but also the sound of his voice.

Wood also identified witnesses who saw someone of similar appearance to Rugg near the Maybee home; he was identified as either a black man or a white man with dark skin. The man also was wearing gloves and carried with him a satchel which was similar in appearance to one Wood had located during a search of Rugg's residence; the satchel had blood spots on it. The fact that the man was wearing gloves was also helpful because the doctors examining the bodies of the murdered women saw an absence of fingernail marks which led them to conclude that the killer may have worn gloves. Wood also realized that Charles Rugg was shrewd; he had the initials 'LRM', Lydia Romaine Maybee, removed from Mrs. Maybee's watch cover prior to pawning it. He also threw the stolen cameo into the East River because it had the same initials. He took similar precautions with the Townsend watch; a gold face watch with a landscape scene decorating it. Rugg had the gold face removed and replaced with a white face. He also had the dials to the watch removed and replaced. It was on the underside of the dials that jewelers inscribed serial numbers identifying the watch. Rugg knew of that and was taking steps to avoid being connected with the fruits of his crimes. Rugg seemed to have the wherewithal to set up others, even as early as the immediate aftermath of a crime so that a false trail could cover his tracks. Since Rugg knew the victims, had dealings with them in the past, such an effort to stage would not be unexpected. For example, he tried to fool Mrs. Townsend into believing that it was Simon Rapeleye knocking on her door. When initially confronted about the Sprague family attack he claimed that a John Appleford actually committed the entry and he had just waited outside. Wood had then arrested Appleford who was not released until several days of questioning cleared him. Detective Wood also suspected that an easy-to-follow trail consisting of boot prints and spittle from tobacco juice leading to John Tappan's house from the Townsend crime scene was actually created by Rugg. In fact, he was able to show that Rugg had access to John Tappen's missing hammer used in the Townsend assault, and the bloody overalls recovered nearby. Charles Rugg was no man to be trifled with, either physically or in his cunning.

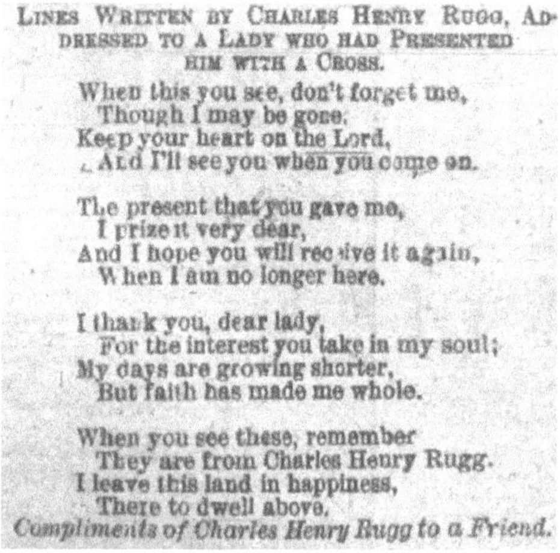

LINES WRITTEN BY CHARLES HENRY RUGG, ADDRESSED TO A LADY WHO HAD PRESENTED HIM WITH A CROSS.

When this you see, don't forget me,
Though I may be gone;
Keep your heart on the Lord,
And I'll see you when you come on.

The present that you gave me,
I prize it very dear,
And I hope you will receive it again,
When I am no longer here.

I thank you, dear lady,
For the interest you take in my soul;
My days are growing shorter,
But faith has made me whole.

When you see these, remember
They are from Charles Henry Rugg.
I leave this land in happiness,
There to dwell above.
Compliments of Charles Henry Rugg to a Friend.

Figure 48 - *"Murderer Rugg in Verse - Rugg died a Catholic. Through the efforts of Father McGuire he embraced Catholicism several months ago. He became very devout and spent half an hour at prayer every morning. A young lady who sometimes visited him with Father McGuire gave him a cross and beads. Rugg directed them to be returned to her after his death, and wrote the poem which was given to her with them."* (Buffalo Evening News, May 19, 1885).

Rugg's trial began on April 22, 1884 with jury selection. It was a lengthy affair. Only a handful of the large amount of prospective jurors was even selected the first day. Ex-judge Busted spent a large amount of time questioning the prospective jurors; having them answer 37 prewritten questions he formulated. A good portion of the questions dealt with uncovering any prejudice they might hold against a black defendant.

Charles Rugg himself appeared indifferent, sitting in the packed courtroom, apparently without a care in the world. "... [Rugg] appeared as unconcerned as the least interested spectator. His hair was greased and carefully parted squarely over the left eye, and his whiskers were growing in the Burnside Style. He wore a dark blue jacket and green and black striped trousers. He had on a blue woolen shirt. His feet were encased in red socks and stuffed in slippers. He was not manacled." (*New York Times*, April 23, 1884). The case was touted at the time as being entirely circumstantial but of such good circumstantial evidence that the net of guilt surrounding the defendant would be hard for him to escape. After several days of testimony and eloquent closing arguments by both sides; with John Quarles closing for the defense, maintaining that one person could not have killed both of the Maybee women, the jury was sent out to deliberate. After about two hours of deliberation the jury returned a verdict of guilty of murder of Annie Maybe. The sentence for the crime was death. Upon returning to his cell Rugg broke down. The work he spent on questioning and gathering evidence against Rugg was Detective Wood's finest moment, the highlight of his career.

After his conviction and as his appeals wound down, Rugg converted to Roman Catholicism. He would frequently be in the company of a Father McGuire. He learned all the prayers. Although he still proclaimed his innocence in the Maybee crimes he said he was prepared for death. He was a very popular figure receiving many visitors, in particular children and females. One account even has him singing religious songs with a group of females who came to say hello. He would be hung on May 15, 1885 in a room of the Queens County Jail known as the '30-day Room.' That morning he put on a new suit of clothes, admired himself in the mirror, was given a Catholic Mass at an altar set up in his cell by Father McGuire, and ate a breakfast of rolls, buttered toast, hard-boiled eggs, and coffee. The death sentence was then read out to him by the sheriff, his arms were pinioned at his sides, and a black cap placed on his head. With Father McGuire at his side he began the procession to the execution room. He turned to a fellow inmate awaiting a sentence of death and told him cheerfully that he would see him soon 'up there.' After reciting the Lord's Prayer the cap was pulled down over his face, the noose was placed over his head and tightened around his neck. Father McGuire placed a crucifix to Rugg's lips. Rugg kissed the crucifix. "The next moment the hangman cut the ropes and Rugg's body shot into the air, swung to and fro rapidly for about half a minute. The usual contortions followed, and in 20 minutes Rugg was pronounced dead." He was 26 years old; an undoubted waste of talent.

The energy and discernment shown by Detective Wood in the Rugg Case gives us an example of what we could assume was the high quality of his work on the Bittenbender Case. It illustrates that the authorities initially took the case seriously, willing to pay for one of Pinkerton's best men to work it. Detective Wood went on to be involved in several more high-profile cases, including murders. These would result in convictions or would otherwise be solved. Detective Wood was soon the number one man in Pinkerton's New York office. In the late 1880s Wood left the Pinkerton Agency and opened up his own detective agency. He was successful and good at what he did. The Pinkerton agency could not locate any of his case files. It *seems* he had taken all of his files with him. On December 26, 1893, the day after Christmas, while with his wife Josie in their Brooklyn home, Detective John Wood suddenly collapsed and died; he was only 47 years old. Josie had his remains transported by rail back to their home town in Auburn and buried on the 29th of December in the family plot at Fort Hill Cemetery. Wood's wasn't the only body buried there that day, Josie had their child Estella's remains taken from her tomb in Brooklyn and brought to Auburn to be buried beside Wood. Estella, had died of scarlet fever 12 years before in 1881; she was only 3 years old. Wood left no descendants. Josie would live on for 30 more years, spending much of it in Brooklyn. As her health declined with age she eventually relocated to Auburn, living with her niece. She passed away in the 1930s and was buried alongside her husband and daughter. Wood's detective agency was sold in 1894 to Mr. Jacob Riis of Newark New Jersey who operated a detective agency there. We have been unable to trace what happened to Wood's files after that.

Chapter 4

Strangers

"They are bad men capable of committing high crimes;
both are Germans of a bad kind."

Warden Michael Cassidy (1886)

I t was Thursday November 4, 1880, Detective John S. Wood, Pinkerton's talented agent, was in his prime. He had just gotten the assignment to take the next train to Stroudsburg, meet the client, the district attorney of Monroe County, get all the facts he could about the crime, examine the scene, and figure out a course of action. November 4 was also the day that the body of Etna Bittenbender was laid to rest in Mount Zion Cemetery, a small hillock just outside of Kellersville in Hamilton Township. Her funeral was held at the Christ Hamilton Church, one of the oldest in Monroe County, along the Bossardsville Pike. The funeral was the biggest in memory; over a thousand people attended. One of the disappointments in our investigation was the absence of records from Christ Hamilton Church for the time period of our case. The fault belongs to Reverend Richard H. Clare, who did not think it was important to record these events in the affairs of his church and congregation. Clare's successor Reverend Joseph R. Focht noted with disgust the 'contemptible laziness' that deprived a congregation of 'the record of her dead from June 9th 1869 almost up to September 1882.' (William Lesh, Materials on Hamilton Township).

November 4, 1880 was also the day Sam Bittenbender paid for his daughter's coffin. The coffin was made by the Brodheadsville carpenter / undertaker William Kresge. It is sad but funny in a way that we have a record of the purchase of her coffin, but no church record of her funeral. Mr. Kresge, unlike Reverend Clare, kept fine detailed records showing that Sam Bittenbender paid him $30 for the coffin on November 4. Well-wishers and others visited the family, offered condolences, and grieved with them. Nothing could comfort Etna's mom; she never recovered from the blow of the devastating loss. She would rarely leave the farm afterwards. She needed more and more help around the home. The stress caused her terrible chronic rheumatoid arthritis. Margaret would live this way for another 30 years or so. Her death certificate records that this pervasive arthritis was a factor in her death.

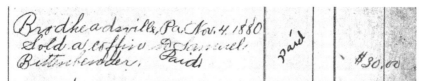

Figure 49 - From the ledger of William Kresge Carpenter / Undertaker Brodheadsville Pennsylvania. I had the pleasure of interviewing Mr. Kresge's grandson, also named William; it was during preparation for the 1968 homicide of Alfred Barnes. Mr. Kresge had been deputy coroner in 1968 and had taken crucial photographs of the crime scene and the victim's body. He would be able to testify to those photographs 47 years later at a preliminary hearing which occurred only several weeks before he passed away. He was 97. The Kresge Funeral Home still continues as a family venture. Courtesy of Colleen Mancuso.

Wood hastily packed, taking with him whatever he needed. He kissed Josie goodbye; held their little Estella in his arms before giving her back to Josie, and left their Brooklyn home to take the ferry to Jersey and then the train to Pennsylvania. By November 5, Wood was carefully looking over the murder scene; starting with the location alongside the road, walking the path, studying the still bloodied stones, studying the murder weapons, the topography, the entire place, looking for some sign or clue. He questioned many people. His arrival was no secret and was the topic of discussion all over the county. Even while the inquest was going on and witnesses were being questioned, Wood was conducting his investigation; often questioning witnesses before and after they testified at the inquest. One of the persons he questioned was 16 year old Wilson Marsh. Wilson, the second child of Jacob and Emma Marsh, lived at the house where Etna was housekeeping and where she was going when she was killed. There were three children born to Jacob and Emma Marsh, all boys. Edward Marsh, eighteen, the oldest had left home the year before to seek his fortune out west. Wilson, the next oldest, worked on the farm and also helped out at Gene Marsh's Foundry. The youngest was 13 year old Curvin.

Wilson Marsh was a very intelligent young man and his claim that he saw 2 tramps on a stone bridge about a half mile up the road from where the body was found was considered a very important clue. "The only persons suspected are two tramps who were seen lurking about the bridge about a half mile up the road from where the body was found. Telegrams have been sent to police officers of the various towns to be on the lookout for suspicious looking tramps. Whether anyone would be able to identify the tramps seen at the bridge is not known." (*Hackettstown Gazette*, November 12, 1880). Wood believed that the sighting of the tramps and the fact that they were so close to the scene, right around the time when Etna would have been heading towards the Marsh home, was a big lead. The accounts are silent as to which bridge Wilson saw the tramps. But they do give some indications. The bridge nearest to where the body was found was not even close to being a half-mile away. Rather, it was only around 100 yards away. Indeed, from the scene one could make out where that bridge was. There were two other bridges nearby; one to the south and the other to the north. The one to the south would be in Sandhill next to the foundry, a little over a mile away. Based on the fact that the accounts talk about the bridge being a half mile 'up' the road from where the body was found, as opposed to 'down' the road, it would seem to exclude that bridge. The only other bridge would be the stone bridge located alongside what is today Effort Neola Road. Although not quite a half mile from the scene, it is over a quarter mile away. The remains of that old stone bridge are still visible today in the woods just past the northern berm of the road. That bridge matches the one where Wilson claimed he saw the two strangers on the day of the murder.

But it was more than just Wilson Marsh's claim to have seen the tramps nearby that got Detective Wood's attention. Wood found evidence all around the murder scene that a tramp or tramps had been staying there. The clues were fresh and intrigued Wood. They fit very nicely with the sighting by Wilson Marsh of the two strangers. Wood was so taken by this evidence that he believed the Tramp Theory seemed the most plausible. "A detective has been employed for several days and endeavoring to unravel the mystery and after carefully examining the many theories advanced and investigating various clues, has come to the conclusion that the murder was committed by tramps. Near where the body of the unfortunate girl was found was a broken sumac bush which has upon it the marks of a knife, where it had been partially severed, and from these marks it was inferred that the cut had been made with a knife blade containing a notch. In the woods near where the murder was committed was found a bed of hemlock boughs which apparently had been cut with the same knife used in cutting the sumac bush, and near this bed of hemlock boughs was discovered a pile of wood prepared for starting a fire, but it had not been set on fire. From these discoveries and the fact that two tramps were seen in the neighborhood on the day of the murder the theory is found that these two tramps were in the woods on the afternoon of the 31st of October, and they committed the terrible deed." (*Honesdale Herald*, November 18th 1880).

Figure 50 - Sumac with leaves of crimson and gold as they appear in autumn. Sumac was apparently used in teas and for medicinal purposes. The branches of a sumac bush or low tree are referred to in the article above as having been cut with a knife which had a notch in its blade. Hemlock boughs with similar knife marks were also arranged nearby for bedding. The final clue confirming that strangers were staying near the crime scene was the discovery of an unlit pile of wood arranged for a campfire.

There were also others who came forward saying that two men fitting the descriptions given by Wilson Marsh were seen hanging out in Stroudsburg a couple of days before the murder. These clues were tantalizing to the detective. As the word spread, strangers all around the area were being detained and questioned. Three of them had been arrested in Monroe County alone. One fellow, Ed Garahan, arrested in Pittston, was even found to have a knife with a notched blade. "On Tuesday a tramp was arrested at Pittston on suspicion of being an accessory in the murder of Miss Bittenbender. A knife was found on his person with a notch in the blade which was supposed to be the knife with which the sumac bush was cut. Further investigation failed to develop sufficient evidence to warrant his being held." (*Wayne County Herald*, from the *Stroudsburg Democrat*, November 18, 1880). Despite the clues, one by one all these men would be released; they either provided alibis or else did not match the description of the men Wilson Marsh saw. By November 13, 1880, Easton's *Daily Free Press* reported that all three of the men arrested in Monroe County on suspicion of the murder had already been released.

The best description Wilson Marsh could give Detective Wood was the same description Sheriff Baker used in the reward posters; one man was around 40 years old and the other between 30 and 35. The older man was bigger, 5 feet 10 inches weighing about 180 pounds. The younger man was smaller, 5 feet 7 inches weighing about 150 pounds. Both men were dressed in old beat-up clothing. The older man, brown-haired, may have had a beard, was wearing a gray 'sack coat', gray pants, and a black soft hat. The younger man, with a clean-shaven face, had on light colored clothing and a faded blue cap. The descriptions were useful. The fact that there were two of them, apparently friends or companions, the age difference between the two; as much as fifteen years or so, along with the height difference of 3 inches and the weight difference of 30 lbs., definitely gave teeth to this description, a basis for comparison; if only the right people could be located. Wood believed that if two men fitting these descriptions could be linked to the scene and each other, chances are the case would be solved.

On Saturday November 13, 1880 two men were apprehended in Portland Pennsylvania. The men were trying to board the train in Portland. The men had the look of tramps. They also had a lot of interesting merchandise on them, merchandise that was presumably stolen. Newspapers printed several different accounts of these men, their whereabouts around the time of the murder, and the suspicion that they had killed Etna. One of the accounts titled: 'A Tale of Two Tramps' provides the following information: "Among the inmates of Lackawanna County Prison are two Tramps arrested for burglary and suspected of something worse. They were captured near Portland on Saturday, 13th inst., at the store of RC Drum and Brother Gouldsboro, from which they carried off several hundred dollars' worth of wearing apparel and miscellaneous articles of value besides $8 in cash." (*Carbon County Advocate*, Lehighton PA, November 27, 1880). The men of course had no identification on them. However, they gave their names as 'John Langfield' and 'Charles Flock'. Mr. Drum's store in Gouldsboro had been robbed on Wednesday November 10. Witnesses saw these men hanging around Gouldsboro for a few days before the robbery. They had abruptly disappeared afterwards. Mr. Drum had gotten an arrest warrant in the name of 'Two Tramps'. According to the *Advocate* article, "After a tiresome pursuit Mr. Drum and a constable captured them on the 13th near Portland and they were brought to Scranton that night" (id). Their guilt seemed clear because they had two large bags of full of Mr. Drum's merchandise. They were incarcerated on $500 bail.

Easton's Daily Free Press provides more information on the capture of Langfield and Flock and also some more details about their activities. "Detective Johnson received the following dispatch from Portland this morning: 'We have two thieves with store goods come and see if you can identify them. Signed J. Moore. Mr. Moore is the ticket agent of the D, L&W Road at Portland."
(*Easton Daily Free Press* November 13th 1880). A couple days later The *Daily Free Press* gave more details in a story titled: 'Important Arrest of Robbers': "Portland November 15th two men were arrested here on Friday last on suspicion of being burglars. Several pair of new pantaloons, two or three new coats, a lot of pocket knives and razors,

handkerchiefs, and other small goods were found in their baggage as well as a fine collection of assorted keys. Constable Decker believing the goods were stolen put the gentleman in the stone cage and telegraphed to Oakland where a store has lately been robbed. The next train brought out the Oakland party, who however did not claim the goods. Some of the old constitutional lawyers thought the birds would have to be let go, but Decker thought otherwise and sent a telegram to Gouldsboro where it was said a store had been robbed. The next day the Gouldsboro party arrived and identified the goods as theirs and the thieves were taken back to Lackawanna County. It was also ascertained that they were the same party that robbed the Oakland store and carried the goods in through this place and stole Beck's horses because they got tired of carrying them. The goods they had in this case were in the bags they stole from Beck and have his name on them. The men are unknown but are of the tramp variety." (*Easton Daily Free Press*, November 15, 1880). The later story seems to be accurate; identifying the goods found on the men, how they were apprehended, as opposed to the dramatic chase printed in the Carbon Advocate. The Easton article also places the men in other locations in the Easton area but unfortunately doesn't give us the dates of the Oakland store 'robbery' or the theft of Beck's horses and bags.

Opportunity is one of the things that you look for in any case. For someone to commit a crime they have to have the chance to do it. Opportunity can answer a lot of questions in a cold case. Opportunity can make or break a case. Opportunity can be of a killer's own design, random, or a bit of both. Sometimes opportunity presents itself without any action being taken by the killer to make it happen. Sometimes the killer creates his opportunity. In a murderous street shooting right on South Sixth Street in the Borough of Stroudsburg, two brothers were gunned down while they tried to change a flat tire on the minivan they were driving. The brothers were clearly the victims of a premeditated shooting. Through careful investigation Stroud Area Regional Police Detective Richard Wolbert was able to locate some video footage at a nearby gas station which showed the brothers getting gas on the day of their murder. They also seemed to have had words with a black male who was later identified as Aaron Tyson age 31. A carefully constructed circumstantial case was developed which showed that Tyson, in the company of two of his friends, had been at that gas station at the same time as the brothers. The brothers had treated Tyson rudely and with disrespect.

Eventually, charges were filed against Tyson, Otis Powell aka 'Damage' 32, and Kasine George 27. Once arrested George gave a confession. He told us that at the gas station one of the brothers had flashed a gun at Tyson. Tyson, upset, reported the incident to Powell. The three men decided they would follow the brothers' minivan. At a favorable time, after the brothers had left the van to enter a bar, George snuck up to the vehicle and stuck his knife into one of its rear tires. Once the brothers returned to their vehicle and began to drive they noticed they had a flat tire. They pulled off onto 6th Street to try to change it. They were being followed; Tyson driving, Powell in the passenger seat with a semiautomatic handgun, and George in the backseat. Powell got out of the car, walked up to the brothers and shot them multiple times at close range. He then walked briskly back to the car and Tyson sped away. George pled guilty to murder in the third degree and agreed to cooperate against the other two who were being tried separately. Powell's was the first to be tried. The evidence was circumstantial. George's testimony was challenged because of his cooperation. I am told that the jury deliberated and initially voted to convict Powell of murder by a vote of 10 to 2. However, one juror in particular, who seemed motivated not so much about the facts of the case, continued to declare Powell not guilty. In a true testament to her determination she wore the others down. After five or six hours of deliberation Powell was declared not guilty; truly an unjust result. Unfortunately for Mr. Tyson he had no such friendly angel on his jury. Following his trial, and using the same evidence, the jury unanimously convicted him of Murder in the First Degree. Such are the uncertainties and vagaries of the criminal justice system. But the way in which these killers created their own opportunity, by disabling the victims' vehicle, rendering them vulnerable to a drive-by shooting, shows the importance of opportunity to any murder. As an aside, the search of the bodies and the van by the police showed that the 'gun' flashed at Mr. Tyson wasn't real but a toy.

For Etna's murderers to have had the chance to do their horrible deed they must have been in a place where they could, without being seen, abduct her, molest her, and then murder her. The handy place for all of that was, of course, in the small patch of woods that bordered her father's fields between Snydersville and Neola. Wilson Marsh could put the killers at the location in the relevant time frame by his identification of them. Detective Wood knew how an identification could quickly solve the case. Did these two strangers, Langfield and Flock, have the opportunity to commit the crime? We know they were caught with Mr. Drum's stolen goods on the morning of Saturday November 13 at the Portland Train Station. We know the merchandise was stolen in Gouldsboro three days before, during the evening of Wednesday November 10, 1880. So in less than three days Langfield and Flock travelled a distance of 30 miles as the crow flies. The men could have traveled that distance on foot, on horseback, or by train.

Langfield and Flock were seen hanging around Gouldsboro a few days before the robbery on the tenth, so that would put them at Gouldsboro around November 7, a Sunday. They were also suspected of robbing a store in 'Oakland'. The only nearby area that bore the name 'Oakland' would have been in Bethlehem Pennsylvania. There's an Oakland drive and a section near the community college called 'Oakland Hills. Langfield and Flock were also suspected of stealing horses and bags belonging to a Mr. Beck. The bags are a big deal because they were full of the Gouldsboro store merchandise and had Beck's name written on them. Mr. Beck's place is listed in the 1880 Census as 103 Delaware Street in Easton; eight miles from Oakland. A thirty seven year old blacksmith, Joseph Beck lived there with his family. His home was actually right along D,L & W Tracks. The line is known today as the 'D&L Trail Lehigh Towpath'. Langfield and Flock were arrested trying to board a D, L & W Train in Portland on November 13. It is important to take note that the old Delaware Lackawanna and Western Railroad D,L & W had stations in all three locations Langfield and Flock were spotted, Portland, Gouldsboro, and Stroudsburg.

Although we don't know the specific dates of the Oakland and Beck burglaries, since Langfield and Flock were in Gouldsboro as early as November 7, they had to hit Oakland and Beck before then; in other words, within the week of the murder of Etna Bittenbender. The old road system could have easily brought the men from the scene of the murder right to the city of Easton. In fact, that route, the old Sullivan Trail, passes to within a mile of the murder scene by Brinker's Mill. One of the routes the men could have travelled, Bossardsville Pike, runs past Mount Zion Cemetery and Christ Hamilton Church. Langfield and Flock could have made the trip on foot in a day; and would have plenty of time, four or five days, to do the Oakland and Beck jobs.

"There are grave suspicions that Langfield and Flock are implicated in the killing of Miss Bittenbender, the young lady who was so cruelly maltreated and murdered near Stroudsburg a few days ago. They were seen loafing around Stroudsburg several days before the commission of the crime, and it is thought the ghastly deed can be traced home to them. Some parties are expected here from Stroudsburg with information, which if corroborated will place the prisoners in a bad light. It is stated that one witness saw them near the scene of the tragedy a short time before the murder was done and that their subsequent movements can be easily traced." (*Carbon Advocate*, Lehighton Pa. November 27, 1880). "It is also said that they answer to and are believed to be the same pair of tramps seen in the neighborhood and at the time of the late Monroe County Murder." (*Easton Daily Free Press*, November 15, 1880). "There were several tramps seen in the vicinity early in the morning and it is supposed that they committed the atrocious crime." (*The Evening Gazette*, Port Jervis November 4, 1880).

It is important to figure out everything we can about Charles Flock and John Langfield. The regular background information proved very difficult to find. They don't appear in any census for the year 1880. The 1890 census was largely destroyed so we couldn't check them there. They have pretty much disappeared from history. This early lead seemed so promising that a detective of Wood's caliber had to pursue it. But there was nothing definitive in the follow-up to the November 27, 1880 article. Nowhere, not in the local *Jeffersonian*, or any other paper are we told specifically what the authorities from Stroudsburg determined. But there is an article, again out of the *Daily Free Press*, a pickup from the *Monroe Democrat*, where the Tramp Theory is criticized: "The tramps have been traced and found to have not been at the scene of the murder at the time... from all the statements there were but two tramps seen and only two have been arrested bearing any close description to those explained by the boy Marsh; his description is very full and would seem from its plainness to have secured the parties if tramps." (The Bittenbender Murder, *Monroe Democrat*, through *Easton Daily Free Press*, December 10, 1880). A couple things from this account stand out. First, it must refer to Langfield and Flock. Second, they fit the description of the men seen on the bridge by Wilson Marsh; 'bearing' a 'close description', to the men described. So why does the article conclude that these were not the same men; that they have been traced and were not at the scene of the murder? Perhaps the Marsh boy could not identify them? It must have been frustration and a difference of theories about the profile of the killers; the tramp versus local theories in conflict again. That is the only way to explain it. Otherwise, our next discovery makes no sense.

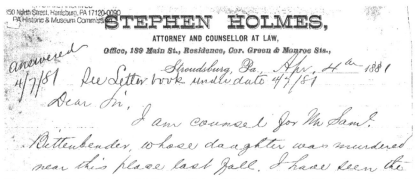

Figure 51 - The beginning of Attorney Holmes' Letter on behalf of Sam Bittenbender to the Eastern State penitentiary.

There had to be something about Langfield and Flock that was left undone and unsettled. By April of 1881, Etna's father had hired a lawyer in an effort to find the killers of his oldest daughter. With the help of

Pennsylvania State Police Corporal Shawn Williams, a lover of history and a top notch detective, we were able to locate a letter written by attorney Stephen Holmes dated April 4, 1881 to the Eastern State Penitentiary in Philadelphia; well after the information about Langfield and Flock should have been vetted. Mr. Holmes, a former district attorney of Monroe County, and among the best attorneys in the county, was specifically asking questions about these guys. For instance, he writes, "I would also like a description of John Langfield and Charles Flock who were sent to your penitentiary last fall or winter from Scranton for robbing a store in Gouldsboro. Please give all the facts known concerning them as they are suspected of being implicated in the murder... If I come to Philadelphia can I be permitted to talk to Langfield and Flock? I give these names as they were given to me and I'm not sure they are correct. SH" (Eastern State Penitentiary, Prison Administration Records, General Correspondence 1878 - 1901).

So based on Stephen Holmes' letter to the Eastern State Penitentiary, there was still the belief, six months after the murder that these men remained under suspicion as the guilty parties; Langfield and Flock require a closer look.

To recap, both Langfield and Flock appear to have been the same men spotted in Stroudsburg days before the murder, and resemble the men seen by Wilson Marsh on the day of the murder, less than a half a mile from the scene; they then commit two burglaries in the Easton area within one week of the murder. By November 7 or 8, they are up in Gouldsboro where they commit another burglary on November 10. They are then arrested on November 13 trying to board a train down in Portland. Their presence around the area and at the dates we've established clearly show that these men had the opportunity to kill Etna. One thing that is troubling about this geography is that when you look at a map of these locations; Gouldsboro, the crime scene, Oakland, and Delaware Road in Easton, the crime scene is just about right in the middle. That means these men would have had to come back through the general area of the scene, western Monroe County, in the midst of all the hysteria and the searching; with everyone on the lookout for suspicious tramps. They would have had to pass through the county, sometime between the evening of November 10 and prior to their arrest down in Portland on November 13. Indeed, they may have passed through the area on their way to Gouldsboro from Easton within a week of the murder. That's a bold reckless route for them to take if they killed Etna. The risk of them being stopped, questioned, and detained would have been high; the men of the Horse Patrol roaming about, all local law enforcement mobilized, and the populace in a state of high anxiety and watchfulness. That sort of recklessness, that boldness, suggests at a minimum, indifference and at the other end an extreme arrogance and disdain consistent with the crime itself. The capture of Etna, holding her for hours, sexually assaulting her, beating her, killing her, and leaving her body on the side of a fairly well-traveled road matches such arrogance. What more can we learn about these men?

Figure 52 – Stephen Holmes

I prosecuted the horrific murder of a drug-addicted prostitute living in Scranton named Deanna Null. She was a pathetic sorrowful woman, almost unaware of her plight. She lived essentially a homeless lifestyle hanging out with the bums or 'tramps' who inhabit the railroad tracks which cross through downtown Scranton. Somehow she met a handsome and enigmatic young man name Charles Ray Hicks. Hicks spoke with a Texas lilt and had an easy going demeanor. Hicks had a good job at the Army Depot in Tobyhanna and drove a Cadillac. He had recently moved to Tobyhanna from his home back in Tarrant County Texas. Hicks and Deanna hit it off; they were seen together partying, doing cocaine, and having a good time. One day Deanna mentioned to a friend that she was going to Tobyhanna with a man she had met. She was never seen alive again.

Her remains were discovered about a week later in a dozen or so black plastic garbage bags. She had been dismembered and her body parts were dumped along the roadside of Interstate Routes 80 and 380. One of the bags had been ripped open by an animal, which retrieved its content, carrying it over the roadway to the opposite lane of travel and leaving it in the snow. It was later identified as the head of Deanna Null. The head was found only a couple hundred yards away from Hicks' own residence in Tobyhanna. Indeed, where he had spread the trash bags containing Deanna's remains was all along the path he would take to and from work every day. The only parts of her body that were not recovered on the roadside were her hands. Her hands were found after a diligent search by the Pennsylvania State Police Forensic Unit, in particular Trooper Tom Slavin, hidden in a plumbing chase in Hicks' own bathroom.

Each hand was meticulously wrapped; coated with layers of laundry detergent, newspaper, and athletic socks so that they were perfectly mummified. Troopers Robert Sebastianelli and Craig Vanlouvender, excellent investigators, brought the charges which included criminal homicide and abuse of a corpse. Hicks was convicted of murder in the first degree and the jury imposed a sentence of death. He remains on death row while a team of federally funded lawyers file voluminous court documents seeking to overturn his conviction and death sentence. I bring up Mr. Hicks because he left the fruits of his evil deed, Deanna's dismembered body, all around where he lived. Perhaps that was not arrogance on his part but rather a need to see and relish the aftermath of what he did. If Langfield and Flock are the men who murdered Etna Bittenbender perhaps their decision to criss cross through the area was born of a similar need.

Both Langfield and Flock were brought to Lackawanna County to stand trial for the robbery of the RC Drum store in Gouldsboro. They were convicted, sentenced to imprisonment, and transported to the Eastern State Penitentiary in Philadelphia to serve their sentences. The Eastern State Penitentiary was a remarkable institution in its day; a very modern incarceration model which stressed work, clean living, and rehabilitation. By 1880 it was a fairly crowded facility. The original design parameters were exceeded and inmates shared cramped quarters. The facility had a pretty good system of record-keeping, much of which today can be found either at the site or at the Pennsylvania State Archives in Harrisburg. Research was undertaken to exhaust those records for any information on Charles Flock and John Langfield. One of the things we needed to know was what the men looked like. Unfortunately, 1880 was before mugshots became a regular feature. But there were descriptive books where the receiving officers were supposed to list the height, the weight, the general appearance of an inmate. They would also record ages and prior occupations and certain other characteristics such as lifestyle, morals, abuse of alcohol, that sort of thing.

From these records we learn that Charles Flock was identified as prisoner A716. He was 52 years old and was sentenced on February 5, 1881 to a prison term of 5 years and eight months. He arrived at Eastern State Penitentiary on February 8, 1881. Flock lists two occupations, an original or initial occupation of a 'Shoemaker' and at the time of his arrest he lists his occupation as a 'miner'. Flock was born and raised in Germany where he attended school until the age of 14. He could read and write. Flock claimed to be married with five children. His use of alcohol was described as moderate.

Prisoner A715 is 'John Langefeld' age 28. He was sentenced to the same term of years as his friend Charles Flock. He also arrived at Eastern State Penitentiary on the same day, February 8th 1881. He too claimed that at the time of his arrest he was a 'miner'. Prior to that he claimed he was 'harness maker'. Like Flock, Langfield was also born and raised in Germany. He too could read and write and attended school there to the age of 14. Langfield was not married and had no children. His temperance was listed the same as Charles Flock 'moderate'. Unfortunately, there is no detailed physical description of the men. However, there is an age difference between the men; Langfield at 28 and Flock at 52, is 22 years difference a good deal greater than the tramps seen by Wilson Marsh at the bridge; one man identified as about 40 years of age and the other between 30 and 35 years of age.

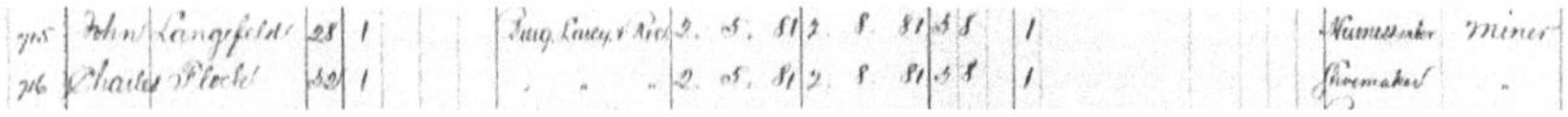

Figure 53 - The Prison Admission Records Eastern State Penitentiary.

Langfield and Flock did not serve out their entire term. Pennsylvania passed a 'Commutation Law' which was meant to ease overcrowding and save money. Under the law both men were released on the same day, April 5, 1886. That day marks their exit from both prison and history. After that day we have been unable to find any definitive record for either of these men; they are simply lost to history. Nor were we able to find out if Attorney Holmes ever had the chance to interview the men or learn anything else about them. But there is an intangible thing, the kind that nags at you, maybe it was a gut feeling, maybe something based upon his extensive experience dealing with inmates. The last known reference to Charles Flock and John Langfield is an entry written by Michael Cassidy, the Warden of the Eastern State Penitentiary, in his Daily Journal. Mr. Cassidy was famous for his knowledge of corrections and inmates. He wrote and lectured extensively on the subject. Something about these men really bothered Warden Cassidy. He uses words unlike those he uses to describe any of the other inmates commuted at that time: "A 715 John Langfield and A 716 Charles Flock were discharged by the Commutation Law, they each served five years and two months, convicted in Lackawanna County of larceny and burglary and receiving stolen goods; they are bad men capable of committing high crimes; both are Germans of a bad kind." (Warden's Daily Journal, Eastern State Penitentiary April 5, 1886).

These 'bad men' Germans of a 'bad kind', men capable of committing 'high crimes', bore a 'close description' to the men Wilson Marsh saw on the stone bridge near the murder scene; men who likely made their camp in the same woods where young Etna was 'decoyed', 'outraged', and 'murdered.' These men were on a reckless crime spree within days of the murder. The spree included 2 or 3 burglaries spread out between Lackawanna and Northampton Counties and involved the men crisscrossing through the area during the height of frenzy and alarm over Etna's Murder.

Chapter 5

Neighbors

"Major Strasser has been shot. Round up the usual suspects."

Captain Renault, Casablanca 1942.

Despite the circumstances showing Langfield and Flock's possible connection to the murder, the investigation was being pulled closer to home, to a local, a neighbor. This man's name was Sam Haney. Surprisingly, the accounts claim that Mr. Haney was arrested and released a total of three times. The last account we have of him needs to be quoted in full:

"The hearing in the case of Samuel Haney, charged with the murder of Miss Bittenbender, near Snydersville, came off as appointed on Friday last. As was predicted at the time of his arrest and imprisonment a week before, it proved a supreme fizzle and he was discharged. Not a single witness was produced against him who knew anything but hearsay talk, and after lying in jail for some ten days he was turned loose upon the world without so much as the expression of regret for having so long and so unwarrantably being detained in limbo. This farce being played with Haney as the chief actor is getting to be monotonous. The public are getting tired of it and the few who are mysteriously sniffing around to scare up something which will place them within reach of the promised reward for the Bittenbender murderer or murderers, should begin to see that they are giving aid to the worse than brute, whoever he may be, by affording him time to so cover up his tracks, so as to make them completely indiscernible. It is true we have mysterious head shakings and insinuations as to what this man has discovered and what is known to that man. If one half the knowledge alleged is true, there is enough known, if presented to an intelligent jury to hang half a dozen men. Against Haney more than against any other man are these insinuations and allegations alleged. If these knowing ones believe what they so much profess to, why not act as men desirous of vindicating the majesty of the law? A horrible shocking and most brutal murder has been committed, which cries from earth to heaven for vengeance. Feelings of parents and relatives have been lacerated beyond conception. Punishment of the crime is sternly demanded and yet these gossipers are silent when they should speak, and dumb when they should be sounding what they know in the Commonwealth's ears. Arrests have been made- some half dozen of them- and opportunity has thus been afforded to detectives, professional and amateur, foreign and domestic, to vent their knowledge, not from the housetops, and in and around bar rooms, but in places where, if still further developments were necessary, it could be retained in secrecy until they were made; but no. There is no desire to be present at the hearing, or if present, to tell anything that would implicate the prisoner. No! Sam Haney is arrested and imprisoned for 10 days to await a hearing, and then left go, without so much as an expression of regret that he had been unjustly detained so long. We are not the apologist for Sam Haney; we know no good of him-we have heard much concerning him that almost leads us to believe him to be a bad man. We have heard stories of him in connection with this Bittenbender murder that are much against him. But these things do not militate against the belief that he should be justly dealt with-do not militate against our right to condemn a farce which has been enacted so long and so bunglingly that if it has any effect at all will only be the effect of enabling the murderer to cover up his tracks and to escape justice altogether. If the evidence in the knowledge of certain individuals is as strong as is alleged against Haney, let the commonwealth have it and proceed to act, and if it convicts him of the murder let him hang for it; if not let him go. It is singular that in this whole concatenation of circumstances, the coolest and most collected man appears to be Sam Haney, whom nearly everybody suspects of having committed the murder. At least let us have no more arrests until something tangible in the shape of evidence is ready to be brought forth to secure his committal, trial, and condemnation if necessary. Let us have rest from this amateur detective bungling." (*Jeffersonian*, Stroudsburg, February 10, 1881).

There must have been something about this guy, something bad for him to be arrested over and over; but exactly what that was remains a mystery. Although his name is repeated throughout the accounts, and the impression left of him is a very negative one, the details of why he was suspected were never recorded. His name could have been written into the inquest findings or the grand jury report, instead the inquest deems the killer or killers as 'unknown'. Evidence of the murder was presented to the December 1880 Session of the County Grand Jury at the old courthouse in Stroudsburg. The Grand Jury did issue a statement on the case urging the district attorney to use all his resources to ferret out the murder; a mandate that was never rescinded. But the Grand Jury makes no mention of Samuel Haney, or any other suspect.

So it is left to us to see what traces of this man's life may still exist to help figure out why people thought he had killed Etna. In June 1880, at the time of the census, Sam Haney was 34 years old married to his wife Sara. Together they had five children, the oldest William Haney was 13 and the youngest John was four. His occupation was listed as a laborer. But the Farm Census for 1880 records him as the owner of a very modest farm. So small and meager was the farm that it doesn't appear adequate to sustain his large family; only 10 acres of land were tilled and the rest, 13 acres, left alone. The estimated value of the farm in 1879 was only $125. Haney had a single milking cow, two pigs, twenty chickens, and ten apple trees. The only other crop recorded was two acres of rye. In 1880, Sam Haney and his family appear dirt poor.

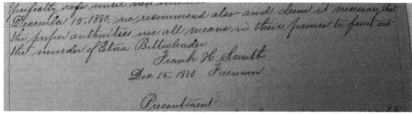

Figure 54 - The above is the Grand Jury Presentment dated December 15, 1880 calling upon the proper authorities to use all means in their power to ferret out the murder of Etna Bittenbender, signed by Frank H. Smith Foreman. It seems an afterthought that this language was placed in the December Grand Jury Session. The words immediately above it and in much more detail admonish the county commissioners for starting to build a bridge over McMichaels Creek at an inconvenient time of year! The few lines devoted to Etna's Murder amount to the only official pronouncement traceable to the District Attorney's office. Perhaps there was still a belief that the guilty party would soon be brought to justice. Its lack of any facts was another disappointment for us investigating the case.

We were able to figure out the location of Sam Haney's home. We had to combine the 1875 map of Hamilton Township with the 1880 census and by plotting all of Haney's neighbors; we determined that the house was on Pensyl Creek Road. In fact, of the houses on that road, Haney's was the closest to the crime scene. In other words, the order in which Haney's house appears, and the neighbors listed, both before and after him on the 1880 census, compared to the 1875 map, which lists certain homeowners, allow us to pinpoint Haney's likely home. We believe this home still stands, a very modest wooden house, painted yellow today. The house stands alongside Pensyl Creek Road three quarters of a mile south of the crime scene. It is a curiously small home.

Haney lists his occupation as a laborer, but we are not told what he does, or who he works for. The whole area was apparently abuzz with rumors of Haney's involvement in Etna's murder, but nobody ever wrote down any details of why he was suspected. From the tone of the *Jeffersonian* Article and the fact that he was arrested multiple times, a couple of things can be considered. First, Haney's reputation had to be very bad. His neighbors considered him the type of person who could commit rape and murder. Perhaps he was overheard talking about Etna in a lewd or troubling way? Perhaps he had a reputation for unwanted advances? Perhaps he made such advances on Etna herself in the days, weeks, or months prior to the murder? The fact that he could also be suspected of murder indicates a reputation for violence. Perhaps that violence was alcohol induced? But certainly his calmness in the face of arrest and imprisonment, as noted in the newspaper, doesn't fit that picture. So why was he arrested multiple times? We've already established that Detective Wood was no slouch. Why did the authorities attempt multiple hearings only for Haney to be released each time?

Maybe there's something about the method and involvement of the Pinkertons that could shed some light on what was going on. At the same time the investigation was focused on outsiders, such as Langfield and Flock; trying to run down witnesses who could identify the men, all this talk around the neighborhood about Sam Haney being the killer had to influence the investigation. When Haney was initially arrested and nobody could say anything but hearsay, Haney gets out. But the talk, the gossip, the scuttlebutt, the innuendo, all increase. The second arrest meets the same fate as the first arrest, but still the consensus from many in the community remains unchanged. Now around this time, January - February of 1881, more than one detective was working on the case. We can't be sure if John Wood was still involved. The county records do not disclose any payments for detective services for the 1881 calendar year. However, the news accounts did mention multiple detectives, from both New York and Philadelphia. These detectives are not named in the accounts. Perhaps that was by design. The Pinkertons had a whole array of investigative techniques. Many of these techniques centered on deception; detectives, operatives, agents, would wear disguises, give false names, and create false impressions about them, all in an effort to elicit information.

The Maybee murders mentioned previously involved that same technique; a detective working with John Wood immersed himself into a suspect's family to become a confidante in the hopes of getting a confession. In the infamous Molly McGuire murder trials, a key witness was a Pinkerton agent who went undercover to infiltrate the Irish gang, learn their secrets, and then use it against them. What if the third time Haney was arrested he was placed in jail alongside someone who appeared to be a fellow inmate but was not? This would explain the lengthy delay of about two weeks between the date of his incarceration and the date of his hearing. In fact, an article out of the *Daily Free Press* of Easton mentions that Haney was still in jail one week after the charges against him were dismissed. Was there a plant spending his time with Haney in a jail cell in Stroudsburg, commiserating with Haney, getting into his good graces to gain his trust, trying to get him to talk about the murder? Something like that would be in keeping with the Pinkerton methodology and could explain that third arrest not as 'amateur detective bungling', but a bona fide investigative technique that didn't pay off.

You know there are always people quick to point out others in the community as the culprits in crimes like this. It's a 'usual suspects' kind of thing; times change but people don't. There are several unsolved but much more recent cold case murders in our community. These often involve a lot of rumor and scuttlebutt, the 'word on the street'; suspects named and inferred but never any proof offered. Usually these suspects are 'colorful' characters with poor reputations, sometimes deserved, and sometimes not so much. In the troubling murder of 20 year old Lee Van Louvender, who was shot to death while out hunting one morning in December of 2004, many people in the community were quick to point to a neighbor who lived nearby. The neighbor could be considered a strange man in his habits, but no evidence could link him to the crime. Nevertheless, the rumors persisted. He wasn't the only one. In the same case another man of a fearsome reputation, was also rumored to be the killer. But all the investigation undertaken showed him to have absolutely no connection to the crime and in fact his fearsome reputation was undeserved. One of the hard-working investigators on the case, Rob Sebastianelli remarked that the man was 'the toughest guy who never got in a fight.' It seemed that if you crossed him he might bring a lawsuit against you in Magistrate Court, but that was it. So it is on that note that we must conclude that even though there was a lot of talk about Sam Haney's involvement there was no evidence.

One of the benefits of a cold case is, ironically, time. It's kind of counterintuitive, but time, the old enemy of a murder investigation is sometimes a friend. In this case, almost 140 years of time is at our disposal, nearly a century and a half in which to chart out the lives of many of these people, witnesses and suspects alike. So although the trail on Sam Haney's involvement in the murder 'fizzles' out in 1881, his name comes up 25 years later. By this time his children are all grown up. He is still married to Sarah. They live in East Stroudsburg, where he owns a general store. He also works in law enforcement. His obituary indicated he worked as a truant officer. In certain court documents he is listed as a constable. The year is 1906 and Haney has just been indicted for rape. The case would go to trial and caused quite a stir in the community. It was standing room only in the courthouse. Not the old courthouse, the one he was brought in for Etna's murder, but the new courthouse, built in 1896 by Italian immigrant brothers. The same courthouse, but with a modern addition, that is still in use today. People wanted to hear the evidence in Haney's rape trial. The accounts mention even young girls trying to get in to hear the sordid details. By this time there was no *Monroe Democrat* paper or *Jeffersonian Republican*. The single newspaper was called the *Stroudsburg Daily Times*. The Times article about Haney's trial mentions the sordid curiosity of the spectators and how the evidence was not fit to print.

The indictment against Samuel Haney was brought by the alleged victim's father, Wesley Bisbing of Pocono Township. The case proceeded from the Justice of the Peace to the grand jury, which issued its indictment. The indictment alleges that: "Samuel Haney late of the Borough of East Stroudsburg County of Monroe and State of Pennsylvania, Constable, on the 4th day of November 1905 at the Borough of East Stroudsburg, did have unlawful carnal knowledge of Rosa Bisbing... a single woman forcibly and against her will ... Haney then and there being a married man and the said Rosa Bisbing not being his lawful wife; and upon the body of said Rosa Bisbing then and there did beget a female bastard child to the great injury and damage of the said Rosa Bisbing..." The case was listed for trial during the November 1906 trial term.

Figure 55 - A View from the balcony looking down into the Courtroom as it looked around the time of Sam Haney's 1906 rape trial. The courtroom would have been packed to capacity in both its upper and lower levels. (Courtesy of Detective Sgt. Wendy Serfass).

The case was moved to December 1906. The *Stroudsburg Daily Times* refers to it as a 'court matinee' "Men, women, and girls swarm to hear the case.' The article states: The Haney case is on and a matinee is being held at the courthouse. Not an available seat is left untaken. The S.R.O sign may as well have been put up early. Women lean over and drink every word in as eagerly as if it were music. Men sit with mouths agape listening lest any word of the filthy evidence escape them. Everybody is on deck and wouldn't miss the show for the world. There are men at the trial who haven't been out of the house all winter. Young girls had to be let out by the tipstaves. Others stayed in the gallery by getting in early. The evidence is not fit to print." (*Stroudsburg Daily Times*, December 11, 1906).

Dr. Werkman who delivered the baby, a Mrs. Charles Judd, Mr. Eugene Heller, a Reverend Ellis, Addison Learn, and Joshua Sebring testified. But since the *Daily Times* felt the evidence was not fit to print, we have no indication of what was said. Despite the public interest and lurid subject matter, Sam Haney was found not guilty. The strangest thing was that nowhere does anyone mention that Haney was arrested in the past on suspicion of murder. It's almost like, in the space of 26 short years, Etna's murder, or at least its details, such as the repeated arrest of Sam Haney, were all but forgotten.

Rosa Bisbing was born on April 11, 1888. At the time she allegedly had sexual relations with Sam Haney she would have been 18 years old. Mr. Haney would have been 57 years old. The child born, a female 'bastard child', was born on July 30, 1906. The child was born in Pocono Township. Rosa is listed as a 'work girl'. The father's information is left blank on the birth certificate with the phrase 'unknown to me' written in the column for 'father.' The next known record for Rosa is that she married someone named Kysic Stellmer and they lived together in East Stroudsburg. The couple had one child, a boy named Kenneth. Rosa passed away from a chronic illness on October 15, 1922 at the age of 34. There is no record of what happened to the baby girl.

Chapter 6

A torn and bloody coat

"Yet each man kills the thing he loves".
The Ballad of Reading Goal Oscar Wilde

There is one name that comes up throughout the entire investigation; one person who is tightly interwoven into the heart of the case. That person is Wilson Marsh, the 16 year old son of Jacob Marsh and his wife Emma. Wilson is the only witness who claimed to see tramps 'lurking' nearby on the bridge the day Etna's body was found. It was this claim that gave rise to the Tramp Theory. Wilson Marsh's detailed description of the two men, the same description which made its way onto the wanted posters, provided the investigators with the only tangible lead; a lead that they pursued vigorously. They arrested numerous 'tramps' in a process called the 'roundup of the tramps'. Every tramp arrested went through a detailed 'tracing' of his whereabouts at the time of the murder; a painstaking process. This endeavor consumed valuable time and effort lasting over a month and into the first week of December of 1880. Ultimately, despite all the arrests, the effort proved fruitless.

Figure 56 -This Photograph appears in the background of the photograph of Emma Marsh. It is believed to be that of Wilson's father Jacob Marsh who passed away in December of 1881and is buried in St. John's Cemetery off Neola Road near the Rees School. Jacob, Wilson's father came from a long line of Monroe County settlers. His grandfather Abraham Marsh served in the Continental Army. His mother Anna Bittenbender was Etna's grand aunt. From RH Marsh.

Who was Wilson Marsh? What do we know of him, his life, and his deeds? He was still just a boy when his cousin Etna was murdered. He was related to Etna on his father Jacob's side. Jacob Marsh and Sam Bittenbender were first cousins. Jacob's mother and Sam's father were brother and sister. So, Wilson's paternal side grandmother was in fact a Bittenbender. That made Wilson and Etna third cousins. According to the 1880 census, Wilson lived with his parents and 11 year old brother Curvin Marsh. The oldest Marsh child was 18 year old Edward, but he had already moved from the area and was living out west. Wilson lived the life of a farm boy. The Marsh Farm wasn't as large or productive as the farm of Samuel Bittenbender. But there was plenty to do. Although his father Jacob is listed on the census as a farmer, Wilson would later tell people that his father was a cooper by trade; that is a maker of casks and barrels. This is consistent with Jacob growing up with Eugene Marsh in nearby Sand Hill where he probably learned the trade in conjunction with the work of the Marsh Foundry.

Wilson's mother was a Rees, descended from a family line reaching back to Colonial times. One of her ancestors was a Colonel Rees who fought in the Continental Army during the Revolutionary War. Abrahm Marsh, Wilson's great grandfather also fought in the Revolutionary War with the Northampton County Militia. The Marsh family attended the evangelical church just down the road from their home. The church was small, but tight-knit, servicing people from northern Hamilton and southern Jackson Townships. It was known in the area as the "Gospel Shop" and was quite an active center for the spreading of the Reform and Evangelical movements affecting Pennsylvania in the second half of the 19th century. Jacob Marsh is actually buried in the small cemetery called St. John's, right next to where the old church was located.

One of the things we look for in cases like this is to reconstruct as much as possible a victim's life, her friends, her family, and other relationships. By all accounts Etna was a beautiful girl, well-liked, from a good family. Her parents were well-to-do and thrifty. At 17 years old Etna was no longer in school. There must have been plans for her future, plans for further education, perhaps as a school teacher, and or plans for her marriage. The stories are not specific. The course Etna's life was to take was not written about in the news accounts. Although these details would have been gathered by the detective and others and would have been sought during questioning before the Inquest and the Grand Jury in December of 1880, those records are lost; but there are clues.

Figure 57 - Etna as she may have appeared based on contemporaneous descriptions.

In addition to her good looks, social standing, and popularity, there was a rumor circulating at the time of her death that Etna was pregnant. This rumor is repeated in the first article of the murder written by the *Jeffersonian Republican* as early as November 4, 1880. In the piece, the local editor uses the word 'enceinte' for pregnant and reports that contrary to rumor the findings of the post-mortem examination proved Etna was not with child. A rumor like that, of pregnancy, usually goes hand in hand with the naming of the alleged father. What exactly was Etna's status? She was single and nowhere is it noted that she was betrothed. Still there must have been some romantic interest of hers. But the accounts do not discuss this aspect of her life. That's a shame because experience teaches that a majority of murder victims know their killer and many are involved romantically with the offender.

By combining some common-sense and life experience with the false rumor of pregnancy and a bit of folk memory, suggests that Wilson and Etna were romantically involved. Third cousins marrying in rural Pennsylvania in the latter part of the 19th century was not uncommon. So the mere fact that there was a blood relation to that degree does not discount the proposition. Also Etna was staying at the Marsh home. Some accounts call her a housekeeper to the Marshes but I believe that is an inaccurate characterization of the status. Etna would have been more of a helper for Mrs. Marsh and perhaps was staying at the Marsh home in recognition of a budding romantic connection between her and Wilson. The status of the two families and the relationship between them wasn't one of employee to employer or servant to master. Rather, it was based on bonds of family and affection.

That brings us to a scrap of folk memory that we found during our research. Several of the old-timers we spoke with recalled their elders discussing the murder from time to time. Whenever the subject would come up the younger family members would question them. Everyone wanted to know who killed Etna. One of the strongest beliefs of the people was that Etna was killed not only by someone who knew her, a local, but also someone with whom she was involved with romantically. We were often told simply that Etna was killed by her 'boyfriend' and, this is important, that her boyfriend then 'moved out west'. Unfortunately, the boyfriend is never specifically named in that folk memory. But we do know that the boyfriend moved out west. There is only one person who fits the bill.

Despite his roots in the rocky soil of Monroe County Wilson Marsh would leave the area; moving far away 'out west'. Wilson left Pennsylvania with his younger brother Curvin within a year after his father's passing in December of 1881. He first settled in Iowa. In 1884 he married Laura Allison in Sac City Iowa. In 1884 Wilson left Iowa and settled in Dakota Territory, more particularly, South Dakota. Young Wilson would make his way to Rapid City South Dakota. There he and Allison raised a family. By 1892 he was joined by his mother. Wilson founded a large and prosperous ranch in South Dakota. The Marsh Ranch became famous for its success, hospitality, and the ingenuity of its founder Wilson Marsh, one of the area's first settlers. Wilson pioneered the use of complex irrigation systems and the ranch grew year by year. He lived a long life and left a lasting impression as a founding pioneer in that section of South Dakota. So by combining the folklore with the history we can safely assume that many of the local people suspected Wilson Marsh of Etna's murder. But there must have been more to it than the belief that Etna and Wilson were in a relationship.

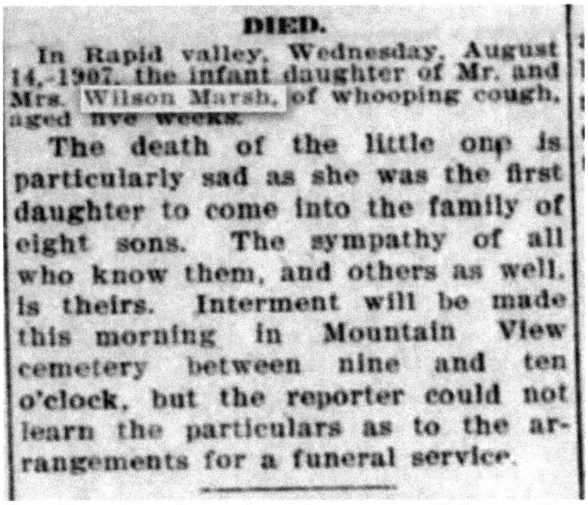

Figure 58 - Wilson's only daughter died in infancy.

DIED.

In Rapid valley, Wednesday, August 14, 1907. the infant daughter of Mr. and Mrs. Wilson Marsh, of whooping cough, aged five weeks.

The death of the little one is particularly sad as she was the first daughter to come into the family of eight sons. The sympathy of all who know them, and others as well. is theirs. Interment will be made this morning in Mountain View cemetery between nine and ten o'clock, but the reporter could not learn the particulars as to the arrangements for a funeral service.

Once again the passage of time can be a friend to the cold case investigator. During the course of a long life repetition is usually seen; habits or traits of character, good or bad, provide some level of predictability. So what does the advantage of time tell us about Wilson Marsh? In defense of Wilson Marsh, there is no evidence that in his long life out west that he ever violated the law, let alone committed a violent assault. The following is a summary of his life out west located at Findagrave.com.

"Wilson was born to Jacob and Emma Rees Marsh in Sciota Pennsylvania. His father was a "cooper' by trade building wooden barrels, casks and tubs. Wilson worked as a carpenter but he wanted to go west. He spent his childhood in Pennsylvania. In 1883 he and his brother Curvin left home, locating in Iowa. Wilson married Laura Allison in 1884 in Sac City IA; they came here from Iowa the following year by stage coach. Wilson and Curvin left Iowa for Dakota Territory, with Laura following in 1885. Later Wilson kiddingly said they walked most of the way because it was so muddy, the horses couldn't pull the stage coach and the passengers had to push. They homesteaded in an area south of present day New Underwood, on what was known as "on the divide" in 1889 near Farmingdale. During the Indian troubles at Wounded Knee, many homesteaders sent their families back east until the problem was over. When Laura returned, they lived on the "Divide" for twelve years' then moved closer to Rapid City in Rapid Valley in 1897, where he lived until last summer. This was the start of the "Marsh Place" one of the best known of the Valley Ranches. The Marsh's built a very elegant house in 1894 and it is still occupied. The house and barns

135

are found at the corner of present day Pennington County Roads 210 and 232 in Rapid Valley. During the early days many a weary traveler was given refreshment and rest at the "Marsh Place". At the height of the thrashing season many people were employed by the Marsh's. There was a "root cellar", for storing potatoes that was large enough to drive a team and wagon into. At the rear of the house and a short distance from the barn in a tent lived an Indian known only as "Little Chief". They helped with many chores around the ranch during threshing and then returned to the reservation. Along the way Wilson found the time to pursue his love of carpentry, helped build many of the early ranch buildings in Rapid Valley and homes in Rapid City. Wilson was very interested in irrigation and purchased the majority shares of the Hawthorn Ditch Co in 1905. The Marsh family continued to be involved in the management of the Ditch until 1980. If you enter the Central States Fairground the head gate can still be seen on the creek.

Figure 59 - Wilson had his share of personal tragedy. His oldest son Elmer, pictured above died as a young man in his twenties of pneumonia. From RH Marsh.

The Marsh Place was one of the best known of valley ranches in those early days. Wilson ran cattle over the prairies and built up a large herd in the early days. He was active in the stock growers association for many years. Laura died in 1932 but he continued to live on the ranch, operating it until 1950 when he came to Rapid City. Because his health was not very good, he made his home with a grandson, Leo Marsh.

Wilson Marsh is survived by one brother Curvin of Rapid City, seven sons, Harry, Rolla, Earl and Clover Marsh all of Rapid City, Corbin of

Fredrickson MO, Ralph of Juneau Alaska, and Frank of Buffalo NY. and 13 grandchildren and 14 great grandchildren. His wife died in 1932. It is because of such men as Wilson Marsh that this West River Empire was built up into the rich country it is today. The pioneers are fast fading from the scene where they were so active for so long, but their works will stand for many years.

From the first time Wilson Marsh saw the possibilities for irrigation in Rapid Valley and later he was instrumental in organizing ditch companies and in developing irrigation, a subject he studied thoroughly and on which he was considered an authority. He was a firm believer in western South Dakota, and although he went through some "tough times", drought, blizzards, grasshoppers, plague, low farm prices, depressions, he never lost his love of the place he lived."

Wilson inserted himself early into the investigation. By doing so he placed himself into the timeline of the murder. He claims to be within half a mile of the crime scene when the body of Etna Bittenbender is discovered by her young siblings. Wilson claims he sees two tramps on the stone bridge nearby the murder scene that very morning. There is no doubt that Detective Wood questioned Wilson, carefully tracing his movements from the time he claimed to see the tramps back to the time on October 31 when Etna would have left her parents' home to go to Wilson's home. Wilson must have explained to Detective Wood where he was, who he was with, and what he did throughout the time period of Etna's absence. Wilson would have certainly provided details and back up, some kind of corroboration, for that whole time. Yet, Wilson was alone at the time he says the tramps were on the bridge. He is the only source for that information. Detective Wood seemed to believe, at least initially, what Wilson was telling him. The crime scene nearby the 'tramp' campsite backed up Wilson's story. So Detective Wood went with it. As a result, tramps, many of them, were arrested, traced, and then let go.

Figure 60 - The remains of the old stone bridge on which Wilson Marsh claimed to see two tramps 'lurking' about on the day Etna's body was discovered. The photograph was taken from Effort Neola Road less than half a mile from the death scene.

"It is now a little over a month since the terrible murder of Miss Bittenbender occurred. Several experts have visited the premises to ascertain by statements and a minute and careful search to get any clue that would indicate who was the guilty one in the dreadful tragedy. Numerous theories and rumors have been afloat, but none yet have warranted an arrest. The tramps have been traced and found to have not been at the scene of the murder at the time, and the general suspicion seems to rest that the deed was committed by someone living in the neighborhood. From all the statements there were but two tramps seen and only two have been arrested bearing any close description to those explained by the boy Marsh; his description is very full and would seem by its plainness to have secured the parties if tramps. (The Bittenbender Murder, *Monroe Democrat* December 1880).

As the tracing of the tramps began to wind down and the process seemed futile, voices were raised, more than one, claiming that the killer had to be local; the focus of the investigation began to look inward, to none other than Wilson Marsh. This shift began as early as the second week of November 1880; "it is thought that the culprit will be caught in a few days, as the guilty party, from the evidence at hand is believed to be known. He is said to be a young man hitherto considered of very good character and high social standing, and his arrest will be a great social shock. (*Easton Daily Free Press*, November 19, 1880). This could only refer to Wilson Marsh. Indeed, the *Jeffersonian* in its November 25, 1880 piece concluded that the' fiend' or 'fiends' were not only acquainted with the locality of the crime scene, but also acquainted 'intimately' with the 'victim of his hellish lust and brutality'. (*Jeffersonian*, November 25, 1880) This reference to an 'intimate' connection between the killer and Etna mirrors the folk memory given to us, that Etna was killed by her boyfriend.

Things came to a head for Wilson Marsh on Monday December 6, 1880. On that date, in the evening, Jacob Felker along with a young man named Ed Marsh, (yes another Marsh), were out in the woods near the crime scene. While there they discovered a coat 'hidden' under a 'low pine tree'. The coat's sleeves were torn; bloodstains bespattered the garment, with long hair clinging to it. The two immediately brought the coat to the authorities. News of the discovery of the coat quickly spread. "On Monday last a coat was found hidden under a small pine tree near the scene of the murder with the sleeves torn and covered with blood. The coat has been recognized as to its ownership and forms an important link in a chain of circumstance which is likely being drawn around an individual who has been from sometime suspected." (*Jeffersonian Republican*, The Bittenbender Case Again, December 9, 1880) The article goes on to describe the confidence of the detectives, their certainty that they had their man and that his apprehension was near at hand. The article also perfectly captures the feeling of the people and the idea that the killer was one of their own and in their midst. "[a] few more circumstances are needed to make a certain case, and these are coming up slowly but surely. May the time for their perfection hasten. A wilful murder has been committed under outrageous circumstances and the blood of an innocent maiden cries aloud from the ground for vengeance." (*Jeffersonian Republican*, The Bittenbender Case Again December 9, 1880)

That cry for vengeance was taken up by everyone, from the farmers, who formed the bulk of the population, to the tradesman, the shopkeepers, the doctors, the lawyers etc. Detective Wood and DS Lee did not stop their efforts. Everyone sought comfort in the thought that the lawmen would catch up to the murderer and that they would '... run him down and secure him for the expiation of his crime and the gallows.' (*Jeffersonian Republican*, The Bittenbender Case Again December 9, 1880). If the lawmen failed the people themselves would bring the gallows, in the form of a lynch mob, to the killer. Lynching, an extrajudicial execution carried out by vigilantes, was not unheard of in northeastern Pennsylvania during this time period. In nearby Northampton County, Bushkill Township a farmhand suspected of killing the couple he worked for and trying to rape their young daughter was lynched. That lynching happened only a few months after Etna's murder. The man lynched was a 27 year old named Joseph Snyder. He was a miner and had been boarding at the residence of Jacob Gogle 38 and his wife Anna 34; they lived north of Bethlehem at Santee Mill.

Figure 61 - Jacob and Catherine Gogle murdered by Joseph Snyder December 26, 1880.

The Gogles had a pretty daughter named Alice who was fourteen years old. Snyder wanted to marry Alice. The Gogles were firmly opposed to it. On Sunday December 26, 1880, the day after Christmas, the family had company over. The friends and Snyder spent time in the parlor singing Christmas Carols together. Later, the company left; except for two girls, friends of Alice, who were going to spend the night. At around 8:30 Snyder went to bed. By 9:00 pm everyone went to bed for the night. But Snyder wasn't sleeping, he was waiting. When he thought everyone was asleep, Snyder, wearing only a shirt, left his room. He had with him an axe. He quietly entered the bedroom of Mr. and Mrs. Gogle. He murdered the couple with the axe as they lay in their bed. "The wife had her head nearly chopped off. The husband had nine cuts, his back being split open. The sight was a terrible one, the smashed and battered skulls of the victims, and the blood spattered on the walls and the ceiling showing that the murderer must have dealt them fearful blows with the weapon he held. He drew the edge across their throats, and rolled up the bloody axe in the counterpane (bed sheets)." (*Allentown Democrat*, December 29, 1880)

Snyder wasn't finished. "He then sought the chamber of the young girl he had professed to love. With her there at the time was a girl named Clara Young, who was paying her a visit, and her younger sister Mary. Snyder here conducted himself in a shameless and brutal manner, ...Clara and Mary crying "murder!" ran downstairs into the room of Mr. and Mrs. Gogle…. The strange silence increased their terror…" (*The New Era*, Lancaster, January 1, 1881) The children in the dark lit a match and saw the bloodied bodies. They fled the room in terror. Snyder locked the children in an upstairs room. He burned his shirt in the kitchen. He pretended that the couple were killed by masked intruders and alerted neighbors. He then slipped away in the confusion.

Snyder was found around 9:00 am by a Bethlehem detective, he had been hiding under sheaves of wheat in a barn belonging to a Captain Ritter. Snyder was brought back to the scene. He admitted his guilt. A crowd of men formed. Over the protests of the detective, the crowd grabbed Snyder. "The crowd seemed determined to hang the man. A rope was thrown over the limb of a tree and the murderer was asked what he had to say. He said 'All I want is time and a trial.' He admitted murdering the man and woman. Finally the crowd began tugging on the rope, and in a moment Snyder's body hung in the air. He drew up his hands and feet convulsively once or twice and then strangled to death. He was hung up about five minutes of eleven. The crowd that hung the man was composed of about 100 or 150 people, while a large number looked on. It was a strange and wonderful hanging. Scarcely a loud shout was heard and nearly every voice was subdued. Yet, there was an earnestness about the whole affair truly wonderful. Not once did the crowd waiver in its resolve to lynch the man, but no unusual language, no unnecessary steps were taken...so quickly did the men lynch the murderer that the coroner's jury was not aware that the man had been hanged until after he was dead, though he was hanged to a tree not 50 feet from the house, and the jury supposed the noise meant nothing more than that which they had heard during the morning." (*Allentown Democrat*, December 29, 1880)

Figure 62 - Illustration of Snyder's Lynching.

The last recorded lynching in the area occurred right in Stroudsburg on March 22, 1894. A black man named Richard Puryear from Mecklenburg Virginia was incarcerated for the murder of a man in Tannersville named Christian Ehler, known as the 'Swede'. Ehler's wife was also shot. The Ehlers operated a general store at White Oak Run. Puryear had been employed as a 'Gang boss' with the Wilkes-Barre and Eastern Railroad. He had regular dealings with Mr. Ehler. He came to the Ehler's house at six pm on a Friday evening; "just as Mr. and Mrs. Ehler and their twelve year old son were sitting down to supper. Mr. Ehler invited him into the room, and the two men held a brief conversation upon common place matters. Puryear stood with his back to the door, which he had meanwhile closed, and as Mr. Ehler turned away to take his seat at the table, the negro, without a word or an instant's warning drew a revolver from his pocket and shot the unsuspecting merchant through his head, piercing the brain and causing instant death. Mrs. Ehler sprang to her feet with a scream of terror and started to the side of her dying husband. Before she had taken the step the fiend turned his weapon upon her and began to fire. The first shot struck her hand which she uplifted in a vain plea for mercy. The second shot entered her breast passing through her right lung and coming back out, after which it embedded itself in the wall. Mrs. Ehler fell to the floor feigning death. The murderer then turned his attention to the boy, who had meanwhile raised a window and was climbing through it in mortal terror. A fourth shot was fired at the boy just as he sprang to the ground, but it went wide of the mark and the lad escaped. (*The Allentown Democrat*, February 28, 1894).

Puryear ransacked Ehler's house, stealing about $35.00 Dollars. He was incriminated by Mrs. Ehler in a dying declaration and by her son who later identified him. Puryear, who had fled was arrested in Blairstown New Jersey about 35 miles away. He would give a written confession. After he was returned to Monroe County there were two attempts to storm the jail involving hundreds of angry men in an effort to lynch him.

Figure 63 - Stroudsburg Times article on the attempted lynching of Puryear. After two attempts the mob succeeded with the hanging.

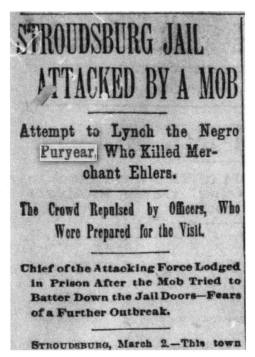

STROUDSBURG JAIL ATTACKED BY A MOB

Attempt to Lynch the Negro Puryear, Who Killed Merchant Ehlers.

The Crowd Repulsed by Officers, Who Were Prepared for the Visit.

Chief of the Attacking Force Lodged in Prison After the Mob Tried to Batter Down the Jail Doors—Fears of a Further Outbreak.

STROUDSBURG, March 2.—This town

Despite or perhaps because of the threats to lynch Puryear, one afternoon he found his cell door mysteriously left open; he quickly got by the sheriff and made a break for it. It is astonishing how quickly a party of men formed to give chase. Puryear ran south crossing Ann Street. He reached the banks of the creek. He was fast. He crossed the water, but was soon caught on the other side and brought back. The *Pocono Record* in 1967 reprinted the story of the lynching which had originally appeared in the *Stroudsburg Times*. It tells the brutal tale of the lynching in great detail. Puryear was actually caught behind Ann Street after he crossed the Pocono Creek. His captor was Benjamin Kuenter another black man who managed to run him down. 'Ben' as he is referred to in the article actually knew Puryear from Virginia where they grew up. He worked with Puryear in the same railroad company. Despite Puryear's pleading with Ben, the latter told him he must die for his crimes. Ben handed Puryear over to the mob. They hung him from a white oak tree moments later. The body would be kept hanging for hours. Motts Photographic Studios of Stroudsburg came out and took a photograph of the hanging body. Onlookers, including children, are seen in the photograph; copies were made in cabinet size and sold as souvenirs. The rope used in the hanging was given to Ben Kuenter who made a nice profit selling pieces of it for .50 cents each. He sold the knot for $1.50.

Figure 64 - The Lynched body of Richard Puryear. After it was taken down it was removed to the jail and viewed by visitors for a couple days. It was eventually shipped to a university in Philadelphia for dissection.

The rope used to lynch Joseph Snyder was also cut up and sold as souvenirs. Apparently, there was a belief that the rope and pieces of the tree limb had magical properties. "Country people for miles around visited the scene of the double crime, and pieces of the bed cord by which Snyder was hanging are in great demand. A piece of the rope two or three inches long will sell readily for a dollar, and those persons who secured a few feet of the cord when the body was cut down have made considerable money by retailing bits of it to the visitors. The rope was originally about forty feet long, but an hour after the hanging its length was reduced to twenty feet, and when the inquest was concluded several feet more were cut off. The limb of the tree over which the rope was pulled is also being whittled off and carried away by relic hunters, many of whom superstitiously suppose it and the rope possess wonderful curative powers in cases of chronic disease." (*New Era*, Lancaster January 1, 1881).

Such a fate would await anyone thought to be guilty of Etna's murder. As for the coat, discovered under the low pine tree, the coat torn and bloodied; yes its ownership was recognized. The bloodied torn coat belonged to none other than Wilson Marsh. That information spread throughout the township and county. The Marsh family and Wilson were made aware of the discovery. Talk of lynching also spread. Indeed, it was reported that Wilson himself was nearly lynched. Instead, he quickly made his way to Stroudsburg. He presented himself to the authorities. Wilson readily admitted that the coat was his. But he denied any role in Etna's murder. He offered himself up for examination. The questioning was conducted in Stroudsburg at the American Hotel on Green Street, now Eighth Street, right next to DS Lee's Law Office.

Wilson was questioned for hours. It is probable that Detective Wood and Lee conducted much of the questioning. Witnesses were also brought in, including Jacob Felker and Ed Marsh the finders of the coat. Wilson claimed that he had taken his coat off, leaving it in the woods, about a week before the murder while out hunting. Those with him backed up his story. " Wilson Marsh who had started the Tramp Story at once claimed it [the coat] and proved that he had thrown it off while hunting with some others a week before the murder was committed. It was found only a short distance from where he had thrown it off. When he was told he was suspected on account of the finding of the coat he had volunteered to be examined. He came to Stroudsburg on Wednesday with those who had been with him when he threw the coat off and those who found the coat last Monday and submitted himself to a thorough examination at the

American Hotel." (The Bittenbender Murder, *Monroe Democrat* December 12, 1880).

Wilson was successful. "The coat belonging to Wilson Marsh was found close by, and at first he was suspected and had a narrow escape from being lynched, but made an explanation which established his innocence." (The Monroe County Crime, *Evening Gazette*, Port Jervis March 1881). Wilson must have been a good communicator; at only sixteen to lay out his defense before seasoned investigators, investigators who no doubt were under a great deal of pressure to solve the case. "All present at the examination are now satisfied that Wilson Marsh is innocent of any connection with the murder of Etna Bittenbender. (The Bittenbender Murder, *Monroe Democrat*, December 12, 1880).

What are the odds that close to the scene of the bloody murder, a coat would be found bloodied, torn, with long hairs sticking to it? A coat not lying upon the ground but hidden under a tree? Not just any coat, but a coat belonging to the only person who claimed to see two strangers lurking on a nearby bridge at the time the victim was found? The person who started the Tramp Theory which led investigators on a fruitless month-long crackdown on tramps? A person whose house the victim was going to when she was assaulted and murdered? Of course that person was Wilson Marsh with whom Etna was believed to have been romantically involved. The odds do seem considerable. Many in our line of work do not believe in coincidences.

But looking at the flip side of things; stuff wasn't adding up. The detective did find evidence of some make shift camp near the scene; Hemlock boughs arrayed for bedding, fire wood stacked to start a campfire, branches from a bush also cut presumably to make some sort of a rustic tea. All the makings of a tramp camp were found. Further, Wilson's descriptions of the tramps he claimed to see was full, plain, and did not vary. He held up well under intense questioning from a bright conscientious detective and well-seasoned district attorney. Also the story of Wilson throwing down the coat a week before the murder while out hunting was backed up by witnesses. It is also significant that nobody came forward to say Wilson wore that coat on the day of Etna's murder. There was also evidence on the coat that apparently did not match the victim. I'm not referring to DNA, which would not have been known until almost a hundred years later, or blood type which was decades from being discovered. I'm talking about hair color; 'the hair on the coat was of a light color while the hair upon the murdered girl was jet-black.' (Bittenbender Murder, *Monroe Democrat*, December 12, 1880)

This apparent inconsistency was too much for Detective Wood. Wood was a stickler about such trace evidence. If the hair didn't match visually, then that, along with everything else, would be enough to unsaddle things. The phrase that the hair on the coat was of a 'light color' isn't clear. While not jet black was it a shade of brown, blond, red, or perhaps gray? Identifying actual hair color from a few random strands of hair is not always easy to do with the naked eye. Is it possible that hair of a black color would fade if subjected to elements like weather, soil composition, vegetation, and pine needles if left exposed or partially buried for several weeks? Why was it assumed that the hair had to belong to Etna in the first place? It was undoubtedly an old well-worn coat; otherwise Wilson wouldn't have left it in the woods never to retrieve it again. Did he ever even mention the coat to anyone before it was discovered? Did others wear the coat? Did they have long hair of a light color? Could the hair have gotten onto the coat at an earlier time and be totally unrelated to the events of the murder? Could the hair belong to one of the tramps? Perhaps one of the same tramps seen by Wilson. Maybe a tramp discovered the coat Wilson left and was wearing it during the murder?

If these conflicting thoughts occurred in the investigation they were not recorded. Instead the accounts claim some sort of setup; that the killer tried to set up Wilson by using his coat as evidence against him. "The consummation of the murder fully shows it to have been committed by a person thinking to throw suspicion from himself, which has thus far been successful. The coat being found only furnished evidence of intent of the murderer to saddle the guilt upon the boy Marsh or the owner of the coat ..." The setup Wilson Marsh theory presupposes that the killer was not a stranger or a tramp. Such an outsider would have no need to frame anyone; his need would be the successful flight from the scene. So any attempt to frame a local could only come from another local. This thinking may help explain why the authorities would re-arrest Sam Haney for a third and final time. But there is an illogic inherent in the whole setup Wilson theory. For one thing, the real killer would know Etna's hair color was jet black. Why would he go out of his way to place long hairs of a light color on the coat? Why would he hide the coat under a tree? Wouldn't that risk the possibility that it would never be found? How could Wilson be set up if no one found the coat? Unfortunately, the setup Wilson Theory creates more issues and less answers.

In order to see, strictly as an amateur, what effect, if any, there is to hair color when subjected to the elements, Detective Kerchner and I came up with the idea that if we left hair of a black color in the elements for several weeks and then retrieved the hair we could see if it lightened or otherwise changed color. We tried to pick an area nearby the scene and characterized by pine trees of the variety we noticed all about the crime scene on the far side of the road from where Etna's body was discovered. The woods in that area are mostly Pine. We located a suitable low pine tree for our experiment. We next found a victim, someone who had long black hair, from whom, with his consent, we plucked some hair for the experiment. A local lawyer, a criminal defense attorney, graciously granted our request. He wore his hair long and it was black. Several hairs were given to us and placed on a woolen pair of gloves with which we hoped to mimic Wilson's coat. We left the hairs under a low pine tree for several weeks. When we retrieved them we noticed no difference in hair color.

So Wilson's account was considered credible. He was believed and cleared. Sam Haney was a third time back in the spotlight. He would be arrested and held only to have the charges dismissed for lack of evidence. But Wilson would come up again as a suspect and this time in an even bigger way. It was about a month after the dismissal of charges against Haney. On Monday February 21, 1881 during the early evening hours, three teenage girls left church in Jackson Township and began walking home. As they walked on the road between fields and alongside stone fences they were attacked by 'half-a-dozen boys and young men'. It was a vicious violent attack. One of the girls, a fourteen-year-old, was thrown over the stone fence that bordered the road and landed onto the field. Another girl, older, 18 years of age, had her dress torn into strips. All three girls were indecently assaulted. Luckily their screams of 'murder!' were heard by several men nearby who arrived and chased off the attackers. The attackers were not strangers from out of the area. Instead they were all local and known. One of them was a 'young man' who had been suspected of being involved in the murder of Etna Bittenbender but 'nothing could be proven against him."

News of the attack spread. People were shocked and angry. "Another outrage in Monroe County'. (*Bethlehem Times*, February 23, 1881). "Up to this time none of the brutes have been arrested, tried, convicted, and sentenced to the fullest extent of the law. The parents of these girls owe it to their families and the community to have them arrested and punished." The connection to the assault of the girls and the Bittenbender Murder was immediately made. Heeding the call to investigate, District Attorney Lee convened a grand jury. Numerous witnesses testified. The grand jury acted as an investigating grand jury. The proceedings were secret as with the grand jury of December 1880. The supervising judge kept no notes of the secret proceeding. On March 2, 1881, five months after the murder of Etna Bittenbender, the grand jury issued a presentment, which is a recommendation, that the district attorney take further action. Certain details are found in the written presentment which give clues to the assaults of the girls and who may have been responsible. Namely, that the allegations involve two townships, Jackson and Hamilton. The assault occurred while the young ladies were coming from church. Several witnesses testified to the assaults. One girl in particular was apparently the main target. The girl is identified as the daughter of a Jonas Murphy. As with the Bittenbender murder the grand jury recommended that the DA investigate further.

There is no record of any arrests. No clear link was ever established between the assault on the girls and the murder; except for this, that one of the assailants was previously suspected in Etna's murder but insufficient evidence was found to prosecute him. So who could that be? We know that of all those arrested or suspected in the murder of Etna Bittenbender only two are locals. Samuel Haney and Wilson Marsh. Samuel Haney was 34 years old at the time of the murder and Wilson Marsh was 16. In earlier articles dealing with the Tramp Theory and the discovery of the coat, Wilson is referred to as both a 'boy' and a 'young man'. Sam Haney is never described by either phrase. So the description of the assailants as half a dozen 'young men and boys' fits Wilson Marsh not Samuel Haney. Also the location of the assault is Jackson Township. The Marsh Residence was located near the Hamilton Township Jackson Township Line. There is also the church connection. The attack occurred as the girls were leaving church. The church known as Rocques Church or the 'Gospel Shop', that evangelical church, is just down the road from the Marsh Residence. Although the structure is in ruins and unrecognizable today, its nearby churchyard contains the remains of Wilson's father Jacob. The church was one that the Marshes attended. The church consisted of parishioners from both Hamilton and Jackson Townships. For these reasons, Wilson Marsh has to be the person alleged to have been part of the half a dozen who assaulted the girls on February 21, 1881.

We were able to locate a Jonas Murphy in the 1880 census. He was born in 1824 and died in 1895. In 1880 he was living in Chestnut Hill Township with his children and wife. His first wife Louise Arnold had died but not before giving birth to his daughter Emma. Emma Murphy was born in 1862. At the time of the assault she was 18 years old. The comparisons between the assault on the girls, including Emma and the murder of Etna Bittenbender are interesting. Of course, the temporal relationship is close, only 4 months apart. Then there is the physical location. The attack on the girls could not have been more than a mile or two from the Bittenbender murder scene. The attacks both involved roadways, Etna's battered body found laying off the roadway, the girls attacked alongside a roadway. The ages of the victims, Emma 18 and Etna 17 are similar. Etna was attacked on a Sunday evening while Emma and the other girls were attacked on a Monday evening. The violence of the attack on Etna is obvious, but what of the violence of the assault on the girls? They were immediately attacked, their dresses torn, one was thrown over a stone fence, and all were indecently assaulted. Remember Etna's battered body was found alongside a stone fence as well. The girls screaming of the word 'murder' alerted others who intervened. What would have happened if the men had not heard them? Both attacks are characterized by a reckless indifference to being caught. With Etna's murder, the location where her body was found could be seen from the road from dozens of yards in either direction. The girls were attacked within earshot of a number of men nearby, who would come rushing to their defense.

The perpetrators of the assault were all local. The killer or killers of Etna were believed to be local. One of the main reasons was the belief that only a local would have knowledge of Etna's plans on that fateful day. Of all the locals, Wilson Marsh should have been well aware of Etna's plans on the day of her murder. After all, she was expected to return to his house before nightfall. Wilson Marsh is the obvious suspect, perhaps even a ringleader in the attack on these girls. Certainly, his alleged involvement warranted another closer and serious look by the authorities.

Figure 65 - A group, mostly girls, from Monroe County posing along a stone fence. A scene helpful for imagining the attack on the girls in February 1881.

One of the strangest things to have happened to us in the course of our investigation was getting thrown out of an open house before a public auction for the estate of a woman who passed away in 2012 named Keturah Elizabeth Feitig. Mrs. Feitig's maiden name was Harps and she grew up and passed away in an old home in Snydersville located right on the intersection of the Easton Belmont Pike and Route 209. The property is a fascinating piece of area history. In addition to the colonial era house, there are tucked into the modest sized lot three other buildings. One of brick was formerly an evangelical church, another building was the town's post office, and the third was the one room schoolhouse. Detective Kerchner and I went to the open house to look over the various items set to be auctioned. We were especially interested in the items of 'ephemera', such as photographs, correspondence, scrap books, ledgers, and newspapers. Many of these items were local and covered the time span of Etna's short life. For instance, there were many editions of the rare *Monroe Democrat* newspaper. This Stroudsburg based weekly newspaper covered much of the events surrounding the murder and investigation. The paper hasn't been preserved. Unlike the *Jeffersonian Republican*, there is no collection available at the County Historical Society. There are only pockets of editions here and there among private persons.

We were also there in search of the portrait of the murdered girl. A portrait described to us by several people, but has been missing for decades. Local historians, residents of the Township have described the portrait, Etna with her long dark hair; surrounded by an ornate oval frame, with golden oak leaves and the initials 'EB'. A frame picked out after her death and meant to memorialize her. Detective Kerchner traced the portrait through the decades to a specific house on the Easton Belmont Pike, just north of Snydersville. People recalled that the portrait hung in the kitchen of the home for many years, well into the 1980s. But the owners passed away, the contents sold at auction. The portrait's trail went cold and detective Kerchner was heartbroken. Although I have assured him that his failure was not due to lack of effort, he remains very sensitive about the subject.

We weren't banking on the portrait being at the open house. But we did think that there was a chance that copies of it, 'cabinet sized', like those of the murdered couple, Jacob and Catherine Gogel, were made. To date we have not found any. But none of that was the reason why we were thrown out of the open house. Instead, we were shown the door because we were asking too many questions; questions about a family secret concerning the possible identity of the killer. We had heard of a rumor that Betty Feitig had spoken to her close friends about a conversation she overheard as a young child. A conversation that she claimed was not meant for her to hear. The conversation was between her mother and one of her mother's friends. The conversation occurred in her Snydersville home. Betty was not more than seven or eight years old at the time. She only heard it one time. She never asked about it. Betty would grow to become a very well educated sophisticated woman. Yet she never forgot what she heard.

Figure 66 - The Harps House in Snydersville. Betty Feitig was born in this house in 1921.

Keturah Elizabeth Feitig was born a Harps in 1921. Her parents were Miles Loyd Harps and Alice Ann (Metzger) Harps. Miles was born in 1886 and died in 1942. Alice was born in 1893 and died in 1979. Her family had deep roots in Hamilton Township. In addition to many family relations, they were very close to the family of Stogdell Lesh. Stogdell was a farmer by trade. He was a simple man but intelligent with a knack for 'mental math'. Stogdell was married to Mary (Fable) Lesh who kept house. The couple had nine children, five girls and four boys. The story of the conversation Betty overhead was told in detail to Betty's long term care provider who we interviewed in depth on two occasions. Betty disclosed this information to her care provider in 2010-2011. Betty believed that she was only seven or so when she overheard the conversation. Since Betty was born in 1921, the conversation took place around 1928, some 48 years after the murder. This would have been in the lifespan of Etna's generation. Indeed, the person implicated in this story was alive when Betty overheard the conversation.

At the Harps home in Snydersville in 1928, Betty's mom Alice, had a friend over one evening. The friend is not specifically named in the story, but it is implied that it was a female, who was a Lesh by blood or marriage. The families were close. In those days social visits were common between friends and neighbors. Betty was playing in another room, out of sight. The conversation suddenly grew hushed, something that peaked Betty's curiosity. She knew they were talking about the murder of Etna Bittenbender. By the tone and subject matter, the perceptive child knew it wasn't meant for her ears. Straining to catch all the words, Keturah heard the women discussing that Halloween night 1880. A bunch of 'them', kids were out 'halloweening or something'. At a 'four way', an intersection, they got separated. Etna was there alone. 'He' raped her, hit her head with a rock; or she hit her head on a rock. He left her dead by a big rock. He came home 'covered' in blood. They asked him how he got the blood on him. There was something not right about him. He was 'Joe Lesh'. The story also touched on a coat. Here it is confused, the witness wasn't sure if Betty said Etna was 'wearing a long coat or that they found a coat hidden behind a rock or something; or maybe they found a piece of a coat'.

There are details in this story which immediately connect to Wilson Marsh. The one connection, the confused stuff about a coat is obvious. We know from the accounts that a coat was found hidden, it was torn, and bloodied with long hairs adhering to it. The coat was believed to be evidence in the case. The coat belonged to Wilson Marsh. The coat was among the items of evidence stored in the courthouse for the day it could be used against the murderer. But the other connection is much more subtle and therefore potentially of more importance. Unlike the coat part of the story, which could be relying on faulty memories of the news accounts dealing with the subject, the part about a group of 'them' 'out Halloweening' brings us right to the February 1881 attack on the girls by the half dozen 'young men and boys', an attack in which Wilson Marsh was believed to have been a participant. The similarities between that attack and the murder have already been discussed. What remains is the real possibility that what happened to Etna on that Halloween night 1880, was the direct result of an attack on her by a group of 'them' 'out halloweening'.

If Joseph Lesh was involved in the rape and murder of Etna Bittenbender there is nothing to suggest he was some kind of ringleader. He was born on October 14, 1867, which made him just thirteen years old at the time of the murder. He was the oldest son of Stogdell and Mary Lesh. Although not well educated; according to the 1900 Census he reached only a sixth grade education, he was a successful farmer who served on boards, including the Monroe County National Bank. By the time of the conversation in 1928, Joe Lesh was over sixty years old. He was married to Lydia Neyhart Lesh and the father of three children, Layton, Mable, and Russell. Joseph passed away in 1945 at the age of 77. His wife died several years earlier. One of his younger brothers, William Lesh, a well-regarded educator in New Jersey, a local historian who was a founding member of the historical society, ironically, wrote at length about Etna's Murder. Certainly, the course of his life, like that of another member of a prominent local family, Wilson Marsh, isn't what one would expect when compared to Etna's brutal death.

But the conversation itself, the fact that it was remembered all those years later, by one who heard it but once, when so young, really captivates the interest. Then there is the content, which seems like genuine memory; the group getting separated at the four way, hitting her in the head with a rock versus she fell and hit her head on a rock, so consistent with some attempt to try to excuse the inexcusable. Then there is the part about Joe Lesh coming home covered in blood and asked where the blood came from. These details seem to come from the mind of someone who was there and took part in it. In any case, the authorities never pursued the investigation against Wilson despite his involvement in the attack on the girls three months later. Something else came along, something bigger, something that seemed to solve the case.

Figure 67 - The Lesh Family circa 1895. At the top row from Left to Right are John Lesh, George Lesh, Joseph Lesh, and William Lesh. The middle row left to right, Mary E. Lesh, Stogdell Lesh, and Mary Fable Lesh. In the front row left to right are Frances Lesh, Lydia Neyhart Lesh, Mirenda Lesh, and Anna Lesh.

Chapter 7

"They call me the devil and a witch"

"The devil's agents may be of flesh and
blood, may they not?
-Arthur Conan Doyle, The Hound of the Baskervilles 1901

The investigation into the attack on the young girls should have resulted in charges against Wilson Marsh by the early part of March 1881. The Grand Jury Presentment was issued on March 2, 1881. We know nothing happened with that case. Neither Wilson, nor any of the other boys and young men alleged to have been the attackers, ever faced the music. Why? Were the investigators using the attack on the girls to get pressure on some of the lesser actors; maybe to 'roll' on Wilson? In other words, to get them to squeal, to give up Wilson in Etna's Murder? Was Jonas Murphy unwilling to have charges brought for the violence used against his daughter? Was such a thing considered too scandalous for Mr. Murphy to put his family through? Perhaps, the families worked it out on their own? We can't find proof of any these as the reason why the district attorney did not move against Wilson for at least his role in the attack on Emma Murphy. But there is one event, a terrible thing that happened in Mid-March of 1881 which may explain why, in the end, they did not go after Wilson Marsh any longer.

The best way to explain this part of the case requires us to go back to August of 1880. During that month, 23 year old Frank Pfeifer left his native New York City to 'sojourn' with his Uncle George Kraft at his farm located in North Kidder Township, Carbon County Pennsylvania. George Kraft was a widow by 1880. He lived on the farm with his children, Sebastian age 25, Catherine 22, and George Jr. 17. Mr. Kraft was a German immigrant, as was his deceased wife. Both of them were from 'Hessedamstatt'. All three of the children were born in America, Sebastian in New York, Catherine and George Jr. in Pennsylvania. Frank

Pfeifer was a very troubled young man. Although only 23, he had a lengthy history of arrests and incarceration. He came from a large family. His parents, Martin and Margreth, had also emigrated from Hesse in Germany. They settled in New York City Ward 20 District 8. The couple had 8 children. Frank was the oldest boy. Years later, one of Frank's sisters would tell the press that when Frank was only 8 years old he was thrown from a horse striking his head during the fall. His sister felt that ever since then Frank was never quite right.

Frank has been described as a large brutish fellow by some of the press accounts. But he wasn't a big man at all; very powerful, but not a large man. Frank did 3½ years in New York's infamous Sing Sing Prison when he was only 19 years old. The prison records describe him at around 5 feet six inches tall, weighing about 140 pounds, with a fair complexion, light colored hair, and gray eyes. Frank had been convicted of conspiracy and larceny. That wasn't Frank's only prison time. Growing up he got into all sorts of trouble, stealing, fighting, robbing, and gambling. His best friend was a guy named Dutch Harmon. Together the police suspected them of an armed robbery during which a night watchman was shot to death. Frank and Dutch usually hung out in the dance hall owned by Frank's mother, known as 'Pfeifer Hall', which had an unsavory reputation.

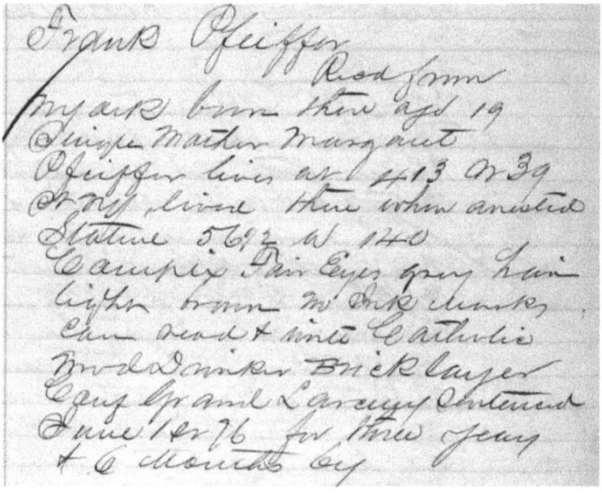
Frank Pfeiffer
Rcd from
my acks born there aged 19
Mother Margaret
Pfeiffer lives at 413 Or 39
St NY lived there when arrested
Stature 5.6½ W 140
Complx Fair Eyes grey hair
light brown No Ink marks
Can read & write Catholic
Mod Drinker Bricklayer
Conf Grand Larceny Sentenced
June 1st 76 for three years
+ 6 months by

Figure 68 - Pfeifer's Intake description from Sing Sing "5 feet 6 and a half inches tall 140 pounds fair complexion grey eyes light brown hair can read and write Catholic..."

"Sergeant C.H. Pless of the 20th Precinct said that he was one of the hardest cases he had ever met with. His father was murdered about nine years ago and strong suspicion was directed toward the son as his murderer, as he had often been arrested for violence toward his parents. The suspicion was strengthened some years afterward, when he was arrested and tried for disorderly conduct before Justice Otterberg on complaint of his mother. He was sentenced to imprisonment for one month, when his mother cried out: "For God's sake, Judge, don't give him such a short time for when he gets out he will kill me as he did his father." His sentence was thereupon changed to 6 months." (Charlie Crowell. Capital Punishment Scrapbook *Philadelphia* Newspaper Article March 1881) Frank's other jail stints in New York had been spent at the prison on Blackwell's Island. Captain Washburn, a cop with the 20th Precinct, recalled that no matter the weather, summer or winter, Frank would swim across the river to his freedom. The good Captain had known Frank for about five years. He was the one to finally get him sent to Sing Sing. But Frank did well there, even getting 10 months off for good behavior. *(National Police Gazette* April 2, 1881)

THE BLACKWELLS ISLAND BRIDGE

Figure 69 - Blackwells Island at a later date. The prison is on the right.

By the spring of 1880, Frank was released from Sing Sing. His mother had since taken in a boarder by the name of John who worked as a black smith. But Frank didn't seem to mind. He was out again, and up to mischief. Burglaries had gotten the attention of the police at the 20th. Frank was suspected. His house was surveilled. He was wanted and slipped away.

It is not until late November 1880 that Frank Pfeifer's presence in the Keystone State is officially documented. Not surprisingly Frank finds himself in a jail cell, one in Wilkes Barre, Luzerne County. "Last Sunday morning about 12:30 o'clock the jewelry store of Charles Forschner was entered by breaking the French plate glass of the door, through which the burglar entered and secured a quantity of tools, revolvers, watch movements, watch chains, silk guards, cartridges, gun caps, and many other things. The thief succeeded in making his exit without being caught, after being seen by some young men who were passing by the store at the time. But the keen eye of Charley Fust, saw in the culprit a young man who was stopping at a farm house about one mile from our borough in Carbon County. Mr. Forschner acting upon the suggestion, procured a search warrant, found his goods, and caught the thief after a long run through the brush, and brought him here. He had a hearing before E.P Tuttle, Esq., on Monday morning, who committed him to the county jail, to await the action of the grand jury." (*Record of the Times*, Wilkes Barre December 2, 1880). The date of the burglary would have been the early morning hours of November 28, 1880, almost one month after Etna's murder. Another article provides some more details; "The thief was discovered while in the store, but by the firing of his revolver scared his would be captors away, and escaped. He was subsequently captured near the house of a Mr. Kraft, about a mile and a half east of White Haven, after a vigorous resistance. He has been in the neighborhood of White Haven about a month and an envelope dropped in the store by him bore the name Frank Edler. He is 22 years of age, about five feet five inches in height and is said to hail from New York." (*The Daily Union Leader*, Wilkes Barre, November, 29 1880). Despite his lengthy record, Pfeifer did not handle his incarceration well. During the evening of Wednesday December 1, 1880, he nearly took his own life. "Frank Keefer, confined to the jail for a burglary committed in White Haven made a desperate attempt last night to take his own life by hanging himself at the door of his cell. Fortunately, he was discovered before it was too late, was cut down and resuscitated after considerable trouble." (*Record of the Times*, 'Tired of Life', Wilkes Barre December 2, 1880). A few of the early news articles got Frank's name wrong, but the fact that Frank tried to commit suicide while in lock up is repeated in articles covering his subsequent trial in Wilkes-Barre. The bad news for Frank would get even worse; he would be indicted for the jewelry store burglary, and the burglaries of two other stores in White Haven. His trials wouldn't take place until the end of January 1881.

It is a rare event that a suspect's own words would be so detailed in an era when court proceedings were not usually written down verbatim. Before Frank's trial he would give a local reporter an interview going over the crimes charged and who else was involved. The article gives us some important clues to compare to the details of Etna's murder. The Article was titled "Another Squeal" and was published on December 29, 1880. The Article begins with; "A few days ago, a Record reporter accompanied by a detective visited the county prison and visited the various occupants of the cells. Among the prisoners is one Frank Pifer, who was arrested for committing a robbery at White Haven, and who subsequently attempted to commit suicide by hanging himself. William Edwards, a tramp, occupies the cell with Pifer, and the reporter heard him remark that he would not if he were in Pifer's place suffer alone." (*The Record of the Times*, 'Another Squeal', December 29, 1880). The reporter began to speak to Frank, urging him to open up. Frank became emotional; he began to cry, and then told his story.

Frank said George Kraft, Jr., his cousin was the accomplice. He explained that he was visiting at his Uncle's farm, which was about a mile and a half from White Haven. He had arrived from New York. One night in November, probably the 28th, he was in a part of White Haven called Jerusalem. He was at a party with his cousin George Kraft Jr, George's girlfriend, and two of George's friends. There was drinking involved. It was late at night. George had told him that there was a store nearby and that no one would be sleeping there. They decided they would rob the store. George went to take his girlfriend home. He promised to meet Frank back at White Haven at a certain bridge. Frank had loaned George his pistol. When George came back, they decided that Frank would enter while George acted as a lookout. George gave the pistol back to Frank. They opened the shutter to a window and Frank went through into the store. While he was inside, George saw a policeman walk by. Luckily the cop went into a lager beer saloon. The first store they hit was the store of Joseph Park. They took cigars, knives, forks, and shirts. They also hit the jewelry store that night. Among the items they took was a small revolver. Frank gave the revolver to George. There was a third store robbed. It was a clothing store. They took scarves and two overcoats right off the rack. The stuff was brought to the Kraft Farm. They kept it quiet from Mr. Kraft. However, George's sister saw them with some of the loot. She said to them, 'For the Lord's sake, what have you done?' The authorities came looking for Frank that Sunday. He fled by jumping from a window and running. He was eventually arrested. Frank claimed that George put the loot in a bag and hid it in the fields so the authorities would think that Frank acted alone. "Pifer told a very long story, but it was all to the same effect. He seemed to feel relieved, that he was not to suffer alone. The same story was told to Detective James O'Brien, who went to see young Kraft, but found he was away from home. On Monday he learned that Kraft was at work for George Dowling hauling logs at a place 25 miles back of white Haven. O'Brien drove there and arrested Kraft, and took him to White Haven. Here he was taken before Squire Tuttle on one of the charges, and gave bail for his appearance at court." (*The Record of the Times*, 'Another Squeal', December 29, 1880).

Frank did a lot of talking, but not about his past. He wouldn't open up about much of his background, the crimes he committed in New York. "He admitted that his character was not good, but said that he was not willing to suffer alone." (*The Record of the Times*, 'Another Squeal', December 29, 1880).

Frank Pfeifer continued to cooperate with the authorities and the press. But Detective O'Brien was troubled by his reluctance to talk about his past. Also, you can be sure that Young Kraft was quick to fill in the authorities about what he knew of his squealing cousin's past. "...There is a chapter in his history which he said nothing about and would seem to indicate that he is not a novice in the profession, but, on the contrary, quite an experienced criminal". (*The Daily Union Leader*, 'An Old Offender', Wilkes Barre January 5, 1881). So the Detective in Wilkes-Barre wrote to the NYPD. On January 4, 1881 Detective Thomas Byones answered.

Figure 70 - White Haven circa 1911.

Based on Pfeifer's confession Kraft was arrested. He too would tell his story. He painted himself as an unwitting victim of circumstance. He compared himself to his criminal cousin and pleaded his innocence. "Kraft was found in his cell and appeared to be quite communicative. He is a slight built, dark eyed young man about 17. He has not the appearance of a thief. He is a cousin of Pfeifer... Pfeiffer and I went to White Haven the night of the robbery. We got into company and drank some and separated. About 12 o'clock he came and asked me if I was ready to go home. I said yes. When about one half mile on our way home, he showed me a lot of goods and asked me to help carry them. I said 'where did you get them Frank!' He answered 'Oh I got them.' I first refused to carry them. He said I should carry them. I refused and told him that if father found it out he would run him away. He said I should go in and keep the dog still, and if father asked where he was, I should say he was coming. I went in and he hid the things." (*The Daily Union-Leader*, 'Interview with Pfeifer's cousin', March 19, 1881).

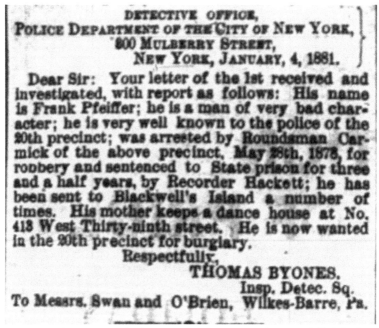

DETECTIVE OFFICE,
POLICE DEPARTMENT OF THE CITY OF NEW YORK,
300 MULBERRY STREET,
NEW YORK, JANUARY, 4, 1881.

Dear Sir: Your letter of the 1st received and investigated, with report as follows: His name is Frank Pfeiffer; he is a man of very bad character; he is very well known to the police of the 20th precinct; was arrested by Roundsman Carmick of the above precinct, May 28th, 1878, for robbery and sentenced to State prison for three and a half years, by Recorder Hackett; he has been sent to Blackwell's Island a number of times. His mother keeps a dance house at No. 413 West Thirty-ninth street. He is now wanted in the 20th precinct for burglary.

Respectfully,
THOMAS BYONES.
Insp. Detec. Sq.

To Messrs. Swan and O'Brien, Wilkes-Barre, Pa.

Figure 71 - The letter written by the New York detective confirming Pfeifer's background and the fact that he was a wanted man.

Both Kraft and Pfeifer would go to trial on January 26, 1881. Kraft's trial was in the morning. Kraft was found guilty of larceny and breaking into the store of S. Parks. Although convicted, the jury issued a recommendation of 'mercy' to the court. Pfeifer, who first pled guilty, then withdrew his plea, was tried in the afternoon. It was a bizarre affair; "The case of Frank Pfeifer indicted for robbing a jewelry store in White Haven last November was called last night. Attorney John Lynch was just leaving the court room, when he was required by the judge to defend Pfeifer as he had no counsel. After consultation with client, Mr. Lynch pleaded guilty. Pfeifer after some reflection stated that he was not quite certain what he had said as he had not recovered from the attempt to hang himself in prison. The plea of guilty was withdrawn and the trial began. At the close of court the case was not finished and will resume this morning." (*Wilkes Barre Record*, January 26, 1881). Mr. Lynch for the defense must have known that he had his hands full. The only way around his confession would have to be a mental angle. With the fact that Pfeifer tried to take his own life shortly after his arrest, Lynch went with a plea of insanity. His first witness was one of the burglary victims, Mr. Jonas S. Parks. Parks told the jury that Pfeifer said he was looking at seventeen years in the penitentiary if convicted. Pfeifer told Parks that he would rather die than serve such a sentence and would kill himself. Lynch also brought up the evidence of his attempted hanging to show that Pfeifer was 'non compos mentis'. But Pfeifer was going to be presenting his own evidence as well. During the trial he asked, "...Deputy James Campbell to take him to the water closet which was done. Pfeifer then took from his pocket a package of what was supposed to be pounded glass, and declared his intention of swallowing it, had he not been prevented from doing so by the officer." (*The Daily Union Leader* Wilkes-Barre January 26, 1881). None of that helped Pfeifer's case. After a brief deliberation the jury convicted him on all counts; believing the defense was a 'put on.' Pfeiffer would also be tried and convicted for the other two burglaries; the jewelry store of Charles Forschner, and the clothing store of Joseph Parks. (*The Record Wilkes-Barre*, January 27, 1881).

Figure 72 - The Luzerne County Prison where Pfeifer tried to kill himself.

The duo of Kraft and Pfeifer were sentenced on Saturday January 29, 1881. Judge Rice showed the recommended mercy to Kraft; who got a sentence of about eight months, which he allowed Kraft to serve in the Luzerne County Jail. Pfeiffer did not fare nearly as well. He was sentenced to serve three and a half years at the Eastern State Penitentiary. During his sentencing, Pfeifer spoke about his background and his motive to confess: "In answer to other questions of the court he said he was in state prison once upon a false charge-he went there innocently-and had been to the work house for drunkenness; there was at present no other charge against him; there was a burglary in a New York saloon, and two boxes of cigars were stolen, one of which was found in his room, but no charge was made against him and none would be. He also stated that he was put down as a notorious thief, but he is not such. He said he made a confession because the officers told him it would go easier with him. He led young Kraft into helping him to commit the burglary at White Haven, and squealed on him because he was told it would make it lighter for him." (*The Daily Union Leader*, Wilkes-Barre January 29, 1881)

Pfeifer's statements were his own attempt to minimize how bad his background really was. For instance, he mentions the burglary of a

166

saloon and the theft of two boxes of cigars as the most recent troubles he had in New York. Pfeifer's version of those events doesn't square with that of Sergeant C.H. Pless, of the 20th Precinct. He recalled that "...a cigar store in Thirty-Ninth Street near Tenth Avenue was robbed and Pfeifer was suspected. The police were on the lookout for him when his mother, who keeps a tenement house at No. 413 West Thirty Seventh Street, called Officer Malone and informed him that her son had purchased a revolver, with which he intended to shoot Officer Biglin of the same precinct. She wished to prevent it and showed the police the stolen goods, which Pfeifer had concealed in his trunk. He could not be captured, however. When next heard of it was in connection with a burglary at Wilkes-Barre." (Charlie Crowell. Capital Punishment Scrapbook, Philadelphia Newspaper Article, March 1881).

The sentence old judge Rice gave him did not seem to bother Pfeifer much. After the judge imposed a sentence of one year and three months for the burglary of the Parks store, Pfeifer said: "thanks". He also thanked the judge for the one year he got for the Jonas store burglary. Finally, after he got another one year and three months sentence, that for the Forschner store, Pfeifer said: "Thank you sir. I am very much obliged." (*The Daily Union Leader Wilkes-Barre*, January 29, 1881).

Looking back, Eastern State Penitentiary was a strange place. The image of a large prison most of us in today's world tend to see is a teeming, noisy place; a society unto itself. Of course, freedom is restricted, but inmates have opportunity to congregate, socialize, participate in programs, and share their thoughts and feelings with others; in short to be part of a human community. That was not how the system was designed under the Pennsylvania Model of Prisoner Reform; the brain child of well-meaning and well to do Quakers. Instead, the idea was that for someone to truly rehabilitate, to reject the sins of one's past life, what was needed was personal reflection; emphasis on 'personal', twenty-four/seven. In other words, the inmate was to be left alone, in solitude, bereft of any social intercourse. The ideal was one prisoner per cell. Food and drink would be brought to the inmate. Iron toilets, which would be flushed at set times, were in each cell. Natural and artificial lighting were design features of each cell. Work could be provided, but it would be brought to the cell. The inmate could not leave the cell. The cell was his world, a world populated by one. The inmate would serve out his entire term in a solitary confinement. Today, such a setting is considered the most cruel type of incarceration, reserved for 'super max' facilities; death row inmates in Pennsylvania. But even these have more chance of interacting with others, than their solitary predecessors of Eastern State.

The solitary theory of confinement was criticized by many. "In the outskirts, stands a great prison called the Eastern State Penitentiary conducted on a plan peculiar to the state of Pennsylvania. The system here is a rigid, strict, and hopeless solitary confinement. I believe in its effects, to be cruel and wrong. In its intention I am well convinced that it is kind humane and meant for reformation...Over the head and face of every prisoner who comes into this melancholy house a black hood is drawn and in this dark shroud, an emblem of the curtain dropped between him and the living world, he is led to the cell from which he never again comes forth, until his term of imprisonment has expired...he is a man buried alive, to be dug out in the slow round of years; and in the meantime dead to everything but torturing anxieties and horrible despair. Every cell has double doors; the outer one of sturdy oak, the other of grated iron, wherein there is a trap through which his food his handed. He has a Bible, and a slate and pencil, and under certain restrictions has sometimes other books provided for the purpose and pen and ink and paper. His razor, plate and can and basin hang upon the wall or shine upon a little shelf. Fresh water is laid on in every cell and he can draw it as he pleases. During the day his bedstead is turned up against the wall and leaves more space for him to work the loom or bench or wheel in there he labours, sleeps, and works and counts the seasons as they change, and grows old." (Charles Dickens 'Philadelphia and its Solitary Prison': Chapter 7 *American Notes* 1842).

If the critics such as Dickens couldn't convince those in power to soften for the sake of humanity, economics could. By Pfeifer's incarceration in 1881 Eastern State Penitentiary was beyond capacity, too many inmates, and too few cells. This trend started after the Civil War and just got worse. By 1881 the prison had 731 cells but 1035 inmates. For that reason 295 of the cells contained two inmates. (ESP Historic Structures Report Volume I pg. 178 1994). The handicrafts industry afforded many of the inmates continued and expanded. For instance, in 1881 the following industries and numbers of inmates engaged in those industries included 'weaving and spinning' 80 inmates, 'shoe making' 133, 'wood work/chair making' 2, 'cane seating' 84, 'cigar making' 12, 'stocking weaving' 200. 'Jobbing miscellaneous' 106, and of course, those who did not work the 'idle' 238. More than a few of these jobs were done outside of the cell. There is also evidence that the guards or 'keepers' as they were called would refer to inmates not by their assigned numbers but their given names. Inmates even communicated with other cells and on occasion were entitled to see family; "prisoners communicated through the sewer pipes, and even fed each other through them when they were punished by being deprived of food...newcomers in the 1880s spent their initial days on the block 4 gallery; inmates could receive supervised family visits once every three months." *(ESP Historic Structures Report* Volume I pg. 178 1994). This was the place Judge Rice sentenced Pfeifer to serve three and a half years. It is probable that Pfeifer, like many repeat offenders, blamed not himself but the system; similar to sentiments set to a poem in the 1840s by an inmate of the Eastern State Penitentiary called George Ryno, a part of which reads:

> Here, after swearing oaths, not loud but deep,
> The wooden headed jurors fall asleep,
> And childless judges have the power to doom
> The friendless prisoner to a living tomb,
> Be sharp, or they'll convict you in a trice-
> More proofs our city's not a paradise.

The Luzerne County Sheriff transported Pfeifer, along with another prisoner, down to Philadelphia. Pfeifer was 'received' by the Eastern State Penitentiary on February 18, 1881 to serve his three and a half year sentence. Upon his arrival he was processed into the prison. He was given prison inmate number A-728.

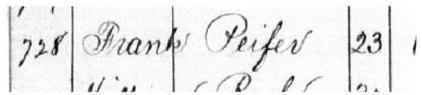

Figure 73 - Prisoner number 728 Frank Pfeifer age 23 from the Reception Records of the prison.

Initially Pfeifer seemed 'melancholy', he started acting crazy, mainly by talking gibberish, nothing violent, just nonsense or 'senseless prattle' as the term the prison authorities used to describe it. "When Pfeifer was admitted to the institution on the 18th of last month, he acted strangely, but the medical examiner concluded, after examining him carefully that he was simulating insanity... It is a common thing for convicts to simulate insanity, and in such cases the opinion of the medical examiners is taken as conclusive. " (*Philadelphia Inquirer*, March 18, 1881). "In cases where the insanity of the convict is undoubted, no other inmate is of course, placed in the same cell with him." (Col. Charles Thomson Jones, Inspector Eastern State Penitentiary, *Philadelphia Inquirer*, 18 March 1881).

Pfeifer was placed in a cell on the ground floor of second block at the easternmost end of the prison. When Pfeifer arrived, he was introduced to his new cellmate, Inmate no. 525, a 49 year old Philadelphian named John McBride; a plasterer by trade. He was married, but had been separated from his wife for 15 years. McBride had been at the penitentiary since September 30, 1880, about five months. He had been the sole occupant of the cell until Pfeifer's arrival. McBride was convicted of aggravated assault, battery, and indecent exposure. He was sentenced to two years. His victim was a child of about twelve named Mary Colligan, 'Little Mary' as she was known in the neighborhood. Little Mary came from a very poor family. One day in early September she was going around from door to door begging in the area of Twenty First and Green Streets. McBride approached the girl and either attempted to or did sexually assault her. A passerby witnessed some of it and alerted a police officer who after a short chase arrested McBride. "Although he stoutly asserted his innocence he was fully identified by the little girl and committed to trial. When Mary's father heard of the attempted outrage he was with difficulty restrained from entering the courthouse and shooting McBride as he stood in the dock." (Charlie Crowell. Capital Punishment Scrapbook, Philadelphia newspaper article, March 1881).

It was reported that McBride had committed the same offense ten years before. It is unlikely that Pfeifer would have been told any details of his cell mate's background. That was against the prison rules. Also, by at least theory, even the guards shouldn't have been privy to such information. Only the Warden and his assistants should have been aware and had access to an inmate's file. The two men seemed to hit it off. By all accounts they got along well.

Figure 74- A Cell occupied by two inmates circa 1872. Both men are employed in shoe making. Take note of the dimensions and the furnishings. Pfeifer and McBride would have occupied a cell of the same design. The men would have had a slate for writing messages to the guards; just like the one pictured on the right edge of the photo hanging on the wall.

One reason they got along so well may have been their work. Pfeifer, who as we know appreciated a fine cigar, worked during the day in the cell stripping tobacco from the stalks. McBride also worked in the prison's tobacco industry. Unlike Pfeifer, McBride was not locked up in the cell during the day, but worked at packing tobacco in boxes. (*Philadelphia Times*, March 17, 1881). Each morning around seven, Keeper McGuigan would arrive at the cell doors with coffee and breakfast. Every morning Pfeifer and McBride would give him a cheerful greeting. After breakfast, McBride was escorted out of the cell to pack boxes full of tobacco, while Pfeifer was left with tobacco plants to strip. So the days passed.

It was Tuesday March 15, 1881. Frank Pfeifer had been at the penitentiary for less than a month. He had been generally in good spirits. Earlier in the day he had told Keeper McGuigan that he felt unwell. However, by dinner time Pfeiffer told McGuigan and McBride that he felt better. In fact, Pfeiffer answered, 'very well' to McGuigan that evening, when asked how he was getting along. McGuigan heard him make a similar reply to McBride. (Charlie Crowell. Capital Punishment Scrapbook, Philadelphia newspaper Article, March 1881).

Figure 75 - A cell block circa 1880. The outer cell doors, made of heavy oak can be seen. They were made to slide open exposing the iron inner door.

Both men ate their dinner together in the cell; it would be their last meal. The various guards made their rounds that night and into the morning;

no unusual noises were heard, no loud sounds. In short, nothing was out of the ordinary. On Wednesday morning overseer McGuigan was making his rounds; inmates 728 and 525 were first on his list. McGuigan had breakfast to serve. It was seven a.m., he unlocked the heavy wooden outer door of the cell sliding it open, exposing the thick iron grated inner door. Right away, McGuigan felt something was wrong. Normally, the process of opening the door to serve breakfast drew a response from Pfeiffer and McBride, a cheerful greeting; McGuigan was struck by the silence. "With the intention of passing some food to the inmates of a cell near the end of the corridor he opened the outer door of the apartment and called them by name. The morning light had not penetrated the cell sufficiently to render objects within distinguishable through the iron grating forming the inner door, and an ominous silence pervaded the place, which from the first was unpleasant, even to the hardened nerves of the keeper. 'John McBride!' he cried. There was no answer. 'Pfeiffer! What's the matter with you fellows?' he continued, somewhat harshly. Still there was a dead stillness." (*Philadelphia Inquirer*, March 17, 1881).

Hearing no sound and not being able to see properly in the dim light, McGuigan decided to go into the cell. "Turning a key in the heavy lock he swung the door open and cautiously entered the prison room. A ray of light streaming in through the narrow skylight revealed to his eyes, with horrifying effect, the body of a man in a kneeling position, a finely twisted rope reaching from the neck of the ghastly object to the crude but strong gas bracket protruding from the wall of the cell several feet above. Intending to cut the cord and if possible save the prisoner's life, Overseer McGuigan made a step forward and was about to make another when he tripped upon some soft object out at his feet and fell heavily to the floor. Simultaneous with his fall a cry for assistance mechanically escaped him, but he had no need to fear either of the occupants of the cell. They were both lifeless. Passing his hand across the face of the form that had tripped him and over that of the hideous object partially suspended from the wall the cold response given to his touch said plainer than words, 'we are dead'. (*Philadelphia Inquirer*, March 17, 1881).

McGuigan immediately called for help and several guards came. Assistant Warden Cassidy was summoned. He instructed that nothing was to be touched; everything needed to be left in place for the coroner's arrival. Lanterns were brought in to better illuminate the condition of the cell. As the sun rose higher more light streamed through the skylight. It was the body the 23-year old Frank Pfeiffer that was hanging from the gas bracket. The body of 49 year-old John McBride was on the floor with the head resting backwards on one of the beds. It was his body that McGuigan tripped over as he tried to reach Pfeiffer. The cell showed signs of a deadly struggle. Blood was on the floor and the walls, furniture was knocked over. The bodies also showed signs of a vicious fight and agonizing death. "...Suspended from a gas fixture jutting out about a foot into the cell was Pfeiffer's body, with his back to the door, the blackened tongue being between the teeth. Three strands of stout dark-colored hardware twine passed up the left side of the neck and it cut deep indentations in the skin. There were but two strands around the throat and those two had cut deeply. Pfeiffer's feet hung in such a position as to indicate that had he so desired he could easily have rested them upon the high iron door sill. A stool about 2 feet high was near his feet and upon this he had apparently stood before adjusting the noose. There was blood upon the hands and upon the soles of the feet, the later proving that Pfeiffer had walked around the cell after the affray. Pfeiffer had a deep cut on his right wrist, which was concealed by a cotton stocking drawn up over the hand." (*St. Louis Dispatch*, Saturday March 19, 1881). It seems that Pfeiffer tried to avoid the pain caused by the twine tightening around his neck, because there was a piece of torn sheeting taken from his bed 'wound around the neck in an effort to keep the cord from cutting his flesh.' (*The Philadelphia Inquirer*, Thursday March 17, 1881).

Pfeiffer also took his time in fashioning the twine into a noose. "The suicide was terribly in earnest when he began his work of death, for to make sure of having a strong rope he ingeniously twisted the heavy twine and sheeting together before attaching them to his neck. His death must have been a horrible one, for there was no fall and the neck was not broken, consequently, it was a clear case of determined self-murder by strangulation." (Charlie Crowell. Capital Punishment Scrapbook,

Philadelphia newspaper article, March 1881). Dr. J.G. Lee, the Philadelphia Coroner's physician examined the body. He determined that Pfeifer's death was caused by, "...suffocation produced by hanging." He also found evidence of blunt force trauma on Pfeifer's arms, as well as the cut on the wrist. He believed those injuries were the result of a fight between him and McBride.

Figure 76 - A heavy iron door sill like the one Pfeifer used to break McBride's skull.

The body of John McBride was also examined by Dr. Lee. At the Coroner's Inquest on March 17, 1881, Dr. Lee testified to the condition of the cell and the bodies. "He found the furniture and effects in great disorder in the cell in which the bodies laid. Directly opposite the grated door lay the body of McBride, the head being partially supported by a mattress. His face was stained with bloods, which had trickled from his nostrils, and on his forehead, above the left eye, were 3 discolored bruises. The palm and back of the right hand were stained with blood, and also there was some blood on the back of his right foot. Around his neck was a tightly tied pair of drawers, numbered 728, the number of Pfeiffer." (*The Philadelphia Inquirer*, Thursday March 17, 1881).

A pair of Pfeifer's 'drawers', that is long underwear, was knotted on the right side of McBride's neck. This showed that Pfeifer strangled him from behind. But there was also a fearful beating to McBride's head. "The post-mortem examination of the body of McBride showed that corresponding to the bruises on his forehead there was an irregular fracture involving the frontal, parietal, temporal sphenoid bones, and the frontal and temporal bones being comminuted. The right orbital plate of the frontal bone was also fractured. The internal examination showed the signs of suffocation in the heart and lungs and air passages, the remaining internal organs being healthy." (*The Philadelphia Inquirer*, Thursday March 17, 1881). Dr. Lee testified that McBride died as a result of "suffocation from a forcible compression of the air passages, complicated by a comminuted depressed fracture of the skull." Nobody could say for sure whether Frank Pfeiffer first bashed McBride's head repeatedly against the iron door sill and then strangled him with the long underwear or whether he strangled him first to unconsciousness, and then broke his skull on the iron door sill.

The investigators examined the cell and its contents. Inside a small box they found a knife used by the inmates for tobacco stripping. The knife was bloody. They believed that the knife had been used by McBride during the fight and with it he cut Pfeiffer's wrist. The investigators tried to figure out a motive for the murder suicide. Was Pfeiffer brought to the point of homicidal violence by something McBride did? They believed it was possible in light of McBride's sexual perversions. The prevailing theory was that McBride attempted some homosexual act upon Pfeiffer which caused the latter to become enraged. McBride "may have acted on the defensive from the first against an assault from Pfeiffer, who may have had an insane outbreak, or Pfeiffer may have resisted an assault which McBride's sentence indicates him capable of attempting." (*St. Louis Dispatch*, Saturday March 19, 1881) "It is supposed that during the night the men got into a quarrel over an indignity offered by McBride and that Pfeiffer turned on him and strangled him and then hung himself." (*Harrisburg Daily Independent*, Thursday, March 17, 1881). After Pfeiffer killed McBride he spent quite some time alone in the dark pondering what to do next. Before taking his own life he left something behind that would undo all the work of those investigating the murder of Etna Bittenbender.

As the dead body of John McBride lay on the floor, Pfeiffer wrapped a sock around his injured and bloodied right wrist. Then he found some twine he had for the tobacco work and he tore his bed sheeting and carefully fashioned the twine and sheeting into a ligature. Then he took two slates, given to the inmates to communicate with the guards, took the slate pencil, and began writing in the dark as he sat at his work table. These would be his last words. Pfeifer's writing was very poor, barely legible. For one thing his adrenaline was still pumping. He found it hard to keep his hand steady. Also, he did not have much in the way of an education. He would start a sentence, try to erase it, and start again. Finally, he finished writing. He left the pieces of slate on the small table, along with a card containing the name and address of a police captain from New York. Pfeiffer then stepped onto the stool, tied the ligature to the gas bracket, placed it over his head, and tightened it around his neck. With determination he kicked the stool out from under him, brought his knees up to his chest, and held himself in place. In that position, he began to lose consciousness. When he passed out his body became limp and all his weight pulled against the twine wrapped around his neck. His body convulsed for a time. The twine cut deeply into the soft tissue of his neck. Deep abdominal respirations could be heard as the body struggled for air. After a time he became still and the cell was silent. Frank Pfeiffer was dead.

When told of McBride's death, Mary Colligan's father was pleased; "it don't make any difference, said he, whether he was killed or killed himself. He was a villainous scoundrel, and the grave is the best place for him." (Charlie Crowell. Capital Punishment Scrapbook, *Philadelphia* news article, March 1881). McBride was mourned by a sister who lived at twenty first and Green Streets. She was described as a woman of 'considerable refinement'; deeply distressed by her brother's death. McBride's body was claimed from the morgue by his estranged wife, they had been separated for fifteen years. She gave him a proper burial in a catholic cemetery. Pfeifer's family decided not to claim him. He was buried in the potter's field.

Chapter 8

The Writing Slates

> "I heard all things in the heaven and in
> earth. I heard many things in hell. How,
> then, am I mad? Hearken! And observe
> how healthily — how calmly I can tell you
> the whole story."
>
> The Tell Tale Heart and Other Writings, Edgar Allan Poe
>
> 1843

The earliest reports of the murder suicide occurred the day the bodies were discovered; March 16, 1881. These reports, mostly published the next day, gave only a few details of the crime; the horror at discovering the bodies, the grotesque descriptions of how they appeared, the signs of struggle, and speculation on a motive. But there were a few accounts that describe another discovery in the cell; words written on a piece of slate. "A small slate is furnished to all prisoners, on which they may write requests or make complaints. On the slate found in Pfeifer and McBride's cell were scrawled the words: "This is the third man I have killed". No signature followed and the words were nearly illegible, as if the writer had repented of his horrible confession and had wished to erase it. Whose writing was it?" (*The News Journal*, Wilmington Delaware 17 March 1881). The problem is that this phrase; "This is the third man I have killed", is different than the words read during testimony at the Inquest into the death of the men. The Inquest happened the day after the bodies were found, that is March 17, 1881. The following day the newspapers reported not one writing slate but two were found lying on a table in the cell. They further identified the writing as Frank Pfeifer's. The slates themselves were collected by the coroner and presented in evidence. "Deputy Coroner Powers described the cell as he found it upon visiting it on Wednesday morning...The witness produced two slates that he found lying on a table used by the prisoners for stripping tobacco upon, together with a small card, the latter contained these lines: "To Captain Washburn, Twentieth Ward Station House, Thirty-seventh Street, between Ninth and Tenth avenue, New York City." (*The Philadelphia Inquirer*, March 18, 1881). The slates were written in an erratic hand making reading it difficult. The words written on the slates are the following:

SLATE 1

"Stroudsburg, Pa,--Miss Elna Bittenbender, Jackson township--Last fall me and my cousin George Kraft. I am--"

SLATE 2 (FRONT)

"I also kill that girl in Jackson County. Cousin George Kraft last fall was arrested his brother. They call me the devil and a wich, so if you all know all the people I have kill, you would be astonished. Go in New York ther you will find out all about me I am sorry for me owen family for I know they use them ruf on"

SLATE 2 (BACK)

"my account. They could not help for that wot I did you can all---You can tell Judge Rice not to send down here any crazy men." (*The Daily Union Leader*, Wilkes Barre March 18, 1881).

There is a lot of stuff to ponder when reading Pfeifer's words. First, are we satisfied that between Pfeifer and McBride, Pfeifer is the author? From the context it seems the writer must have been Frank Pfeifer. Only he had a cousin named George Kraft. He mentions that fact twice in his short statement; First on Slate 1:"... me and my cousin George Kraft...", again on Slate 2, "Cousin George Kraft..." Also on Slate 2 is written:"...Go in New York ther you will find out all about me..." McBride was from Philadelphia. We have no evidence that he ever lived in or carried on activities in New York. However, Pfeifer was born and raised in New York, and had an extensive criminal record there. There is also the reference on the back of Slate 2, a message to "...tell Judge Rice not to send down here any crazy men"; Pfeifer, not McBride, was sentenced in Wilkes Barre by Judge Rice. The reference to 'crazy men' also refers to Pfeifer not McBride. Pfeifer's defense to the burglary charges in Luzerne County was insanity. The judge and jury rejected the defense, but Frank is, in his way, telling the judge that he was wrong. In other words, Frank Pfeifer is claiming his own insanity.

Some of the news accounts also mention the handwriting is Pfeifer's. This could refer to comparing known writing samples from Pfeifer and McBride. There is a very interesting article published in a now defunct New York newspaper that contains a reporter's interview with some of Frank's family, including his Mother. She mentions that the last letter she received from her son was on March 6, 1881, ten days before the murder suicide. (*Truth*, The Cherry Hill Horror, Saturday March 19, 1881). So the likelihood of having comparable writings to analyze was good. Finally, the condition of the bodies shows that Pfeifer wrote the words. Pfeifer is the one hanging, partially suspended, his drawers are tried around McBride's throat, and there is blood on the soles of Frank's feet consistent with him being the last man alive. Certainly that is supported by that very first writing referred to in the earliest accounts, the one described as barely legible and nearly erased; "this is the third man I have killed.

Once we were satisfied that Pfeifer was the author, the hard part began; what to make of the words? What exactly was he trying to tell the world? One article describes the writing as 'incoherent'. That's not quite accurate. Overall, Pfeifer is taking credit for killing multiple people, and in particular a girl, who he appears to identify as Etna Bittenbender. He is connecting his cousin George Kraft to the killing, but Pfeifer takes sole credit for her murder, saying: '**I** also kill that girl...' not '**we**' kill that girl. He is telling us that George has a brother who was arrested in the fall of 1880. For some reason the arrest of George's brother, who Pfeifer doesn't specifically name, is connected to the killing of the girl. Pfeifer suggests his motive for killing Etna and the others comes from being evil and insane; 'they call me the devil and a which', and 'tell Judge Rice not to send down here any crazy men'. He wants to be believed. Pfeifer not only urges the reader to find out all about him by going to New York, he even leaves a card with a New York police captain's name and address on the same table as the slates. He doesn't show any remorse for killing the girl, killing McBride, or anyone else. He only seems saddened that because of him the authorities treated his family harshly; 'I am sorry for me owen family for I know they use them ruf on my account. They could not help for that wot I did' He also may have cursed the reader, but that is not clear because the phrase is incomplete; 'You can all---'

The writings become easier to follow when we add the phrase reported in the first accounts to the writing on Slate 2 and separate each thought to its own line; by doing that we get:

> **This is the third man I have killed.**
> **I also kill that girl in Jackson County.**
> **Cousin George Kraft last fall was arrested his brother.**
> **They call me the devil and a wich.**
> **so if you know all the people I have kill, you would be astonished.**
> **Go in New York ther you will find out all about me.**
> **I am sorry for me owen family**
> **for I know they use them ruff on my account.**
> **They could not help for that wot I did.**
> **You can all--**
> **You can tell Judge Rice not to send down here any crazy men.**

But what about the words on Slate 1; the tone is quite different from the longer writing on Slate 2. I believe that the writing on Slate 1 was Pfeifer's first attempt to explain himself. He tried to be formal, but his lack of education made it hard to finish so he abandoned the effort and instead wrote the Slate 2 statement as if he was actually speaking to us. In fact, it helps to speak out loud his words on Slate 2, pausing briefly between each line. However, Frank's first attempt, his writing on Slate

1, is crucial to establishing Etna Bittenbender as, 'that girl' he claimed to kill, his victim:

Stroudsburg, Pa.
Miss Elna Bittenbender, Jackson Township
Last fall me and my cousin George Kraft.
I am--

The connection between Pfeifer's words and Etna's murder was testified by Deputy Coroner Powers at the Coroner's Inquest into the murder/suicide held in downtown Philadelphia on March 17, 1881; "Witness here explained that he had been informed the Elna Bittenbender referred to had been feloniously assaulted and murdered near her house last fall, it being supposed at the time that the killing had been done by tramps. A cousin of the woman was subsequently arrested and tried for the crime but was acquitted." (*Jeffersonian Republican*, Stroudsburg March 18, 1881).

The Stroudsburg newspaper added a cryptic follow-up to the Philadelphia dispatch; "In another column will be seen an account of the murder and suicide of two tramps in the penitentiary at Philadelphia. According to confession and circumstance it would strongly appear that one of the persons was connected with the Etna Bittenbender murder in this county in November last. The facts are not conclusive but they may point the way to the guilty persons. At the time of the murder it was strongly believed by some that the crime was the work of tramps, and a clue to the probably guilty party was partially fixed, but for want of encouragement by interested persons it was never worked up, and finally dropped. The error in not following up the clue now seems very clear." (*Jeffersonian Republican*, Stroudsburg March 18, 1881). A frustrating article for us because it lacks detail, is hard to follow, and seems to contradict an earlier article which claimed that the tramps 'have all been traced.' But one thing is clear, within two days of the death of Frank Pfeifer, the authorities in Stroudsburg, like District Attorney DS Lee, were on notice of Pfeifer's 'terrible confession'; what was their response?

Pfeifer's naming of George Kraft in connection with Etna's murder immediately brought young Kraft under scrutiny. "The Kraft mentioned in the memorandum is now in jail here, for burglary committed in White Haven. (*Record of the Times*, 'A Desperate Scoundrel', Wilkes Barre March 19, 1881). Wilkes-Barre's other newspaper, The *Daily Union Leader* beat the *Record* and scored an interview of George Kraft, the only one we know ever took place. In their piece of March 19, 1881 called; '*Interview with Pfeifer's Cousin. - What George Kraft has to say about Pfeifer*', Kraft defends himself from any thought he or his cousin Frank had anything to do with Etna's murder. "The recent allusion to George Kraft in the confessions of Frank Pfeiffer, the convict murderer and suicide, led a *Union-Leader* representative to seek an interview this morning with Kraft...Kraft was found in his cell and appeared to be quite communicative. He is a slight built youth, dark eyed young man about 17."

In an interview of this type, with someone who may have been involved in a murder, patience is the byword. The best interviewers of this type of investigation tend to be patient, great listeners, they can relax those they question; all the while the answers they are getting are being analyzed even as the next question is being asked. While this is going on the interviewer is gauging the body language, subconscious movements, and emotions of the subject. In essence, a top interviewer is a form of human polygraph. Sadly, the reporter's interview of Kraft is a hollow affair. You can tell from reading the article Kraft is asked questions that must have been on the order of: "Did you and your cousin kill that Bittenbender girl?", "You were in the area last fall, right?", "Well you knew about the murder didn't you?" etc. It's even sadder that none of the Monroe County investigators or authorities appear to have questioned Kraft. But it's all we have, so a careful examination of this article is required.

Kraft said he first thought Pfeifer to be bad news and crazy only after they were locked up together awaiting trial on the White Haven burglaries. This is problematic because, as you know, he and Frank were the perpetrators of several burglaries together during the latter part of November 1880. Nonetheless, Kraft states the following: "Before getting in to the prison, I never thought he was crazy, but when he attempted to hang himself, I thought he was out of his head." It was also during their time incarcerated together that Kraft claims Pfeifer told him about assaulting his own mother and how his father died; "While in jail here before going to the penitentiary, Pfeiffer told me and others, that at home in New York he used to whip his mother. She had him arrested and after being in prison a couple of days she would relent and get him out. One day when he was whipping his mother his father told him to stop. He then told his father to shut up or he would club him. The father after that carried a revolver to protect himself against Frank's assaults. Soon after that there was a funeral next door to their house, and Frank had a gang of his associates' playing cards and drinking beer. Someone wanted to go out and his father reached in his pocket for the key and while pulling it out it caught in the trigger and he shot himself in the leg from the effects of which he died." (George Kraft Interview, *Union Leader* March 19, 1881). It will be remembered that the New York police suspected Pfeifer of killing his father. This belief was in part based on his mother's own words to a judge when she objected that a sentence of one month was too short and that once Pfeifer was released he would kill her, just like he killed his father. There must have been a great earnestness in her words and demeanor, because the judge increased the sentence to six months, which was probably the maximum for the charge.

Much of Kraft's statement to the reporter is so self-serving that his credibility suffers for it. For example, even after he is convicted of burglary and serving his sentence, he tries to put all the blame for the burglaries on Pfeifer. It gets to the point where Kraft claims he was not even aware that Frank committed any burglaries that night until they were nearly half way home on their walk from White Haven and Frank asked him to help carry the loot. It is only then that Kraft claims to see the stolen goods; boxes of cigars, overcoats, scarfs, watches, a revolver and other accessories. Such a claim being made to a seasoned detective, like Craig VanLouvender, Shawn Williams, or Robert Sebastianelli, would be great material for them to use skillfully against Kraft to start getting him to come clean. Those kinds of opportunities must be followed up with skill and perseverance. Oftentimes, clear falsehoods from a suspect, even though they don't involve the crime under investigation, will serve as a catalyst to get the suspect to start telling the truth about everything. So we must take the words of Kraft with caution, that's why corroboration, which is the backing up of a story, is so important in our line of work.

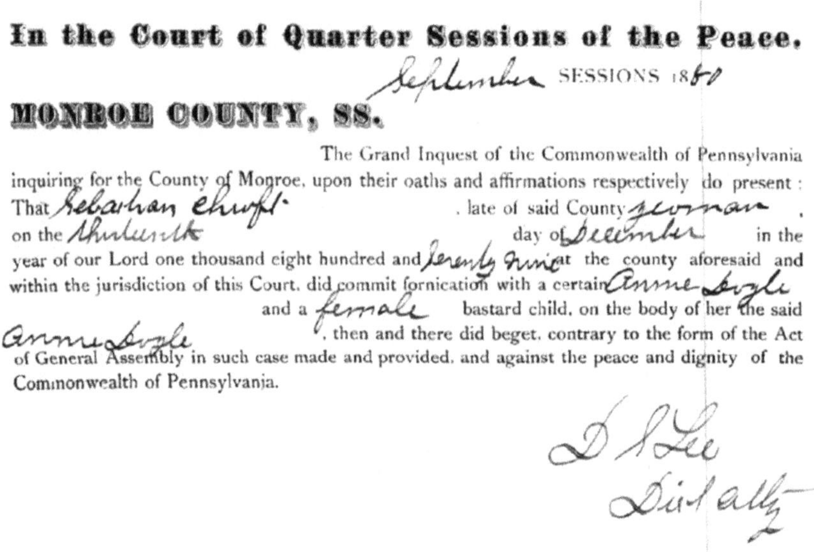

In the Court of Quarter Sessions of the Peace.

September SESSIONS 1880

MONROE COUNTY, SS.

The Grand Inquest of the Commonwealth of Pennsylvania inquiring for the County of Monroe, upon their oaths and affirmations respectively do present : That *Sebastian Kraft* . late of said County *German* , on the *Thirteenth* day of *December* in the year of our Lord one thousand eight hundred and *Seventy Nine* at the county aforesaid and within the jurisdiction of this Court, did commit fornication with a certain *Anne Boyle* and a *female* bastard child, on the body of her the said *Anne Boyle* , then and there did beget, contrary to the form of the Act of General Assembly in such case made and provided, and against the peace and dignity of the Commonwealth of Pennsylvania.

D S Lee
District Atty

Figure 77 - The Indictment charging Sebastian Kraft with committing fornication with Anne Boyle and the resulting birth of a 'female bastard child'.

There is information from Kraft that is corroborated and backs up parts of Pfeifer's writings. One of the important ones has to do with Frank Pfeifer seeming to throw in a random fact in the middle of his mea culpa like; '**Cousin George Kraft last fall was arrested his brother**'. Did George have a brother? Was he arrested in the fall of 1880 like Pfeifer claimed? The answer to both questions is yes. Sebastian Kraft, George's only and elder brother, was in fact arrested in the fall of 1880. More precisely it was September of 1880. The charge was 'fornication and bastardy', a crime back then, and a way to get child support. The crime occurred around December 13, 1879. Sebastian Kraft was indicted and pled guilty on September 27, 1880. His 'victim' or complaining witness was an Irish girl named Anne Boyle. Anne had in September of 1880 given birth to a little girl. Anne must have lived in Monroe County, or the fornication occurred here, because the charges were brought in Monroe County by DS Lee, District Attorney. The case was called in Stroudsburg, in the Court of Quarter Sessions, the criminal court of the time, in September 1880, a little more than a month before Etna Bittenbender was murdered.

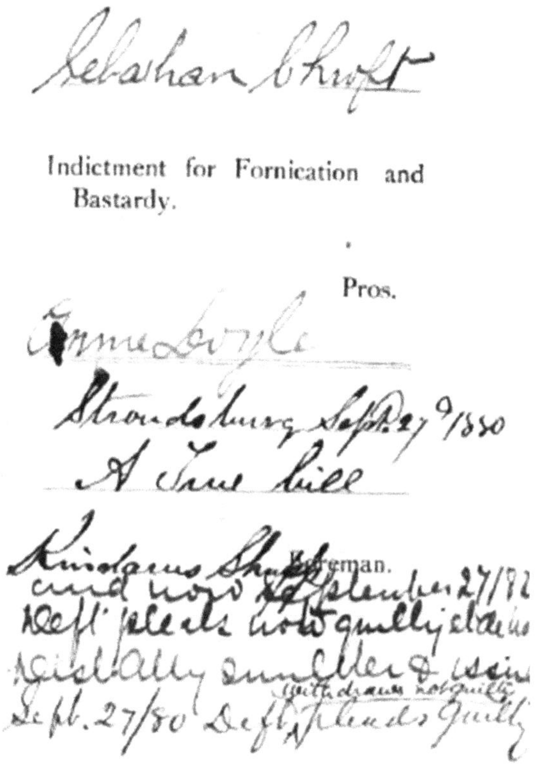
Sebastian Kraft

Indictment for Fornication and Bastardy.

Pros.

Anne Boyle

Stroudsburg Sept. 27/1880

A True Bill

Foreman.

Figure 78 - The Indictment of Sebastian Kraft for Fornication and Bastardy dated September 27, 1880.

So how did Frank Pfeifer know? What connection did it have with the murder? And why did Pfeifer mention it? Kraft's answer does little to advance the case, and even less to shed light on why Pfeifer mentioned it. Kraft acknowledges he had an older brother and that he was charged in September of 1880. Sebastian had to go to court in Stroudsburg. He was accompanied by a friend of the family named James Woodring. Kraft claims that he, his brother Sebastian, Mr. Woodring, and Frank Pfeifer made the journey into Monroe County in September of 1880. Frank Pfeifer drove the team of horses. The group got a couple miles near to a place called 'The Pocono Switch'. There, Sebastian and Woodring walked the rest of the way to the 'Switch' and took the train to Stroudsburg so Sebastian could attend court. Meanwhile, Kraft says that after feeding the horses, he and Frank returned home to Carbon County. Kraft adds that neither he nor Pfeifer ever set foot in Monroe County again.

In George Kraft's own words: "I never was in Stroudsburg in my life, and was never in Monroe County but once and that was in September last. It was in company with my brother, Pfeifer, and Mr. Woodring of White Haven. We went to within about two miles and a half of Pocono Switch when we stopped and fed the team, my brother and Woodring walking on to Pocono Switch to take the train going into Stroudsburg to be in attendance at court. Pfeifer remained with me, we drove back home to Carbon County, about a mile and a half from White Haven...Pfeifer came to my father's house in August, and was not away from there at any time except when he drove my brother and Mr. Woodring over to take the train. (George Kraft Interview 19 March 1881).

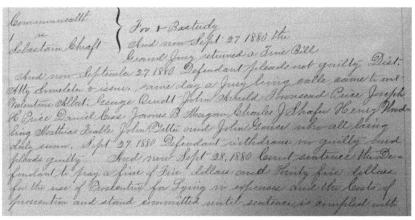

Figure 79 - The Court Summary showing that after a jury was selected; Sebastian Kraft changed his mind and pled guilty. He was fined $5.00, ordered to pay Miss Boyle $30.00, and to pay the court costs. Sebastian was further ordered committed until payment in full.

The reporter was not satisfied with Kraft's explanation. There is a hint of frustration in his article. Clearly he thought there was more to it than George Kraft was admitting. Certainly the fact that Pfeifer wrote about it on the slates meant it was meaningful to him. Perhaps, it got them, Kraft and Pfeifer, familiar with the area of Jackson and Hamilton Townships so that they returned a month later? The proximity between their route of travel and the murder scene itself was the one fact the reporter took from the interview. "The only thing in Kraft's revelations is that when he alludes to his trip with Pfeifer and the others into Monroe County. The road leads through Jackson Township, the place where Miss Bittenbender was murdered. Pfeifer refers to Jackson in his confession." (George Kraft Interview March 19, 1881). This wasn't quite true. The murder happened in Hamilton Township, but it was very close to the Jackson Township line; so close was it to Jackson that even a local could mistake the location as part of Jackson and not Hamilton Township.

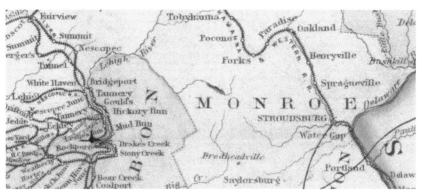

Figure 80 - A close view of an area map circa 1880. Kraft lived a mile and a half east of White Haven. The Pocono Switch was right at the railroad spur at 'forks' near the Southern boundry of Coolbaugh Township, Monroe County. The route they took went through Chestnuthill and Jackson Townships.

The reporter asked George Kraft whether he knew Etna Bittenbender. George was quick to deny that he ever met her, knew her, or ever saw her. "I never knew Emma Bittenbender and never saw her. I never was in Stroudsburg in my life, and was never in Monroe County but once and that was September last." (George Kraft Interview, March 19, 1881). However, it was hard for George to claim that he never heard of Etna's murder. He admitted that he heard about the murder and provided a name. "I have heard Louis Praetorius, of Chestnut hill, Monroe County, talk about Miss Bittenbender being murdered sometime during the fall."

(George Kraft Interview, March 19, 1881). A couple things about George Kraft's answer are interesting. The claim that he was never in Monroe County 'but once' caught my eye. Absolutes in certain details of a story always give an investigator a reason to pause and reflect. Absolutes about details such as never being in a place, especially a large and adjoining county, are easily vetted. Lying about such matters can be considered 'consciousness of one's guilt'. Sure even an innocent person who is afraid of being wrapped up in a murder may lie out of fear; but it usually feels different to the investigator.

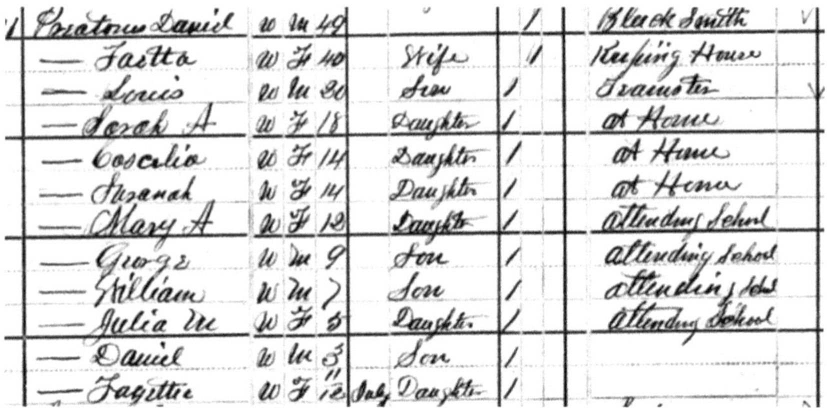

1	Praetorius David	W	M	49			/	Black Smith
	— Fastta	W	F	40	Wife		/	Keeping House
	— Louis	W	M	20	Son	/		Teamster
	— Sarah A	W	F	18	Daughter	/		at Home
	— Cecelia	W	F	14	Daughter	/		at Home
	— Susanah	W	F	14	Daughter	/		at Home
	— Mary A	W	F	12	Daughter	/		attending School
	— George	W	M	9	Son	/		attending School
	— William	W	M	7	Son	/		attending School
	— Julia M	W	F	5	Daughter	/		attending School
	— Daniel	W	M	3	Son	/		
	— Fayettie	W	F	11/12 July	Daughter	/		

Figure 81 - From the 1880 Census the Praetorius family. Louis the oldest son was twenty, Cecilia or Cathsilia, Kraft's girlfriend was 14.

Kraft's answer has that other feel, like he is hiding something bad. The piece entitled 'Another Squeal' published in Wilkes-Barre's 'The Record of the Times' recounts Pfeifer's confession to the White Haven Burglaries and his 'squealing' on Kraft as his accomplice. Parts of Pfeifer's account were quoted in Chapter 7. The circumstances of Kraft's arrest by Detective O'Brien instantly throw into doubt George Kraft's claim of being a homebody. "The same story was told to Detective James O'Brien, who went to see young Kraft, but found he was away from home. On Monday he learned that Kraft was at work for George Dowling, hauling logs at a place some 25 miles back of White Haven. O'Brien drove there and arrested Kraft, and took him to White Haven." Twenty five miles 'back' of White Haven; where could that be? Remember that the newspaper reporting this was based in Wilkes Barre, which adjoins White Haven to its immediate western edge. So from the Wilkes-Barre vantage, a location to the 'back of White Haven' must be to the east of it. Now remember when the detective went to arrest Kraft in the latter part of November 1880, he wasn't home. Instead, the detective had to travel twenty five miles east of White Haven, where Kraft was working, take him into custody, and bring him back to White Haven to present him to the Justice of the Peace. That distance and direction would put Kraft's arrest by Detective O'Brien somewhere in the west end of Monroe County. This means that within weeks of Etna's Murder, young George Kraft is not only working in Monroe County, but in the same general area of the county in which the murder took place.

Then there is the Louis Praetorius clue. The fellow is from Chestnut Hill Monroe County according to Kraft. Chestnut Hill Township is in the west end of Monroe County and shares borders with both Jackson and Hamilton Townships. Praetorius is the guy who Kraft claims told him about Etna's Murder in the fall of 1880. It turns out that an examination into Mr. Praetorius reveals deep ties to not only George Kraft but also Jackson Township; the place repeatedly mentioned by Pfeifer on the slates; **"I also kill that girl in Jackson County"** and; **"Miss Elna Bittenbender Jackson Township last fall…"**

In 1880, at the time the census takers recorded information, which was spring into the summer, Louise Praetorius was twenty years old living with his family in Northern Kidder Township Carbon County, the same neighborhood as George Kraft. There were many brothers and sisters. One sister, Cathsilia caught George Kraft's eye. She was 14 years old he was 17. At the time of the White Haven burglaries, November 1880, George and Cathsilia were seeing one another. In the article called 'Another Squeal', Pfeifer mentions that on the night of the burglaries, Pfeifer, Kraft, and his friends went to a party in a part of White Haven called 'Jerusalem'. There was drinking involved. It was at this party that Pfeifer and Kraft decided to pull off the burglaries. George had to first take his girlfriend home and then come back and meet Pfeifer on a bridge. As Pfeifer explains; "I left the party to go on ahead…before robbing the store Kraft took his girl home from the party and promised to meet me on the bridge." ('Another Squeal', *Record of the Times*, Wilkes Barre December 29, 1880). That girl, Cathsilia Praetorius, would become George Kraft's wife shortly after his release from prison.

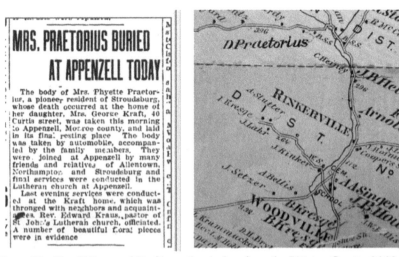

MRS. PRAETORIUS BURIED AT APPENZELL TODAY

The body of Mrs. Phyette Praetor-lus, a pioneer resident of Stroudsburg, whose death occurred at the home of her daughter, Mrs. George Kraft, 40 Curtis street, was taken this morning to Appenzell, Monroe county, and laid in its final resting place The body was taken by automobile, accompan-led by the family members. They were joined at Appenzell by many friends and relatives of Allentown, Northampton and Stroudsburg and final services were conducted in the Lutheran church at Appenzell.

Last evening services were conduct-ed at the Kraft home, which was thronged with neighbors and acquaint-ances. Rev. Edward Kraus, pastor of St John's Lutheran church, officiated. A number of beautiful floral pieces were in evidence

Figure 82 - The Obituary of Kraft's mother in law from the Pittston Gazette 26 Nov 1917 alongside a close up of an 1875 map of Jackson Township. The surname Praetorius appears as does the town of Woodville (Neola), which is named in the Inquest as part of the description of the crime scene; "On the public road from Snydersville to Woodville about two miles from Snydersville." Kraft and through him Pfeifer are thus connected to our murder location.

The Praetorius family had deep roots in Jackson Township. They were among the pioneering families of that section of Monroe County. The 1870 census shows the family living in that Township. A section of the Township Map from 1875 lists one of the larger landowners as 'D. Praetorius'. George Kraft's future mother in law would one day pass away in his home in Pittston Pennsylvania. She would be buried in a small cemetery in Appenzell Jackson Township, just up the road from the scene of the murder.

So Pfeifer and Kraft had the opportunity to commit the murder. The attempt of young George Kraft to deflect and deny not only doesn't square with the facts, it raises serious questions about his credibility. The young men had the means, connections, and opportunity to have roamed around the area during the fall of 1880. People who had a strong interest in solving Etna's murder certainly felt that way. Some of them would seek out George Kraft in his jail cell to get the truth out of him. One of them was Etna's uncle. We are not certain which of Etna's uncles it was. Etna had three uncles on her dad's side; Aaron, Christopher, and George Bittenbender. George was her father's twin. George owned a store in Snydersville. It was George who sent the telegrams out to the surrounding areas within hours of the discovery of her body. It was probably George, who after reading Kraft's interview in the *Daily Union* travelled to Wilkes-Barre. "An uncle of Miss Bittenbender, who was murdered in Monroe County last fall and whose name was recently mentioned in Pfeiffer's confessions, was in the city today in company with another gentleman. They called at the office of the *Union Leader* to interview the representative whose talk with George Kraft, Pfeifer's cousin, was published a few days since in this journal. The uncle had seen a copy of the paper containing the interview and he wished to ascertain if anything further had been revealed." (*The Daily Union Leader*, Wilkes-Barre March 24, 1881).

During their conversation with the reporter, Etna's Uncle talked about Louis Praetorius. He said he knew the Praetorius family and intended to speak with them about their connections to both Kraft and Pfeiffer. Etna's Uncle strongly suspected that Pfeifer and Kraft returned to Monroe County after their trip in September. He wanted answers. After speaking with the reporter, George and his friend went to the Luzerne County Jail to question George Kraft. However, the warden there, a fellow named Gilchrist, would not allow them to see Kraft. "He and his companion went up to the county jail, but at the suggestion of Warden Gilchrist, they held no conversation with Kraft." (*The Daily Union Leader*, Wilkes-Barre March 24, 1881). It's a shame they weren't allowed to question Kraft. It is fairly certain that Kraft's story would have changed. It is probable that they spoke with Louis Praetorius or his family, but what they were told is unknown. One thing seems clear, both Kraft and Pfeifer, through their association with Louis Praetorius and other members of that local family could have learned details about Etna; where she lived, her looks, her work at Jacob Marsh's house. They also could have become familiar with the various paths and routes between the Bittenbender Farm and the Marsh Residence.

Despite the grand jury mandate, that the district attorney use all his resources to ferret out the murder, by the end of March 1881, little if any investigation seemed to be going on. In fact, the last event of note was the attack on the girls in Jackson Township, in which Wilson Marsh was involved. Certainly, no work in interviewing Kraft, travelling to Philadelphia to read Pfeifer's confessions, interviewing people like Louis Praetorius, Sebastian Kraft, Pfeifer's cell mate from Luzerne, and Mr. Woodring went on. It seems like Etna's family was left to use their own resources if they wanted justice. "Stroudsburg, April 3. Since the death of Frank Pfeifer, who committed suicide in the Eastern Penitentiary and made disclosures concerning the murder of Etna Bittenbender, implicating himself and George Kraft, little has been done to ferret out the mystery, though the Monroe County authorities intend investigating the connections of the accused with the crime." (*The Times Philadelphia*, 'The Penitentiary Suicide, The Monroe County Authorities and the Bittenbender Murder', Monday April 4, 1881).

This inaction did not sit well with Etna's family. Her dad, as you may recall from a previous chapter, hired an attorney and former prosecutor named Stephen Holmes. Holmes' letter dated April 4, 1881 to the Eastern State Penitentiary included multiple requests for information and help from the prison authorities. Holmes wrote: "I have seen the account in the newspapers of the confession of Frank Pfeifer who hung himself in the penitentiary a few weeks ago. I would like to have a full and accurate description of this man Pfeifer and all the facts that are known concerning him, particularly concerning his whereabouts and doings last fall... Please state whether the pieces of slate on which Pfeifer's confession was written have been preserved. We hope that they will be well taken care of and the writing itself preserved as it may be of great importance if Kraft is brought to trial. He is now in jail at Wilkes-Barre on another charge and will probably be arrested for the murder on expiration of his present sentence. (Eastern State Penitentiary General Correspondence 1878-1901). Of course, the slates had already been taken by the Coroner of Philadelphia and used at the Inquest. It is unknown what happened to them after that. Kraft was never arrested for murder at the expiration of his Wilkes-Barre sentence. There is simply nothing to show us that the district attorney followed through with any efforts to investigate the Pfeiffer/Kraft connection to Etna's murder.

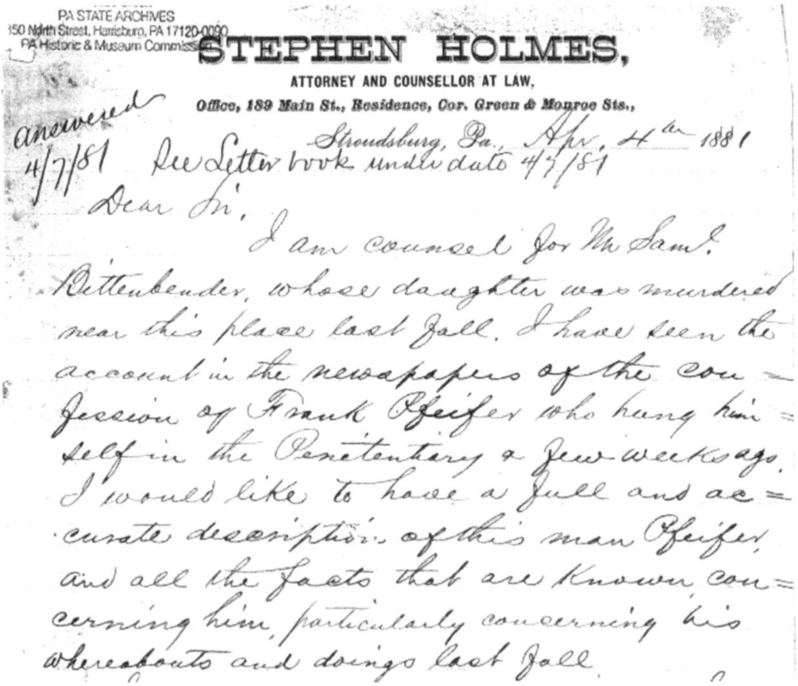

Figure 83- A portion of Mr. Holmes Letter of April 4, 1881.

Following through with Attorney Holmes' desire to find out everything he could about Frank Pfeifer led us back to New York City 1880, his hometown. Luckily we found a story that ran in an oddly named New York newspaper called '*The Truth*'. The reporter, taken with the account of the murder suicide he read in the Philadelphia newspapers, and aware of Frank Pfeifer's New York connection decided to pay Frank's mother a visit in the hopes of asking her about her son. The article was printed on March 19, 1881, only three days after her son's death. The resulting interview gives us a great deal of insight into Pfeifer:

"Mrs. Pfeiffer is a very respectable German lady. She has two daughters married to respectable citizens of the neighborhood. She lost her youngest daughter, age 19, last December. Her husband died five years since. She has still another son about 13 years of age. He is a good boy and attends school regularly. His mother tearfully said she trusted that he would make amends for his brother's terrible history."

Mrs. Pfeifer and Frank's sisters all spoke at length with the reporter. They all thought Frank was insane and said that Frank himself would at times say there was something wrong with him. Frank's oldest sister Susanne, who would have been about 31 years old, remembered a time when Frank was just a boy and he fell from a horse injuring his head. She thought that accident was responsible for his problems. They told the reporter that Frank was upset to find out his younger sister Amalia had died last December. In his last letter to his mother, which he wrote on March 6, 1881, he said that the news of his sister's death made him feel like he had no reason to live anymore and that he would end his life. Despite his past, Frank's mother and sisters claimed he was a very affectionate person. "Mrs. Pfeifer is as yet undecided as to what disposition she will make of her unfortunate son's remains. She owns a cemetery lot where her husband and daughter are buried, and will probably inter him there. Mrs. Pfeifer needed no arguments to convince this reporter that she was a good mother. She wept bitterly as she thought of her son's horrible end. She asserted that she did not deem him responsible and forgot and forgave him for the suffering he had caused her." (*Truth*, 'The Cherry Hill Horror', Saturday March 19, 1881).

There was some information shared about Frank's movements in the fall of 1880. The time frame of Frank's departure from the City given by his mother to the reporter does not jive with the facts. She told the reporter that Frank left home for Pennsylvania in November. Of course, if true that would mean he could not have killed Etna. However, Kraft says it was August. There is no reason to doubt Kraft's story that Frank went with him to Monroe County in September when his brother had court in

Stroudsburg. Although, there is an account of Frank's arrest for the White Haven burglary which says Frank was in White Haven for about a month. The article gives the wrong name, but must be referring to Pfeifer. "He was subsequently captured near the house of a Mr. Kraft, about a mile and a half east of White Haven, after a vigorous resistance. He has been in the neighborhood of White Haven about a month, and an envelope dropped in the store by him bore the name Frank Edler. He is 22 years of age, about five feet five inches in height and said to hail from New York." (*The Daily Union Leader*, 29 November 1880).

Household Members:	Name	Age
	Martin Pfeifer	42
	Margreth Pfeifer	41
	Susanne Pfeifer	21
	Cathrine Pfeifer	16
	Frank Pfeifer	14
	Helena Pfeifer	12
	Barbara Pfeifer	10
	Amalia Pfeifer	8
	Martin Pfeifer	2
	Anna Pfeifer	4

Figure 84 - A close up of the 1870 Census for the Pfeifer Family of New York Ward 20 District 8.

Frank's mother was appalled by the thought that he was involved in the murder of Etna Bittenbender. "Mrs. Pfeifer said that he was out with his cousin George Kraft. She could not believe that he had been concerned in that horrible affair." Mrs. Kraft gave a reason for why Frank left New York that was different than that of the New York police. Instead of mentioning a warrant for burglary, Mrs. Kraft said that Frank left New York because he had a problem concerning a girl. "He had got into some trouble about a girl of the neighborhood. This was the immediate occasion of his departure." (*Truth*, 'The Cherry Hill Horror', Saturday March 19, 1881). It's too bad that the girl is not named nor is there anything specific about the trouble.

Mrs. Pfeifer and Frank's sisters were certainly sincere in their sadness over his violent death as well their belief that Frank suffered from some type of mental illness. But their love for him just underscores how little even their assessment of his character, looking to his past through grief stricken lenses, paints Frank as anything but unstable, troubled, and violent. This brings to mind Frank's own words written on the slates; "They call me the Devil and a which." There again his words are corroborated. The police who dealt with him in New York certainly did not hold back their assessment of the man. Even before his death and before any possible connection to the murder of Etna was known, the New York authorities told Wilkes-Barre detective O'Brien that Pfeifer was a 'very bad man'. The police would provide the details of Frank's crimes after his death. These include the strong suspicion he shot to death his own father and the murder of a night watchman during a robbery at the Harlem Railroad Yard on Thirtieth Street. Add those to Pfeifer's killing of his cell mate, John McBride and you have three murdered men. This corroborates another part of his writing; "This is the third man I have killed."

Frank Pfeifer also tells us, with some braggadocio; **"so if you know all the people I have kill, you would be astonished".** To have killed three men is bad but not astonishing. But Frank doesn't say you would be astonished to learn of all the **men** I have killed. Unlike the third man killed phrase, this language is gender neutral, '**people**' not just men. Frank must be including women in this part of his writing. Yet there is no specific reference to Frank Pfeifer killing women in New York. This brings us to his mother admitting that Frank left the city because he was in trouble concerning a girl from the neighborhood. It seems Frank had quite a few problems with girls. Among the records kept by the Eastern State Penitentiary, there is a note claiming that Pfeifer assaulted multiple females; "...one Prisoner No. 728 killed an associate and then committed suicide. He was of unsound mind on admission but never during imprisonment developed paroxysmal tendencies. Note-- Prisoner No. 728, of whom mention is made, came from Luzerne County. After the murder and suicide authorities of Luzerne County informed the prison authorities that the prisoner is believed to have killed his father and feloniously assaulted several females before conviction to this prison..." (1881 ESP Annual Report Physical and Mental Condition Upon Admission).

There is but one obvious source for the Luzerne Authorities to believe Pfeiffer sexually assaulted several females before his incarceration there. That source is Pfeifer's cousin George Kraft. At the time the Luzerne County Authorities provided the Eastern State Penitentiary with the information concerning Pfeifer assaulting several females, George Kraft was still serving his sentence in Luzerne County. Finally, there is the opinion of Captain Washburn of the 37th Street Station House. Pfeifer left his name and contact information in his prison cell alongside the writing slates. The Captain would tell the press; "I have no doubt he killed the Bittenbender girl. It would be just like him." (*National Police Gazette*, April 2, 1881). Of all the possible motives, rape is the most likely for Etna's murder. As we know she was not only raped, but raped in a secluded location nearby before being brought to the scene where her body would be found. It was only after the rape that Etna was brought to the road and beaten to death with stones and a club. Outside of recognizing that he was thought of as "the Devil and a wich" and suggesting he was insane, Pfeiffer never writes down reasons for any of the crimes he admits to. Instead, he just simply tells what he did; "**I also kill that girl in Jackson County.**"

What of Kraft's involvement? Pfeifer specifically includes him throughout his writings. Remember Frank Pfeifer's words; "**Last fall me and my cousin George Kraft.**" Through the advantage of time we can trace the course of George Kraft's life as we did with Wilson Marsh, Samuel Haney, Charles Flock, John Langefeld, and Joseph Lesh. Originally, it was hard to figure out which George Kraft was the right one. There were so many George Krafts throughout Pennsylvania and elsewhere. He was only 17 when incarcerated. Furthermore, the next big data dump was the 1890 Census. But that unfortunately was largely destroyed by fire; we almost gave up. Finally, with much persistence and after years into the investigation we found the right George Kraft.

George Kraft was released from prison in August of 1881. He was never charged, arrested, or as far as we know, even questioned by the Monroe County Authorities. Kraft married Cathsilia Praetorius in 1882. He was 19 and she was 16. In September 1888 he became a trainman on the Lehigh Valley Railroad. After two years as a trainman he was promoted to a fireman on the railroad. He served in that position for two years and seven months and then was promoted to the coveted position of engineer on the railroad. That would be in 1894. Kraft would hold the position of veteran engineer for many decades with the Lehigh Valley Railroad. "During his long term of service he has had all the runs on the Wyoming Division his service as engineer has been in the passenger division with runs from Coxton to Jersey City, Coxton to Easton and in late years from Coxton to Lehighton. More recently he had piloted the John Wilkes and was in charge of that train on its maiden run from Coxton to Lehighton"(*Pittston Gazette*, Pittston Pennsylvania August 5, 1940).

GEORGE M. KRAFT.

Figure 85 - Kraft's only son (adopted) died in France during VVVI of pneumonia.

Life had its share of tragedy for George Kraft. One of the earliest was the horrible death of his father George Kraft Senior. Ironically, the elder Mr. Kraft was struck by a locomotive in 1891 while walking the tracks looking for coal near his home. He was hard of hearing and didn't realize a train was approaching. Mr. Kraft was living with his son George on Canal Street in Wilkes Barre at the time. His mangled body was taken home to his son who was then a railroad fireman. George himself was seriously hurt the year before when working as a trackman he was squeezed between two cars. He was carried home suffering in much pain but did recover. (*Wilkes-Barre Record*, Wilkes-Barre Pennsylvania April 28, 1890).

Kraft was still living on Canal Street in October 1892 when his wife Cathsilia left him. In an incredibly embarrassing article published in the Sunday news in Wilkes-Barre it was explained that "Mrs. George Kraft is the wife of a good honest fireman on the Lehigh Valley Road and the couple, who have been married for about five years, lived together until about a month ago on Canal Street. Kraft was a good husband providing his wife with all the money necessary to keep the house properly and dress herself but she evidently tired of his company and received and encouraged the attention of a young man living nearby. About a month ago she left her husband and the town, first collecting all the money and valuables she could and going without giving a reason. Shortly afterwards the young man went away also and now the neighbors connecting their previous intimacy with the fact of their going away believe they have a eloped and now are living together somewhere." (*Sunday News*, Wilkes-Barre October 2, 1892).

The separation didn't last long. Mrs. Kraft was a very social person and there are numerous articles of her entertaining friends and family, including George's brother Sebastian at the couple's Curtis Street home in Pittston. By 1895 the couple had relocated from Wilkes-Barre to Pittston where they would spend the rest of their lives.

The couple had no children of their own but adopted two, a son (George Mathieson) and a daughter (Maggie Gill). The son served in France in World War I. There, at the height of the influenza pandemic, also known as the Spanish Flu, the young man was stricken ill and died a few days later. His body was brought back home for burial. Their daughter eventually married and bore children before she passed away in 1938. Cathsilia Praetorius Kraft passed away in February 1939. She had been active in Saint Mary's Roman Catholic Church in Pittston and a member of the Altar and Rosary Societies and an organizer of the Auxiliary to

Fort Pittston Post Veterans of Foreign Wars. She died in the family home at 40 Curtis Street in upper Pittston. Her obituary describes her as "a prominent and widely known resident" of the community. A year later George retired from the railroad. The article commemorating his career credited him with 52 years of continuous service on the Lehigh Valley Railroad. (*Pittston Gazette*, Pittston Pennsylvania, August 5, 1940).

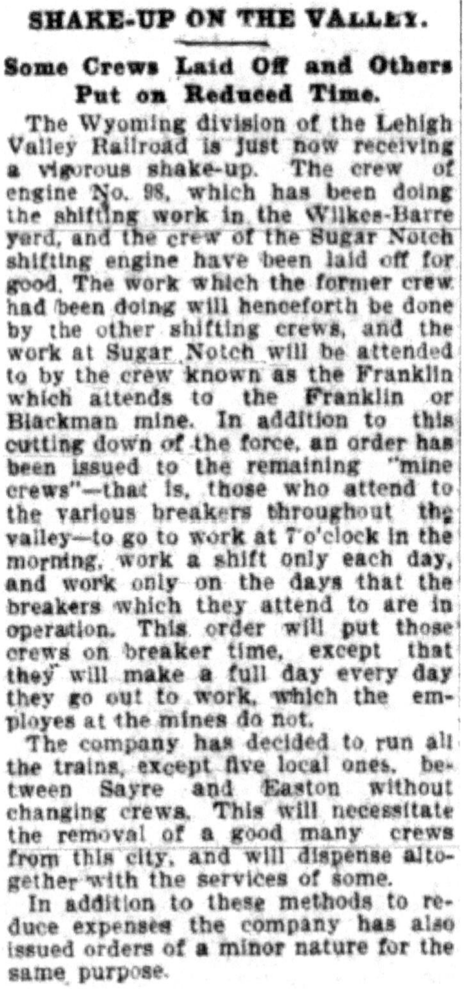

SHAKE-UP ON THE VALLEY.

Some Crews Laid Off and Others Put on Reduced Time.

The Wyoming division of the Lehigh Valley Railroad is just now receiving a vigorous shake-up. The crew of engine No. 98, which has been doing the shifting work in the Wilkes-Barre yard, and the crew of the Sugar Notch shifting engine have been laid off for good. The work which the former crew had been doing will henceforth be done by the other shifting crews, and the work at Sugar Notch will be attended to by the crew known as the Franklin which attends to the Franklin or Blackman mine. In addition to this cutting down of the force, an order has been issued to the remaining "mine crews"—that is, those who attend to the various breakers throughout the valley—to go to work at 7 o'clock in the morning, work a shift only each day, and work only on the days that the breakers which they attend to are in operation. This order will put those crews on breaker time, except that they will make a full day every day they go out to work, which the employes at the mines do not.

The company has decided to run all the trains, except five local ones, between Sayre and Easton without changing crews. This will necessitate the removal of a good many crews from this city, and will dispense altogether with the services of some.

In addition to these methods to reduce expenses the company has also issued orders of a minor nature for the same purpose.

Figure 86 - The Wyoming Division of the Lehigh Valley Railroad was the division Kraft worked in. This article is about a restructuring which effected many employees of the division including the crew of engine 98. Kraft survived the restructuring and continued to work for the railroad until he retired in 1940. (Wilkes-Barre Weekly December 11, 1897).

George Kraft passed away on October 12, 1949 in his Curtis Street home. He died of a sudden heart attack. He too was active in Saint Mary's Roman Catholic Church and was a member of the Holy Name Society and the Brotherhood of Locomotive Engineers. He was survived by a granddaughter Mrs. Mary Krantz English and a great-grandchild James J. English, both of whom lived with him at his home on Curtis Street. So there is nothing in his long life which showed any further criminal activity. The only time it seems George committed crimes was the month or so during the fall of 1880 when the 17 year old was in his Cousin Frank Pfeifer's company.

Chapter 9

Remnants

"Energy cannot be created or destroyed;
it can only be changed from one form to
another."

Albert Einstein

Persistence is a trait that serves the cold case investigator well. You can't give up; there are always angles to check out, stuff to look into for any cold case. For investigators without experience in cold cases this isn't an easy thing. There is this pull to close a case or move on to other investigations. Sometimes the investigator thinks they have reached an impasse and won't look at a file again unless a game changer of some kind comes to them. This is usually a failing proposition; hoping someone comes forward and brings the case together. It is another way of giving up on a case. But it happens, I've seen it; and when it does the investigation is for all practical purposes over. I have seen it with the case of Ed Yale, who claimed his wife Joan died from an accidental fall down the stairs of their home in Smithfield Township in March of 2001. The scene was suspicious from the beginning. Mr. Yale's story did not add up. The autopsy was inconclusive; perhaps it shouldn't have been. Then Mr. Yale refused to answer any more questions without his lawyer agreeing. Of course, it is a rare thing for a lawyer to let his client answer questions. The investigation ground to a standstill. The lead investigator did not know where to turn. Almost every day he would drive by the Yale residence, reflect on the fact that it concealed a murder, shake his head, and hope that maybe one day the truth would be brought to light. The years passed and he retired. The younger guys, who had been rookies at the time of Mrs. Yale's death, would every once in a while, usually when someone wanted to clean out the evidence room, warn about discarding the evidence; 'leave that stuff be', they would say, 'that was a murder you know'. We reopened the investigation and through the efforts of the Investigative Grand Jury, an in depth review by highly qualified forensic pathologists, and a team of persistent investigators, led by Craig Vanlouvender and Rob Sebastianelli, Mr. Yale was finally charged and fifteen years after Joan's death, convicted of her murder.

In the 2001 Halloween murder of Helen Biank the investigation did not for a moment let up. Troopers Mark Holtsmaster, Pete Gutowski, and Barret Township Police Chief Steve Williams, working closely with myself and Assistant District Attorney Mike Rakaczewski investigated the case from every angle. There were about half a dozen suspects at the onset of the case; each with a motive and the opportunity to have done the deed. The case was entirely circumstantial and involved evidence collection and witness interviews covering multiple states, document analysis, forensic testing, fire scene reconstruction, fingerprint analysis, timelines, and ballistics. All these disciplines played important roles in eliminating the possibilities down to one man, Mark Miller, who had his marriage proposal rejected by the victim that Halloween morning. Charges were brought. The case was ready for trial. At that point, with a jury pool awaiting selection, Miller caved and pled guilty to murder. After six years of constant investigation the case was finally cleared up. Like I said, you need persistence in this line of work.

It is a shame that the investigation into Etna's murder did not show that level of persistence. There was some good detective work done in November and into the early part of December 1880 by Detective John Wood of the Pinkerton Agency. But there is no evidence that Wood continued on the case after Wilson Marsh was questioned in early December about his bloody coat. The county records show no detective payments in 1881, not a penny. Outside of the initial grand jury involvement into the attack on the girls in Jackson Township nothing further seems to have been done. It is hard to tell because the murder suicide in Eastern State Penitentiary happened soon after. But one thing is clear, as late as the first week of April 1881, three weeks after the murder suicide, no Monroe County authority or agent had bothered to interview George Kraft. Indeed, we cannot find any effort by the District Attorney or other county officials to investigate Etna's murder after February of 1881. The investigation seems to have been left to Etna's family, her Dad's lawyer, and the newspapers. There was no professional police force then; yet with such a horrible crime one would expect the authorities of that time to have been made of more determined stuff. The timeline of the investigation is laid out in the insert below:

TIMELINE
Sunday October 31, 1880

- **Approx. 4:00 pm** Etna Bittenbender leaves her parents' home and walks toward the residence of Jacob and Emma Marsh a little over a mile away.
- **Approx. 6:00 pm** Reverend Gilbert riding on Greenview Drive hears the faint cries of some 'little girl'. Coming from down toward the creek. He does not investigate.
- **Evening hours:** several people pass along Pensyl Creek Road, without seeing anything unusual.

Monday November 1, 1880

Early morning hours:
- Samuel Bittenbender passes the scene hauling a load of wood, one of Etna's uncles and 'several others' pass the scene; no one notices anything unusual.

Approx. 9:00 am
- Etna's siblings discover her body.
- Wilson Marsh claims to see two tramps (drifters) 'lurking' on a bridge near the scene.

11:00 am
- The Inquest begins at the scene.

Afternoon/Evening:
- The Post Mortem Examination is performed

---

under the lead of Dr. John Mutchler of Stroudsburg.

5:40 pm
* George Bittenbender sends telegrams to surrounding areas alerting authorities to be on the lookout for suspicious persons.

Thursday November 4, 1880.
* Etna's funeral takes place at Christ Hamilton Reformed Church.
* A tramp is arrested on 'suspicion'.
* Detective John S. Wood of the Pinkerton Agency arrives in Stroudsburg from New York.

Wednesday November 10, 1880.
* Reward posters for the tramps described by Wilson Marsh are distributed.
* The 'Germans' Charles Flock and John Langefeld are arrested in Portland for burglaries.

Friday November 12, 1880.
* Edward Garahan, a tramp is arrested in Pittson on 'suspicion'.

Monday November 29, 1880.
* Frank Pfeifer is arrested at the Kraft residence for the White Haven Burglaries.

Wednesday December 1, 1880.
* Frank Pfeifer tries to hang himself in his jail cell in Wilkes-Barre.

Monday December 6, 1880.
* A torn bloodied coat belonging to Wilson Marsh is found hidden near the crime scene.

Wednesday December 8, 1880.
* Wilson Marsh is questioned in Stroudsburg and 'cleared' of suspicion.

Saturday December 11, 1880.
- Coroner's Inquest is filed ruling Etna was murdered by a person or persons unknown.

Wednesday December 15, 1880.
- The Grand Jury urges the DA to use all resources to ferret out the murder.

Sunday December 26, 1880.
- Pfeifer is interviewed in jail by a reporter and Detective McBride.

Monday December 27, 1880.
- Kraft is arrested somewhere in the West End of Monroe County for the White Haven burglaries.

Tuesday January 4, 1881.
- NYPD confirm that Pfeifer is wanted for burglary in New York.

Monday January 24, 1881.
- Samuel Haney arrested on suspicion of murder for the second time.

Tuesday January 25, 1881.
- Kraft is found guilty of burglary with a recommendation of mercy by the jury.

Wednesday January 26, 1881.
- Pfeifer found guilty of multiple counts of burglary; during a recess in the trial he tries to swallow 'pounded glass'.

Thursday February 3, 1881.
- A justice of the peace dismisses the charges against Haney for 'want of evidence'.

Saturday February 5, 1881.
- Langefeld and Flock sentenced to Eastern State Penitentiary.

Friday February 18, 1881.
- Pfeifer arrives at Eastern State Penitentiary.

Monday February 21, 1881.
- Three girls are attacked by 'half a dozen young men and boys', in Jackson Township, one of whom was Wilson Marsh.

Wednesday March 2, 1881.
- Grand Jury issues presentment recommending DA investigate the assaults on the girls.

Tuesday March 8, 1881.
- Langefeld and Flock arrive at Eastern State Penitentiary.

Wednesday March 16, 1880.
- Pfeifer and McBride found dead in their cell; also found are writing slates containing the last words of Pfeifer.

Thursday March 17, 1881.
- Coroner's inquest on the murder suicide.

Saturday March 19, 1881.
- George Kraft is interviewed by the press in his jail cell in Wilkes Barre.
- Margaret Pfeifer and Frank's sisters are interviewed by the press in New York.

Thursday, March 24, 1881.
- Etna's Uncle arrives in Wilkes-Barre to speak with Kraft.

Monday April 4, 1881.
- Attorney Holmes representing Samuel

> Bittenbender writes to Eastern State Penitentiary
> for information on Pfeifer and Langefeld/Flock.
> This is the last known investigative activity.

There are consequences to failure for a district attorney, even if that failure was beyond his control. In the case of the Bittenbender investigation, David Stokes Lee's failure to secure a conviction for the crime no doubt played a role in his political fortunes. Certainly, there was the belief that a lack of effort, or ability was responsible. Lee had been DA since 1872. Terms then were three not four years. Lee had a history of winning even where the election was hotly contested. That ended in the general election of 1881. Lee was crushed; the lowest vote getter of the three running. Exactly how much his defeat had to do with the anger and frustration over the failed investigation can only be guessed, but it was clearly substantial.

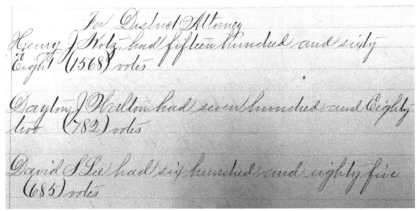

Figure 87 - General election returns for November 8, 1881, a year after the murder. Lee made a dismal showing despite being the long-term incumbent. His political career picked up decades later when he made a successful bid for state senate.

This is a good place to bring up an ongoing effort of our investigation. Almost from the beginning of our collaboration we wanted to know 'where are the Bittenbenders?' In particular, where are the descendants of Sam and Margaret's other eleven children? Perhaps if we found them we could learn important details of the murder and its investigation kept alive by living descendants. Most families have at least one member interested in its history. Detective Kerchner was hopeful that the descendants might be in possession of historical documents relevant to the investigation, or might recall family stories handed down over the generations. They may be in possession of family records, such as letters, scrapbooks, diaries, photographs, baptismal certificates, newspaper clippings and so on. They might even have that portrait of Etna which he sought for in vain.

Family researchers generally find it most helpful to begin with the most current census and work backwards as a strategy for locating people in earlier generations. However, for this investigation, we knew the names of the people connected to the 1880 homicide. We wanted to contact their living descendants. In the case of Etna Bittenbender it would be 1880.

Figure 88 - A Census recording sheet from the 19th Century.

Census records may include the name and age of the husband, wife, children and any others residing in the household. Census records may also include occupations, health conditions and education. Census records are updated every ten (10) years (beginning in 1790). The 1880 Census was the first census to list marital status, street name and house number in addition to the birthplace of people's parents. So the 1880 census, the year Etna was murdered, is a good place to start. Unfortunately nearly all of the 1890 census was destroyed as a result of a Department of Commerce fire in 1921, resulting in a large information deficit. However, we were successful in tracking down some of the people of interest through 1950. Then we used obituaries, newspapers and other public documents to bring us up to the current date. The 1880 census was carried out under a law enacted March 3, 1879. Additional amendments to the law were made on April 20, 1880, and appropriations made on June 16, 1880-16 days after the actual enumeration had begun.

Etna - A Murder Out of Time

The new census law specifically handed over the supervision of the enumeration to a body of officers, known as supervisors of the census, specifically chosen for the work of the census, and appointed in each state or territory, of which they should be residents before March 1, 1880.

Each supervisor was responsible for recommending the organization of his district for enumeration, choosing enumerators for the district and supervising their work, reviewing and transmitting the returns from the enumerators to the central census office, and overseeing the compensation for enumerators in each district.

Each enumerator was required by law "to visit personally each dwelling house in his sub-division, and each family therein, and each individual living out of a family in any place of abode, and by inquiry made of the head of such family, or of the member there of deemed most credible and worthy of trust, or of such individual living out of a family, to obtain each and every item of information and all the particulars." In case no one was available at a family's usual place of abode, the enumerator was directed by the law "to obtain the required information, as nearly as may be practicable, from the family or families, or person or persons, living nearest to such place of abode."

The 1879 Census Act also provided for the collection of detailed data on the condition and operation of railroad corporations, incorporated express companies, and telegraph companies, and of life, fire, and marine insurance companies (using Schedule No.4 - Social Statistics). In addition, the Superintendent of Census was required to collect and publish statistics of the population, industries, and resources of Alaska, with as much detail as was practical. An enumeration was made of all untaxed Indians within the jurisdiction of the United States to collect as much information about their condition as possible.

In 2013 while researching historical records, Detective Kerchner attended a historical society meeting in Chestnuthill Township. After talking with a number of attendees Eric met with a Bittenbender who happened to be involved in genealogy research. They had in their

Michael Mancuso and Eric J. Kerchner

possession a softbound booklet titled "DESCENDANTS OF JOHAN CONRAD BITTENBENDER – MONROE COUNTY PIONEER". The booklet consisted of 112 pages containing Bittenbender family records starting with immigrant JOHAN CONRAD BITTENBENDER, from Psaltzburg Germany in 1717, arriving in Philadelphia on the St. Andrew on October 27th, 1738. Johan was around 21 years old. He married Maria (surname unknown) and had four children, George, Christopher, Jacob and Conrad. Johan was killed by Indians in a raid on the settlers on May 2nd, 1757. One of the survivors of the raid was Phillip Bossert or Buzzard, of whom David Christine the District Attorney of Monroe County is a direct descendent.

Several generations after Conrad we find Etna Bittenbender's parents listed on page 42. Samuel Bittenbender (born September 3rd, 1833) and his wife, Margret Newhart (born September 22nd 1836). Sam and Margaret had twelve children, including Etna (born September 22nd, 1863, the same birthday as her mother. Etna was murdered on October 31st, 1880). Records through 1984 are included in this booklet. Using the Bittenbender ancestry booklet as a guide, several dozen living descendants of Johan Conrad Bittenbender were located and contacted. Detective Kerchner sent dozens of letters to the descendants explaining the reason for contacting them and including newspaper accounts and other information, all in the hope that one or more of them would be able to give us information and answers. Through the process he was able to speak to several descendants. Unfortunately, none of them had anything new or different to add. And also, the portrait remains missing.

In March of 1886 Stroud Township resident Lewis Swink, sometimes incorrectly written as Schwenck or Schwenk was accused by his 18 year old daughter of having 'illicit' relations with her for over four years. In her complaint, the young woman claimed that the incestuous acts began when she was only fourteen. She claimed that Swink subjected her to continuous intimidation in order to keep her compliant and prevent her from speaking out. "...Schwenck was charged with criminal intimacy with his daughter aged 18, which relation had been continued for four years. The girl finally made a confession, on the strength of which a

212

warrant was issued for Schwenck's arrest. Before the constable arrived Shwenck slipped over to a neighbor, borrowed $60 and fled." ('A special from Easton', *The Parsons Daily Sun*, Kansas May 19, 1886,). A review of the docket for the May 1886 Monroe County Grand Jury confirms that a 'true bill' for the charge of 'Incestuous Fornication' was issued against Lewis Swink, on May 25, 1886.

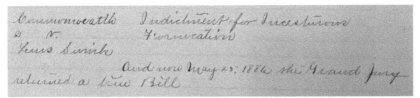

Figure 89 - The acceptance by the Grand Jury of the Incest charge against Lewis Swink.

The Swink family was long resident of Stroud Township, Monroe County. Lewis Swink, born in 1848 came from a large family; his parents were Charles and Sara Swink. In the 1880s, before the accusations made by his daughter, Lewis farmed property in the Township. He had married Mary Ann Hohenscheldt of McIlhaney near Brodheadsville in Monroe County's West End. The couple had a number of children. The oldest was their daughter Sarah, born November 22, 1868; she was the 18 year old who came forward with the incest allegation. A couple months after Sarah came forward, and a week before the Grand Jury approved the charges, Mary Swink, Lewis' wife, met with Detective James Simmons of Easton Pennsylvania and wrote out an affidavit containing a startling further accusation against her husband.

"Facts are given by Schwenck's wife, who has made an affidavit giving all the principal points necessary to work up the case. She claims that on the night Miss Bittenbender was murdered, Schwenck came home with his clothing bespattered with blood. He told his wife that he had murdered Miss Bittenbender, and threatened to kill her if she divulged the secret." ('A special from Easton', *The Parsons Daily Sun*, Kansas May 19, 1886). "He told his wife all about the crime and why he committed it, but threatened to kill her if she ever divulged the secret. Several months ago Schwenk was charged with incest with his daughter aged 18, which relation had been continued for four years. The girl finding herself unable to longer hide her shame, made a confession, on the strength of which a warrant was issued for Schwenk's arrest. Before the constable arrived Schwenk slipped over to a neighbor, borrowed $60, and skipped since which time he has not been heard from. Mrs. Schwenk, fearing that he would return and murder herself and her daughter for exposing him, left their home and took up their abode with Mrs. Schwenk' mother, near Bangor. She has made her affidavit against her husband, she says so that he may be arrested and punished." (Easton Pa May 19, *Appleton Post*, Appleton Wisconsin 20 May 1886)."

The records show that the case against Swink for incest went no further than the grand jury stage. This is consistent with the reports that he went missing after learning that he was to be arrested for the Incest charge. The reports of the Bittenbender angle to the Swink story gave it a lot of exposure. The story was even printed in the *New York Times*. Stroudsburg's newspaper, the *Jeffersonian*, issued a strangely worded counter to the story entitled 'An Outrage.' The paper claimed on 'good authority' that the story was fabricated by an attention seeking detective; "Inquiry into the facts concerning it strikes us as though there is considerable false coloring in the affair, as we are authoritatively informed that Mrs. Schwenk, (as they call her), but it should be Swink, never made any such confession, nor has she gone to Bangor, Northampton County, to live with her mother, when in fact she has not been away from her home in a couple of months. She is still on the property and has commenced farming the land she occupies. The whole affair is a very good sensational got off by some slow homespun work of a detective to gain notoriety." (*Jeffersonian Republican*, Stroudsburg, May 20, 1886).

So where is the truth in this story? As another example of bizarre events in this case, the local newspaper claims the whole story is bogus. But Mrs. Swink is not blamed; rather the onus is put on the detective. A couple of things come to mind; Swink was actually charged with incest, a fact not mentioned in the *Jeffersonian* Article. Second, Swink himself was missing, and the Bittenbender angle to the story only came out after those two things happened. In other words, Mrs. Swink only came out with the revelation of her husband's confession after he was on the run. So what does she have to gain by coming out with it? The paper is silent on what authority they are using to claim she is still on the property and has not relocated; the *Jeffersonian* article side steps that issue simply blames detective Simmons with making it all up. To do that would mean he had to outright lie about Mrs. Swink swearing out an affidavit.

So we looked into the detective and his work. James Simmons was born in Easton Pennsylvania on April 23, 1845 to Charles and Rachel Simmons. He served in the Civil War, attaining the rank of 1st Sergeant Seymours Battery Company 5th US Artillery. By 1880 Simmons was employed as a detective, married to Harriet, with one son, Chester age twelve. He worked as a detective till at least 1910, living on Ferry Street in Easton with his wife. Detective Simmons passed away three years later on December 7, 1913. His death certificate still lists his employment as 'Detective'. We read multiple news articles showing that Simmons was very actively involved in many different investigations throughout his lengthy term of service without any evidence of poor performance, lack of credibility, unprofessionalism; in short anything approaching the level of chicanery laid against him by the Jeffersonian.

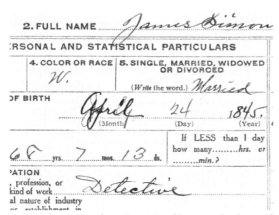

Figure 90 - An excerpt from Detective Simmons death certificate.

So there is no evidence even hinting that Simmons was making up the story. That doesn't mean the story is true. It is similar to the version overheard by Better Feitig, when Joe Lesh returned home at night wearing bloody clothing. Certainly, Mrs. Swink could have fabricated the allegations in an effort to keep an abusive husband from coming out of hiding; or a way to protect her daughter from the shame of publicly testifying about the years of incest; or perhaps to explain her own failure to stop the abuse of her daughter Sarah? All of those are possibilities. Once more, Lewis Swink is never named as a suspect by the investigators. Nor has this accusation against Swink for the murder of Etna passed into any oral history that we found.

What about Lewis Swink? He seems to have truly disappeared. He is not even named in his father's 1901 will; suggesting he was already dead by that time. There is no record of him after the May 1886 indictment. Sarah, his abused daughter, married Horace Reimel in 1888. Sarah spent the rest of her life in Northampton County. She passed away in 1927. Her mother Mary stayed in the area for a number of years. Several of her sons relocated to Greeley Colorado. At some point, around the turn of the century, Mary went to Colorado to be with her boys.

There is a family memory of sorts gleaned from a query on a genealogy website that poignantly touches upon the trauma suffered by Swink's family as a result of his actions:

> "I am looking into what happened to a particular relative and circumstances surrounding his death. His name is Lewis Swink (no middle name known) born 1848 or 49, I believe in Monroe County PA. He married Mary Hohensheldt in Stroudsburg PA and supposedly died in 1886. His father was Charles Swink born 6/3/1825 died 11/8/1901 and his mother was Sarah born 11/11/1830 died 1/17/1906. He was not mentioned in his father's will so I assume he had died before then. His children traveled to Colorado about 1890, Ervin, Charles, Milton, Frank, and Allen; but refused to speak of him. My Grandmother is very curious as to what happened and why no

one would even mention his name. She has asked me to find out what I can. Eventually Mary (the mother) was brought to Greeley Colorado where she died in 1917." (PaRootsweb September 16, 2003).

Another bizarre event touching upon the murder of Etna was reported in June of 1924 in a piece published in the East Stroudsburg paper '*The Morning Press*'. The article recounted the disappearance of a man named Frederick L. Davis. Davis had told people that he would be going hiking out of state to Texas. He bought a number of camping items at local stores. He started off at the Pocono Creek. There he pitched a tent and set camp. The next day he was nowhere to be found. Much of his gear was left behind. There were reports of a dark stranger seen the evening of the disappearance. The stranger was driving a Ford with New York license plates. "At 7 O'clock Wednesday evening a short dark visaged man with a foreign accent appeared on the scene. He is believed to have driven into a parking space about 50 yards from Davis' tent." (*The Morning Press*, East Stroudsburg, June 7 1924). There was a great deal of concern and speculation that this stranger may have killed the missing Mr. Davis. There was also speculation that Davis may have went with the man voluntarily, or involuntarily. It was odd that he left most of his belongings behind. It was also ominous that a strip of cloth from his tent was cut off and missing; perhaps he was strangled with it? Or perhaps he killed himself?

The County Detective, a fellow named Shafer was at the scene interviewing some ladies who had been doing their wash nearby. Shafer also interviewed the students and their teacher who had a picnic nearby. But the most bizarre discovery at the scene was the partially burnt remains of a notebook. "Although someone had attempted to burn a notebook left by Davis, the book was found charred but legible, because the fired notebook had been extinguished by the heavy rain of Wednesday. Written on one of the pages was the following: "I have found the slayer of Etna B., but will not tell. 'Look this up'. The Etna B. referred to is Etna Bittenbender, who was mysteriously murdered at Snydersville over 40 years ago." Davis also noted that he made a visit to the cemetery Etna is buried at. With the papers Detective Shafer found a photograph of Etna's Grave. There was other weird stuff also, for instance 'snapshots of women and girls with their faces cut out.'

The article identifies Frederick L. Davis as living in East Stroudsburg but formerly of Bangor Pennsylvania. It also mentions that Davis had worked at the Dery Silk Mill in Stroudsburg.

No one knew what to make of the references to Etna. "The mysterious inscription regarding Davis' cognizance of the slayer of Etna Bittenbender is so cryptic that almost any deduction is possible." We also did not know what to make of Davis' Notes regarding Etna. By all appearances this Davis fellow seems like an odd duck. Maybe he thought he knew who killed Etna. But exactly why he wrote that is unknown. But we are pleased to report that Fred Davis was to reappear. We located records of him well into the 1930s still in Monroe County. In the 1930 Census the 41 year old Davis is lodging in Stroudsburg at the home of James and Blandemia Schach, he is employed back at the silk mill, and is still unmarried. In May of 1934 Mr. Davis applied for veteran's compensation benefits for a brief stint of service in the army during the summer of 1918 and into the winter of 1919.

Who knows what motivated Mr. Davis to photograph Etna's grave and write his little secret down and then try to burn the writing. Certain places affect people in different ways. Many people believe that there are some with a greater degree of sensitivity to their surroundings than that of an average person. I have also heard it said that energy does not just disappear, but lingers on; perhaps as a remnant of what once was. In the course of life a person could experience a number of things, odd happenings, feelings of Deja vu, sounds without a recognizable source etc. In fact, one prosecutor I work with, a level headed guy, took a ride to Etna's grave to see it for himself. He later complained of having a sleepless night during which, at one point, he saw a female figure watching him from the foot of his bed. He felt paralyzed; a feeling he had never before experienced. He felt the visit to Etna's grave was responsible. I often find it very helpful to visit a crime scene, even a cold case scene. When I was preparing for trial in the Mark Miller prosecution, I visited the crime scene. Although Mrs. Biank had been murdered in her Barret Township home six years before and the place set on fire, it remained intact. It was boarded up but I had permission to be there. The place was locked in time to that tragic Halloween day back in 2001. Everything was left in place nothing disturbed, even the burnt couch upon which Helen's body was discovered by a firefighter crawling through the smoke. I am not sensitive when it comes to things like this; but there seemed to be an energy there that you could almost touch.

There was another time when Troopers Craig VanLouvender, Jim Wheeler, and I were in the woods visualizing a horrible murder that happened there several years before; again as part of trial preparation. The murder was during the winter, we were there in the summer so it was difficult to find that spot where the victim's body lay. We couldn't quite find it. Then I noticed my brother, Rich Mancuso, who came along to keep me company, staring down at the ground. We walked over and there on the ground, only a couple feet away, staring up at us was a big black crow. The crow was calm, docile, and looked healthy. We realized that the spot where the crow stood was precisely the spot where the murder victim's head rested when his body was discovered years earlier. As we left the scene, the crow remained as if keeping vigil. That was strange.

This all brings to mind a controversial subject in law enforcement, the use of psychics to aid in the investigation. Some of my colleagues are dead set against it, no pun intended, others embrace it whole heartedly. I don't like either extreme. I believe using a psychic has its place and time. The place is very incognito; where you can't be seen, the time rare, when you have nothing to lose. Under those conditions and with a psychic who you believe to be sincere, it really is a no lose proposition. During the course of my career I met a young man who I believe is a sincere psychic. Alex Curcio is his name, a fine young man with a shy, quiet, and unassuming demeanor. Alex believes he has an extra sense that allows him to see and hear impressions of things that have happened. I don't know precisely how things come to him. He seems to rely on the sense of touch and will often close his eyes and look down as he describes the images he receives. He has given aid to us on a few cold case and missing person investigations. While nothing is one hundred percent, there have been times when Alex has said things that would prove not only to be true, but also left us at a loss to explain it away as coincidence.

One time was when we were investigating the sudden disappearance of 88 year old Joseph DeVivo, World War II veteran and well known former school teacher. We brought Alex over to the Devivo residence. Mr. Devivo had disappeared from his Stroud Township home; his bed sheets turned down, his heating pad on and warm to the touch, his new Chrysler was missing from the garage. Rico Herbert was arrested by the authorities in North Carolina driving the car. He had been interviewed but denied any knowledge of DeVivo's whereabouts. None of that was known to Alex. The lead detective, Richard Wolbert from the Stroud Area Police Department, had brought some of Mr. DeVivo's personal effects for Alex to hold. Alex held one of the items, a baseball cap emblazoned with information from DeVivo's war time service. Alex closed his eyes and concentrated. One of the first things he said was that Mr. DeVivo was dead. He knew we needed to find him. After a further quiet time concentrating with the hat still in his hands Alex told us that the remains were 'out of state'. Alex added that the body was partially submerged in water. Then Alex said something even more unusual. Something that he said would happen soon. He told detective Wolbert that he would get a call later in the day from the guy's mother saying he wanted to talk. Hours later, Herbert's mother called the station to advise that her son wanted to speak to the authorities. The detective flew to North Carolina. He sat with Herbert who admitted to putting Mr. DeVivo's body in the trunk of his car and driving to South Carolina. There, at a place called Lancaster, Herbert dumped the body. Based on Herbert's description, the badly decomposed remains of Joseph DeVivo were located in a wooded area, partially submerged in a small creek.

It was Sunday September 16, 2012 about three in the afternoon. The location was off Pensyl Creek Road on property owned by Tom Bilheimer, the land where the body of Etna Bittenbender was found by her little brothers and sisters nearly 132 years earlier. Detective Wendy Serfass of the Monroe County District Attorney's Office had transported Alex to the scene. Over the years, Wendy has worked closely with me in the many homicide cases I have brought to trial, as well as those which end as guilty pleas, and numerous equivocal death investigations. She is very experienced with all the issues involved in murder investigations and prosecutions. Indeed, she has participated in more murder trials than any detective, state or local, that I know.

Detective Kerchner and I discussed asking Alex to help out in a cold case we were looking into. Although Kerchner was appropriately skeptical, we agreed not to give Alex any details about the case. I also thought it best that only Wendy accompany Alex. Wendy at that time knew practically nothing about the murder of Etna Bittenbender. That was by design. I didn't want Kerchner or me to somehow influence the outcome by inadvertently disclosing details during the session. Maybe some remnant of the horrible crime still lingered there. Something Alex could sense. In other words, maybe Alex could be a witness to the murder. A little over an hour and half later, I received a phone call from Wendy. Her usually piercing voice was now louder and took on a shrill excited tone. She had just taken Alex back to his car after his visit to the Bittenbender crime scene. She couldn't believe the things he was telling her. The experience was 'overwhelming'. She said Alex seemed at times to feel the victim's pain. She proceeded to tell me disturbing details of the murder. The details seemed to be from both Etna's experience and that of her killers.

Detective Serfass wrote a report of the session that very day. She captured Alex's words, the images he described, and the emotions of the moment.

"They were waiting for her, watching her and her family'. Alex pointed across the road to the patch of woods and up the hill. 'To the right, at the top of the hill, there was a large oak tree. They were hiding behind the oak'. There were two of them, 'two guys hiding behind the tree and waiting'. They knew where to hide and wait for her. When she entered the woods Etna heard the sound of whispers and of footsteps in the underbrush. She became anxious. At one point Alex began to hold his chest and had shortness of breath. He said he was 'feeling a lot of bruises' in his chest area. He then asked if there was a stream nearby. At another point he seemed uncomfortable and asked Wendy if she, Etna, was 'touched'. Alex hesitated to describe the touching but alluded to it being sexual. Wendy did tell him that she thought the victim was 'violated'. Alex then said 'it was horrible for her because she never experienced that before'. He said she was 'fearless'. He said, 'her family found her right'; and asked if it was the next day. Alex then said, 'I feel the night coming and going'. He said he felt she 'held on for her family to find her and that she took her last breath soon before her family came.'

Like a witness to the dreadful deed, Alex continued to describe the fearful, vicious, and brutal attack on Etna. "....[s]he was horribly bruised, beaten badly. He said they took her over to the stream'. The stream was drawing him to it. Alex then said, 'and they brought her back out by the road because they were proud of their accomplishment and wanted her to be found'. He said the attackers were 'not right in the head'. He asked if there was a coal mine in the area and said they were 'dirty like that.' He was picturing them and they looked 'dirty like someone who works in a mine or something.' He said that one person was familiar to the family, but the other guy was not from this area; he came from away.' Wendy saw Alex holding his chest and experiencing some shortness of breath as he described what he saw. Alex continued; 'she was taken down by the stream because it was still light'. Alex went over toward the stream. As he looked down onto the stream he complained of having a very uneasy feeling there. He felt that many bad things happened there. He did not feel comfortable and asked to leave.

Over the course of the next few weeks, Alex was brought to the Bittenbender Farm House, the old fields surrounding it, the one room school house, and Etna's grave. These visits were recorded and Alex provided many additional and some tantalizing details.

Figure 91 - A class photograph from 1890 of the Rees School. Three of Etna's sisters and one brother are depicted here. Courtesy of Mr. Bob Wallingford, Appenzell Pa. and David Marra Assistant District Attorney. From the collection of the late Claire Wallingford.

Figure 92 - A close view of the Class Photo, depicted here; from left to right are Anna Bittenbender, Jennie Bittenbender, and Alta Bittenbender. Alex described Etna as a beautiful girl, black haired, who was wearing a white or light blue dress with some kind of apron, similar no doubt to the outfits her sisters Annie and Jennie are wearing. What are the odds that Alex's description of Etna matched information we only received years later?

Chapter 10

Closing Argument

"No man can walk out from his own story"

Rango 2011

T hings started to come together the more we dug into the details. Slowly at first, then by fits and spurts the picture started to emerge. Would we finally be able to solve the murder of Etna Bittenbender? This was a question that was personal for both of us. We discussed the various theories that were culled from the facts we found. We played devil's advocate with each other's reasoning. We called upon our colleagues for their insights, and played devil's advocate with them. The threshold question for us was to define the degree or level of proof necessary to identify the guilty. Everyone had an opinion. But opinion not based on fact and a flawless analysis was meaningless for us. Yet we knew that the underlying investigation was flawed from the start, official records were scant and bare bones. Thank goodness for the extensive and detailed press coverage. Although the news accounts were spread out over many sources, once collected and analyzed they provided the structure upon which we could reconstruct the crime and maybe, just maybe solve the mystery.

One of the duties of an assistant district attorney is to carefully review the facts of a case to see if charges should be filed. This is a core prosecution function; one which any prosecutor or police officer would understand. It is a function we take with all seriousness. We are guided by the mandate that we seek justice in all we do. The seeking of justice is the basic concept behind my job as a prosecutor. After six years as a public defender I took a job as assistant district attorney. My former colleagues were very gracious. They gave me a fond farewell which included a certificate commemorating my work with the public defender, and a coin. The coin bears the phrase; "Justice Justice thou shalt pursue." I could not think of a better more fitting object, a symbol, upon which to base my career as a prosecutor.

In deciding whether criminal charges should be filed the U.S. attorneys, the 'feds', do not use probable cause to arrest as the standard. Instead, the assistant U.S. attorney decides if the charges can be proven beyond a reasonable doubt. In other words, they determine whether the case would result in a jury verdict of guilty. A jury system is our way of ensuring that only the guilty are convicted. That is why the jury consists of twelve people who should be objective and free of bias. Both sides participate in the selection of the jurors. Rules exist that allow the parties to find out about juror's backgrounds. The rules also allow for the 'striking' or removal of prospective jurors during the jury selection process. The jury's verdict must be unanimous; all twelve must agree on guilt or innocence. If not a hung jury mistrial results and a retrial is required. Also, the jury is told over and over during the course of a trial that a defendant is presumed innocent, the defense has no obligation to prove anything, it is the prosecution which bears the burden of proving guilt, and unless guilt is shown beyond a reasonable doubt the jury must find a defendant not guilty. Still no system is perfect, but when everyone follows their obligations our system is the fairest in the world.

Our way of deciding to file charges is different than the feds. If I based the approval of homicide charges on the belief that they *would* result in guilty verdicts at trial, I wouldn't have approved at least half of the cases where guilty verdicts resulted. This is not to say that I personally had any doubt as to the guilt of those I have tried. Rather, I realize how difficult it is to convince a jury of twelve everyday people, faced with the gut wrenching duty of sitting in judgement that they should convict. So instead we evaluate whether a case is strong enough to be submitted to a jury. In other words, is there enough evidence that the question of a defendant's guilt should be decided by a jury? Or, by way of shorthand, are the charges supported by 'PC', probable cause?

Figure 93 - Sam Haney 1848-1912 close up from a family portrait circa 1895. Considered a bad man by many of his neighbors Haney seems to have been used as an early and frequent scapegoat. However, the case against him was entirely built on the accusations and rumors of tipsters. Whenever it was time to 'put up' all the DA had was 'hearsay talk'. Photo from Diane Krol.

The probable cause standard is the one we would use in solving the murder of Etna Bittenbender. We felt comfortable and at home deciding who, if any of the suspects warranted charges for the murder. We also needed to assess what evidence would be admissible. One option was to strictly limit the evidence to that admissible under rules of evidence, such as those adopted in our state of Pennsylvania. However, we concluded that would be unfair. For example, with several suspects we had a lifetime of 'good character' evidence. If we discounted such evidence as, strictly speaking, not relevant, then we could not factor in the lifetimes of several of the men under scrutiny, such as Wilson Marsh, George

Kraft, or Sam Haney. No, we believed that information about their lives would be utilized. It really came down to a question of how much weight to give that type of evidence. On the flip side there was also evidence of 'other bad acts'. We had an abundance of that evidence. Frank Pfeifer's entire life was one prior bad act after another. His cousin George also involved himself in those nasty White Haven burglaries. Wilson Marsh was certainly among the half dozen who assaulted the girls coming from church that February evening in 1881. The Germans Langenfeld and Flock were on a veritable crime spree all around the time frame of Etna's murder. Sam Haney would face rape charges involving a young female some thirty years after Etna's murder. We felt all these had potential relevance to solving the mystery. Again it was a question of how much weight we would give this evidence.

The last category of potential 'evidence' we needed to decide whether to use was the 'readings' of the young psychic Alex Curcio. This was tough for us. We saw practically first-hand the uncanny connections the kid psychic laid out. How many of them matched what we knew, would know, and even connected to the lives of those under consideration. That kind of stuff is hard to ignore. Yet of all the 'evidence' this was the most unreliable and inadmissible. But to ignore it or pretend it didn't happen was wrong. After all, we knew the use of psychics has a limited role in the investigation of cold cases. So we concluded that the findings of Alex would be highlighted as they pertain to the murder and its suspects; but we would not rely upon them for our conclusions. With these thoughts in mind Detective Kerchner and I set about to 'wrap things up'.

The case against Sam Haney is a strange one. The only real fact we uncovered was that Haney lived less than a mile from the crime scene along Pensyl Creek Road at Sand Hill just outside of Snydersville. However, quite a few others lived in Sand Hill as well, including the Justice of the Peace Eugene Marsh. Haney was the only suspect repeatedly arrested for the murder. He was arrested up to three times for Etna's murder. Yet every single time the charges against him were dismissed for lack of evidence. The then thirty four year old Haney stood up to the pressure with incredible calmness and stoicism not in line with the rumors of his bad character. After the third dismissal of the charges the local newspapers expressed the general sentiment that enough was enough. Whatever the basis was for the authorities to go after Haney it is lost. Based on the result the evidence couldn't have amounted to much. The surviving record leads us to speculate that the case must have been based entirely on Haney's bad reputation; a reputation that could have involved excessive drinking, extramarital sex, and maybe some antisocial personality traits. Some back up for these thoughts came from the notorious rape trial involving the young Rose Bisbing and her infant child. Although Haney was found not guilty, the evidence was so depraved it was considered not fit for printing in the newspapers. So in the end we must conclude that the case against Sam Haney was in fact 'a fizzle'. We find no basis to charge Mr. Haney for the murder.

Figure 94 - Haney Clan circa 1895. Back row left to right: William Haney and wife, Walter Haney, Calvin Haney and wife, Ed Haney, Stroud King. Middle row left to right: Herbert Haney (Sam's son), Herbert's wife Emma Jane Cronk, Sam Haney's wife Sarah Marvin, Sam Haney, A. Bess, Ed Haney's wife, Sara Haney King. Front row: Ben Haney (Sam's grandson), unknown boy holding dog, Ruth Haney (Sam's granddaughter). Photo and identifiers from Diane Krol.

Next up are Charles Flock and John Langenfeld. The two Germans described by Warden Cassidy as Germans of the worst kind; men capable of committing high crimes. It is inferred that these guys fit the description of the men Wilson claimed to see on the bridge. We say this because Wilson's descriptions contain an age range might be consistent with Flock, 52 years old, and Langenfeld, 28 years old. But we have no other details of their appearance. For some reason that information, the physical description of the men, was not filled out by the penitentiary when the men went through intake to serve their sentence. The lawyer Holmes, hired by the family, sought to interview the men in 1881 at the penitentiary. That fact coupled with the news account that these men appeared consistent with the description given by Wilson was enough to keep them in play as suspects. But it is plain to us that for whatever reason Wilson was not actually able to identify them as the men he claimed to see that November morning on the stone bridge.

We tracked the movements of Langenfeld and Flock as they committed crimes in Gouldsboro and the Easton area. We showed how they travelled through Hamilton Township on their way to their next caper. Based on their movements they would have the opportunity and the means to do the deed. However, their modus operandi or MO doesn't fit the crime. These men were sneak thieves with an eye toward stealing stuff they could fence and make a quick turn around on. For them to commit such a senseless and violent crime without any financial incentive is a stretch. Also, the sheer recklessness of the rape and murder of Etna, the time spent on the grisly deeds, would require these men to have lingered around for hours after the murder, presumably to view the aftermath. That level of depravity doesn't fit what we could learn of these men. They do not, without more, appear to have committed any serious or violent crimes after their release from the penitentiary in 1886. At least they are never mentioned again. We therefore find no basis to charge them for the murder of Etna Bittenbender.

The real choice is between Wilson Marsh and the duo of Frank Pfeifer and his younger cousin George Kraft. For both choices we felt there was enough evidence and information upon which to decide if one or none should have been charged for Etna's murder. We were also favored by the fact that the decision between Wilson Marsh on the one hand and Pfeifer/Kraft on the other was along the familiar lines of the local theory versus the tramp or outsider theory of the murder. This allowed us to use much of the same reasoning employed by the original investigators but focused more on the specific suspects, Wilson Marsh for the local theory and Pfeifer/ Kraft for the outsider theory.

Figure 95 – This pair of photographs are close ups of two portraits depicting Wilson Marsh on the left and George Kraft on the right. These are the earliest portraits we have been able to locate of the men. They are from the late 1890s to early 1900s. We have been unable to locate a photograph of Frank Pfeifer. These men, Marsh, Pfeifer, and Kraft are the ones in serious contention. Photo of Kraft courtesy of Mr. James English. Photo of Marsh from RH Marsh.

The first place to start is at the basics, the murder weapon. This item of evidence is of great importance. A club three feet in length with a knot on its business end. This description is significant. It is not described as a stick or a branch, something which could easily have been lying about the wooded ground and used at the spur of the moment, but as a 'club'. The Oxford English Dictionary defines a club as: a heavy stick or staff used as a weapon. Thin enough on one end to be grasped by the hand. Increasing in thickness and weight on the other end..." (*Oxford English Dictionary* pg. 533 Oxford University Press 1971). In other words, we are talking about an object fashioned into a weapon. Not a piece of wood or tree used as a weapon but a proper club; a weapon personal and familiar to its possessor.

Such an object tends to stand out as something easily seen and easily remembered. If the owner of the club was a local, a teenager like Wilson Marsh, it would be easy to connect him to the club. Just like the torn and bloodied coat was instantly recognized by other locals as Wilson's coat, so to would the ownership of the club. The weapon was not whittled into existence as the culprit held Etna in the woods before killing her. The object was brought to the scene before Etna was attacked and after she was raped it was used to kill her. Yet nobody associated Wilson Marsh with the club. He is never mentioned as ever being seen with such an object. Therefore, it's fair to assume that the weapon was brought to the scene by someone else, an outsider.

A club is a very primitive, cheap, but effective weapon. It has existed for thousands of years over numerous cultures and groups. Indeed, violence through the use of clubs, cudgels, and fighting sticks was a characteristic feature in the New York City of the 1870s and 1880s. The increase in the weapon's use was traced to the heavy Irish immigration. Gangs such as the infamous Five Points Gang of New York favored these types of weapons. Street fights between Irish Catholics and Protestants frequently utilized clubs and fighting sticks. Frank Pfeifer grew up in that time and place. Frank ran in criminal circles and undoubtedly was familiar with and used clubs as part of his thug life. It is significant to remember Frank Pfeifer's own story about his father's death. His dad bought a gun to protect himself from Frank after Frank threatened him when he tried to intervene and stop Frank from beating Mrs. Pfeifer. What was the actual language of Frank's threat against his father? Frank threatened to '*club*' him if he tried to intervene. In short, the discovery of this murder weapon at the scene indicates the presence of an outsider. This by itself tends to exclude Wilson and include Pfeifer/Kraft.

As an aside we must mention that a second weapon was also located at the scene. This was described as a large pointed stone with blood on it. The Coroner's Inquest also found that both the club and stone were used to murder Etna. Perhaps the fact that multiple weapons were used shows more than one person was involved in the murder. Certainly, we can recall many murders in our own experience where that was the case. In this case that is more problematic. Remember that the club was found broken into pieces. It is plausible therefore that the same person who wielded the club and broke it during the murder, then chose a rock at hand and continued his murderous efforts. So the mere presence of multiple weapons was not an important piece of evidence, standing alone to suggest multiple killers.

Figure 96 - Detail from "Frank Leslie's Illustrated Magazine", July 1870 showing a violent large scale conflict in New York City between club wielding Irish Catholics and Protestants.

Another big factor for us was the sheer viciousness of the attack, its extreme brutality, targeting the head and face of the once good looking girl, multiple blows, all lethal. This was overkill. This level of violence bothered us. It speaks of intense hatred and rage directed toward the victim and meant to despoil her beauty. Which of the remaining suspects has shown in their lives such a rage as this? In his long life we find no evidence of such behavior by Wilson Marsh. The closest thing hinting at such a mindset is his involvement in the February 1881 attack on the girls leaving church in Jackson Township. But a careful review of that event and the murder shows entirely different mindsets were involved. The rape and murder was planned and involved a period of stalking or lying in wait, as well as knowledge of the victim and her plans. As noted, weapons were used in the murder. The victim was alone and isolated. By contrast the attack on the three girls by the half dozen boys and young men occurred more by circumstance than design. No lying in wait occurred. The group of girls was seen on the road and engaged by the boys. No one was armed. Indecent proposals were made and rejected. After that things became physical but no blunt force trauma is described. No hitting, kicking, punching, or choking took place. The girls were assaulted, they were thrown to the ground, clothing was ripped, but the assault never approached the murderous. In fact, no injuries to the girls were ever documented. Further, the attack on the girls was noisy and loud. A group of men were within earshot and quickly intervened. The only sounds overheard in Etna's case were apparently faint cries for help ultimately dismissed and ignored by the good Reverend Gilbert. So while Wilson's involvement in the attack on the girls was unquestionably a criminal act of violence it is of a substantially different nature and degree than the murder of Etna Bittenbender. So different are they that it would likely not be admissible in court to prove Wilson was connected to the murder.

In the long life of George Kraft we find even less signs that he was capable of such violence. It simply does not exist. The single mark on him was the White Haven burglaries he committed with his cousin Frank Pfeifer. But these were not crimes of violence but property crimes. The targets were stores that were closed for the night. No one was present during the commission of the burglaries. Frank Pfeiffer is a totally different story. He exhibited murderous rage in his relatively short life.

The murder of his cell mate McBride was brutal. Pfeifer strangled McBride to death or near death. Pfeifer repeatedly bashed McBride's skull against the large iron door sill of the cell until he fractured it in multiple places. This assault was sustained and murderous, similar to what happened to Etna. Pfeifer's history of violence included multiple assaults against his own mother. She stated in court that she feared he would kill her. Pfeifer is also mentioned as being violent and feloniously assaulting numerous females. His violence against females may supply a motive in the overkill directed against Etna. Pfeifer also tells us that we would be 'astonished' to know all the people he has killed. So the sheer brutality of the murder is consistent with Pfeifer.

One of the most depraved aspects of the murder was that Etna's body appears to have been displayed by her killers. The displaying of Etna's body is seen in its placement alongside the public road and the well-used path. She is lying on her back with her head resting on a stone. Her deadly injuries are brutally apparent. One could see right inside her skull and her brains are oozing out. Why did her killers choose to display her body in this manner? The fact is that this was by design and required thought and effort. She could have easily been murdered in the same place of isolation where she was raped. Instead, there was a decision to move her and make a display out of her. The placement of her was designed to shock people. This is in keeping with Frank's claim that people referred to him as a devil and a witch. This also brings to mind the very first reading Alex had at the crime scene. He told the detective, without knowing anything about the case, that they brought her out to the road because they were proud of their 'accomplishment' and wanted her to be seen. Perhaps they were excited by the prospect that Etna's body would be found by her own family? After all, November 1 was the first day of the new school year.

The fact that her murdered body was arranged for display instantly brings to mind the claim made by Wilson Marsh. That the very morning the body is discovered by Etna's siblings two strangers or tramps are seen 'lurking' nearby on a bridge. Did the killers hang back to observe first-hand the reaction to their handiwork? That would be consistent with the whole reason behind displaying her body by the road. Such recklessness would also be consistent with a sick twisted pride in such an 'accomplishment'.

Figure 97 - Wilson Marsh born February 18, 1865 died February 5, 1951 age 86. Seated at the far right is his wife Laura Allison Marsh who he married in Iowa in 1885. Marsh's brother Edward was married to Laura's sister. Also depicted are five of their eight sons, Elmer, Harry, Rolla, Earl, and Clover. Based on the ages and birthdates of the children this photograph was taken around 1896. Wilson would have been around 31 years old. The photograph was taken in South Dakota. Photograph from RH Marsh.

At first we doubted Wilson's story about seeing two tramps nearby. However, there was independent verification made by the detectives that a tramp camp was discovered in the patch of woods near the crime scene. Hemlock boughs arranged for bedding and firewood set up for a campfire but never ignited were located. So the presence of outsiders at or near the scene at the right time was in fact established. But were they the right outsiders? Were they Frank Pfeifer and George Kraft?

Wilson Marsh provided the authorities with his best description of the tramps he saw on the bridge. We know he observed them during the morning hours. We do not know how close to dawn, to the break of day the sighting was. Of course, lighting conditions could have affected the accuracy of his description. We also do not know how far away Wilson was from the outsiders. The description suggests that Wilson was too far away to even make out if one of the men had a beard or not. Wilson describes one of the men to be about 5 feet 10 inches tall approximately 180 pounds, forty years old with brown hair. Wilson added that he 'did not see a beard but the man may have had one'. The inability to make out whether the man was bearded or not indicates that lighting or distance hampered Wilson's ability to accurately give a description. The other man was shorter, about five feet seven inches tall, 150 pounds and about thirty years old. This man had a 'smooth face' and wore light colored clothes. Wilson doesn't mention the second man's hair color; another indication of the poor quality of the identification.

Figure 98 - George Kraft was a Fourth Degree Knight of Columbus. George was born September 1863 and died in 1949 at age 86. George married Cathsilia Praetorius in 1882 in White Haven. In 1885 they indentured Margaret Gill an orphan from the Lourietown Home, Lausanne Township Pennsylvania. George started with the Lehigh Valley Railroad in 1888 and retired as a Locomotive Engineer in 1940. In 1896 he fostered George Mathiesson out of an orphanage in New York. Both George Mathiesson and Margaret Gill were raised by Kraft and Cathsilia as their own children. George Jr. died in France of the influenza in 1918. Margaret Gill died in 1938. Kraft's wife died in 1939. Courtesy of James English.

The descriptions are vague at best. How do they square with Pfeifer and Kraft? The ages are clearly off, 30 and 40 years old versus 17 for Kraft and 23 for Pfeifer. But witness descriptions can be notoriously inaccurate. This is true even under optimal conditions. Also, it wouldn't be far-fetched for some effort at disguise to have been involved. It is interesting on that topic to add that Alex Curcio described the killers as very dirty with blackened faces, like miners. We do know what Pfeifer and Kraft looked like. The news accounts and his prison records tell us that Pfeifer was around five feet six inches, blond hair, grey eyes, and fair complexion. Kraft is described as dark haired with dark eyes and a slight frame. The photographs of George Kraft are from later in life, middle and old age. But they show him taller than Pfeifer. Kraft appears about five feet nine or ten inches. So on balance, the taller man described by Wilson is around George Kraft's height and also dark haired. The other man is light complexed and shorter, which is consistent with Frank Pfeifer. However, because of its vagueness, the descriptions on balance do not move the needle in either direction.

Another circumstance pointing to outsiders is the whole time frame of the crime; specifically, the huge gap between the time of the abduction and the time of the murder. Etna was abducted shortly after 4 in the afternoon on Sunday October 31. The blood found just inside the wood line near the edge of the fields locks the time of the attack in. She was assaulted practically as soon as she entered the woods. We know she was 'decoyed' that is taken to a place of isolation nearby and raped for a time. Her cries are heard two hours later at 6 pm. Her body is discovered the next morning by the road. But people passing the road at that spot at 8 and 9 pm did not see her. Also, her dad and uncle passed by early the following morning and did not see her. It seems she was yet to be displayed. This is likely why the accounts never mention rigor mortis. She was not dead long enough prior to her discovery for rigor to set in. The length of time she suffered is the single most disturbing thing about her murder. This brings up one of the most poignant images described by the young psychic to Detective Serfass during that first 'reading.' Alex described Etna 'hanging on' hoping she would be found. He felt her suffering from an injury to her chest and ribs making it difficult to breathe. Alex sensed that the night came and went and that right around dawn, shortly before being found by her family, Etna died.

Figure 99 - Wilson Marsh later in life. From RH Marsh. The closest Wilson came to being charged was after his torn and bloodied coat was found near the crime scene. It is a tribute to his fast thinking that he immediately appeared for questioning and after a thorough examination was cleared of all suspicion in the case. Although we weren't there we can say that Wilson must have demonstrated he was telling the truth when he claimed he threw down the coat a week before the murder while hunting. No doubt there was a bit of an Indian summer that fall. What we find more interesting is the fact that the coat had been moved from where Wilson threw it down and now was torn, bloody, and had light colored hairs adhered to it. Could it have been used in the murder? Did it play a role in decoying the victim? Did it help muffle her faintly heard cries of help? Several times during his readings Alex asked the detectives whether they ever found something used to cover Etna's face and head. Alex repeated that the attackers threw something over her to keep her from seeing. Could they have used Wilson's coat which they found lying nearby? We know the color of Frank's hair was light brown.

This time frame meant the killers were with the victim for up to twelve hours. A local like Wilson Marsh couldn't spend so much time unaccounted for. He would have no way to prove his whereabouts, no alibi. Recall the conversation Emma Marsh, Wilson's mother, had with Etna's sisters as they arrived at school that morning; 'the woman of the house asked the girls where their sister was. They replied she left home on Sunday afternoon to come over, and being informed she had not been there the girls started back to inform their parents...'' Such a conversation makes no sense if both Wilson and Etna were unaccounted for the whole night. Rather, it seems plain that Wilson detailed his whereabouts to the authorities and that his alibi was corroborated. On the other hand, a stranger or outsider would have no need to account for his whereabouts. He or they wouldn't be missed by anyone nearby. They would have the ability to spend as much time with the victim as they could get away with. There only concern was if someone, by chance, were to discover them with the victim.

So far we have seen that the weapon was brought from the outside. The presence of outsiders near the scene was documented by the investigators. The sheer brutality of the murder is only consistent with the suspect Frank Pfeifer, an outsider. The body was displayed only a short distance from the Marsh home, which is not consistent with Wilson being the perpetrator. The 12 hour gap between the victim's attack/abduction and her murder would not have been feasible for a local like Wilson to be unaccounted for. The gap in time is therefore further evidence of an outsider. This brings up one of the biggest problems with the outsider theory; a problem that the original investigators were not able to overcome. How did outsiders learn about the victim and her movements?

The strongest evidence to support that a local like Wilson killed Etna is due to the fact that she was attacked as soon as she entered the woods from her father's fields. In other words, someone was waiting for her, someone who had to be familiar with her movements. What evidence is there that outsiders like Pfeifer and Kraft could know such details about

Etna? The starting point for the answer is in Frank Pfeifer's own words, his death note; the writing on the slates.

Figure 100 - George Kraft and his wife Cathsilia Praetorius Kraft circa 1900 along with their adopted daughter Maggie Gill and two orphan children in front. "I cannot picture grandpa Kraft being what the info says; He never said anything to me about criminal behavior. ... the Krafts were active in many social and religious activities, well liked, never in trouble with the law. He must have learned his lesson after being arrested since he married and settled down two years after the burglary event remained employed, raised two children who were orphaned, was very religious... I think Frank Pfeifer led him astray for a short time but I can't see him involved in a murder." Courtesy of James English grandson of Maggie Gill.

In all, the writing on the slates consists of 117 words, of which nearly half involve the murder of Etna Bittenbender, either directly or by offering sources of corroboration. One of Pfeifer's most telling efforts to corroborate his claim of killing Etna Bittenbender is by informing the reader about the arrest of Sebastian Kraft in the fall of 1880. "Cousin George Kraft last fall was arrested his brother." Similarly, Pfeifer brings up the fall of 1880 again; "Last fall me and my cousin George Kraft." Based on the examination of court documents and the interview George Kraft had while incarcerated its plain that Pfeifer is talking about an event which occurred one month before the murder. Sebastian travelled to Stroudsburg at the end of September 1880 to attend court. For part of the way Pfeifer and George Kraft accompanied him. However, Sebastian went on to Stroudsburg without them. Where did Pfeifer and George Kraft go? George Kraft claims they went straight home to Kidder Township Carbon County never to set foot in Monroe County ever again. We know that to be false.

By the fall of 1880, George Kraft had extensive ties with Monroe County. Remember that at the end of November 1880, he was arrested by Detective O'Brien of Wilkes-Barre while at work inside Monroe County. George had a close relationship with the Praetorius family of Appenzell, Jackson Township Monroe County. At the time of the White Haven burglaries he was dating one of the Praetorius girls, Cathsilia Praetorius, who he would marry in 1882. He was close friends with Cathsilia's older brother Louis Praetorius, who at the time was living in Monroe County in Chestnuthill Township. In the fall of 1880 Etna Bittenbender's entire world centered practically right at the boundary between Jackson and Hamilton Township. Both the Bittenbender farm and the Marsh home were within one mile of each other. Both locations are also only about a mile away from Appenzell, the home of the Praetorius family. Unless at church Etna could be found at either house, or on her way to the one or the other.

There is another aspect to Etna. One never explicitly mentioned but there anyway. Etna was an attention getter in the small community. Whether by design or just her nature, people paid Etna attention. She was tall, 'stylish', 'beautiful', 'quite the belle in her section', a very popular young lady. Pfeifer must have first laid eyes on Etna during the time he and George struck out on their own in Monroe County after leaving Sebastian and Mr. Woodring at the Pocono Switch. This probably happened when they visited George's friends among the Praetorius family in Jackson Township. This is why Pfeifer felt it important to write about the first time he travelled to Monroe County. Pfeifer's preoccupation with Jackson Township is evidenced on the slates. He writes at one point; "I also kill that girl in Jackson County." At another point he identifies Etna by name; "Miss Elna Bittenbender, Jackson Township last fall me and my cousin George Kraft." After Pfeifer saw

Etna that September of 1880, he must have asked about her. At that time it would be an easy thing to learn about Etna. Everyone would know she was keeping house for Mrs. Marsh. They would know to which family she belonged, where her father's farm was. And of course, the road and well-worn path would be plain enough.

During the course of our investigation we interviewed a young woman named Julia Gumm. She lived at what was the Hobbs farm located on Neola Road just down the road from the Rees Schoolhouse. Her great grandmother was a Hobbs. Ms. Gumm told us a family story. According to it Julia's great grandmother was one of the last people to see Etna. Her great grandmother recalled seeing Etna leaving the Marsh home that Sunday morning heading down the hill in the direction of the stream. Of course, this would have been when Etna was going to spend the day with her family. If Pfeifer and Kraft saw her walking from the Marsh place to her father's farm earlier that Sunday then all that was needed was to wait around awhile. They could have walked the path in the woods and waited just inside the tree line. This is what the psychic Alex first told Detective Serfass; that there were two of them waiting behind a big oak tree. They had been watching her and her family. She didn't know them, but saw them in passing on an earlier occasion somewhere in town.

So the addition of that little bit of knowledge, knowledge Pfeifer was trying to articulate in the slates, that he and Kraft encountered Etna in September of 1880 is all that is needed to overcome the difficulty of how outsiders would know the victim's habits. You see both Pfeifer and Kraft were neither tramps nor true outsiders. Rather Pfeifer, through the connections his cousin George had to Monroe County and in particular the locale of the crime, knew everything that was needed to successfully lie in wait for his victim.

Frank Pfeifer killed Etna Bittenbender. He tells us that. He tells us how he came about her. He tells us why he did it. He offers us the chance to learn all about him in New York. He tells us this not during a police interrogation. He tells us this voluntarily without prompting. He tells us at a time when he is alone at night in his cell, the dead body of his cell mate lying next to him. He tells us this as he is preparing to end his own miserable life. Pfeifer is sick and tormented but his words ring true. Even months before, when he lays out his confession to the White Haven burglaries, Pfeifer is consistent and detailed. He spells out how he entered the store while Kraft acted as a lookout. He talks of the plan he and Kraft hatched at the party in Jerusalem. How Kraft has to first bring his girlfriend home and then meet up with him. Pfeifer describes the loot and how he and Kraft brought it back home from White Haven.

George Kraft's stories, both about the activities of he and Pfeifer, as well as his role in the White Haven Burglaries do not ring true. Kraft can't even admit that he was a willing participant in the burglaries. He tries to claim that he only became aware that stores in White Haven were burglarized during his walk home with Pfeifer. He claims suddenly, about halfway there, that Pfeifer asked him to carry some of the loot. It is only at that point that he sees the loot and learns of the crime. On its face his story is absurd. He fares the same when he tries to minimize his relationship with Pfeifer. He denies learning of Pfeifer's crimes in New York. He claims only after he is imprisoned that he learns Pfeifer's story about the death of his father. And of course, Kraft denies his own connections to Monroe County. The latter denials and omissions about his knowledge of the people and places in question is strong evidence of a guilty mind.

Is George Kraft also a murderer? That is the question. Pfeifer, as honest and demented as he is, never says Kraft killed her or helped to kill her. Pfeifer says that 'I' killed the girl. Not 'we killed the girl. So we should take Pfeifer at his word, him and only him actually killed Etna. But that is not enough to answer the question of Kraft's guilt. One can be charged and convicted of murder without being the actual slayer. It is an ancient feature of the law. One used many times in the prosecution of murder. That is accomplice liability. Kraft could be charged and convicted of Etna's murder if he was Pfeifer's accomplice. Simply stated, an accomplice is a helper. An accomplice does have to have the intent to aid the slayer in the commission of the offense. In other words, Kraft had to actually help Pfeifer do the deed. The help doesn't have to be pivotal. The aid does not have to be essential for Pfeifer to commit the killing. It just has to help make it easier. For example, if Kraft lent a hand to prevent Etna from fleeing that might be enough. Certainly, a jury would have to decide the question. The crime is of such a nature that implicitly it has to involve at least two people. The abduction in the woods, taking her to a place of isolation, the rape, the passage of time, moving her to the road, and the killing itself, are acts that lend themselves to the need for an accomplice.

There is an even easier way to charge Kraft for his role in the murder. A way that doesn't require the prosecution to prove Kraft had the intent to aid Pfeifer in the commission of Etna's murder. The way is to charge Kraft with felony murder, known in Pennsylvania today as Murder in the Second Degree. Felony murder would require that a killing occur in the course of a felony such as a rape, a robbery, a kidnapping etc. If that happened, then all parties to the underlying felony are guilty of felony murder. Kraft vehemently denied that Pfeifer had ever left his Kidder Township home after they returned from accompanying Sebastian to Monroe County. The fact that Kraft at all times puts himself with Pfeifer makes it hard for him to argue that Pfeifer acted alone, that at some point Pfeifer left the Kraft residence for several days. By his own words Kraft ties himself to his homicidal cousin. The bonds are tight and should have been tested by a jury.

The charges against Kraft would be for accomplice liability to murder and felony murder. Pfeifer's confession would probably be admissible as a statement against his interest. Along with that, Kraft's false denials about his ties to Monroe County would sketch out the case against him. Kraft might try an alibi, but if it only included family members, a skillful prosecutor could take it apart. There might also be witnesses who put Kraft in Monroe County with frequency. I would not even be surprised if some of Etna's family members would claim to have seen Kraft around the area.

Figure 101 - George Kraft Lehigh Valley Railroad Engineer. For much of Kraft's career he worked as a locomotive engineer at the Coxton Yard in West Pittston. In the 1890s a pivotal moment in Kraft's career occurred there when he was in charge of the crew of Engine 98. At that time he survived a massive downsizing and reorganization of the railroad during which many crews were laid off or phased out. Over a hundred years later in 2013 Alex Curcio leaned on the corner of the wooden schoolhouse. The same one Etna's sisters were going to when they encountered Emma Marsh, turned back home, and found their sister's battered body. After a bit Alex opened his eyes and told Detectives Serfass and Kerchner that of the two killers, one did not live that long. But the other one did. He lived a long time. He moved out west to Pittsburgh or a place that sounds like that. Alex added that toward the end of his long life the man thought often about the murder. He dwelled on it. He reflected upon it. While Alex laid out these images he said he kept seeing a number associated with this man. The number kept repeating. The number was 98.

Kraft was only seventeen at the time of the murder. He was the same age as Etna. Pfeifer was 23 and undoubtedly much worldlier than Kraft. It is also likely that Pfeifer had a great deal of influence over his younger cousin. The worldly, sophisticated, older cousin from New York certainly knew how to influence the youngster Kraft. In fact, throughout his long life the only time Kraft violated the law was during the fall of 1880, the same time that he was under Pfeifer's influence. This is consistent with another of the psychic's comments. Alex stated that only one of the two really did the crime. The other one was definitely just a follower. Nevertheless, both were proud of their accomplishment.

This case has been for us a long journey, a sort of Odyssey out of our own time and into another time long gone, certainly not familiar territory. But the inhumanity and depravity of the murder of Etna was all too familiar. Indeed, we have journeyed many times into the darkest inner recesses of the human soul in order to ferret out, to solve a murder and seek justice by the result. We have been privileged to do so. This unsolved murder haunted us for far too long. In a way it was a stain on the Office of the District Attorney. Yet despite the shortcomings of the original investigation and the long passage of the years, in the end, when all the pieces were assembled and carefully considered, the mystery was unraveled and the truth emerged. By that process a once forgotten and murdered farm girl, cut down in the prime of her life has been given a voice and the recognition she and her murder deserve. It is our hope that by this work the dead may rest easier.

Index

Curcio, 219, 238
Delaware River, 6
devil's advocate, 225
Devil's Hole Road, 44
direct evidence, 2
DNA, 6, 17, 19, 51, 80, 147
DNA profile, 6
drug dealers, 14
E. David Christine, Jr, viii
Easton, 23, 27, 50, 57, 68, 82,
    107, 108, 111, 112, 113, 114,
    126, 138, 152, 200, 213, 215,
    230
Effort Neola Road, 19, 105
Emma Marsh, 31, 33, 53, 104,
    240
Eric J. Kerchner, v
Exchange Principle, 17
Felony murder, 245
Fenner, 15, 48, 78
First Assistant District
    Attorney, 1
Five Points Gang, 232
Fleming, 27, 29, 89, 90, 93
Flock, 108, 111, 112, 113, 114,
    117, 118, 121, 125, 199, 206,
    208, 209, 228, 230
Ford Thunderbird, 6
Foul Murder, 25, 61
Frank Pfeifer. *See* Pfeifer
Frantz, 27, 29
Freemore, 17
George Kraft. *See* Kraft
Germans, 103, 119, 206, 228,
    230
Gilbert, 58, 60, 62, 69, 205,
    234
Goucher, 17

Gouldsboro, 108, 109, 111,
    112, 114, 117, 230
grand jurors, 6
Guinther, 24
Gupta, 5
Hamilton, 1, 7, 9, 15, 16, 23,
    26, 29, 31, 33, 48, 60, 67, 69,
    70, 77, 78, 103, 112, 124,
    132, 149, 150, 153, 189, 191,
    206, 230, 242
Hamilton Township, 1, 7, 9,
    16, 23, 26, 29, 31, 33, 48, 60,
    69, 77, 78, 103, 124, 150,
    153, 189, 230, 242
Haney, 21, 121, 123, 124, 125,
    126, 127, 128, 129, 148, 150,
    199, 207, 228
Harps, 27, 29, 152, 153, 154
high crimes, 103, 119, 230
Holmes, 114, 118, 194, 195,
    208, 230
homosexual, 6, 79, 80, 176
Huegel, 3
hung jury, 226
Inquest, 14, 16, 18, 19, 48, 52,
    57, 69, 78, 133, 179, 195,
    205
Investigating Grand Jury, 6
Jackson Township, 242
Jeffersonian Republican, 23, 25,
    30, 48, 50, 82, 127, 133, 139,
    140, 152, 183, 214
Julia Gumm, 243
jury, 2, 6, 7, 12, 14, 43, 45, 53,
    55, 100, 110, 116, 122, 123,
    127, 142, 149, 160, 164, 181,
    194, 204, 207, 214, 226, 245
jury system, 226